Markets with Chinese Characteristics:
Economic Liberalism in Modern China

Before the First Opium War, from 1839–1842, China had long had substantial commercial activity. After Europeans forced the country to open up to the West, one of the Western ideas to which China was exposed was economic liberalism. This way of thinking had never cohered as a doctrine in China, even though aspects of it can be found in older Chinese thought.

After 1842, many influential people in China came to see economic liberalism as the key to saving China. Similar claims would be made at various times for social Darwinism, women's rights, Christianity, and ultimately Marxism, under which economic liberalism was tarred as nothing more than a façade for colonial exploitation. After 1949, under Marxism, China was driven to extreme. Then, in desperation, its leaders awkwardly harnessed economic liberalism in practice to Marxism in theory. This harnessing of liberalization unleashed prosperity and substantial social changes, beginning in the late 1970s. But today the leaders of the Chinese Communist Party (CCP) want, above all, to maintain power, and they fear that China now has too much economic liberalism.

About the author:

Evan Osborne is a professor of economics at Wright State University. He reads and writes Chinese, and has published on Chinese history from the late Qing to the present. He has also done work on ethnic conflict and more general social conflict, and on the economics of art, empirical analysis of litigation, development economics, and sports economics.

Markets with Chinese Characteristics: Economic Liberalism in Modern China

Evan Osborne

CL Press

Published by CL PRESS
A project of the Fraser Institute
1770 Burrard Street, 4th Floor
Vancouver, BC V6J 3G7 Canada
www.clpress.net

Markets with Chinese Characteristics
Evan W. Osborne

© 2024 by CL Press

ISBN: 978-1-957698-13-7

Cover photo: Wikimedia, "Shanghai Bund seen from the French Concession": https://upload.wikimedia.org/wikipedia/commons/a/a1/Shanghai_Bund_seen_from_the_French_Concession.jpg

Cover design by Joanna Andreasson
Interior layout by Joanna Andreasson

Searchable PDF of this book, with color in figures,
open access, free: https:://clpress.net/

Contents

LIST OF FIGURES AND TABLES

Preface

This book was a labor of love, but it would have been impossible without the generosity of others. Li Weisen and Feng Xingyuan were my co-authors on the paper that prompted this project. Prof. Li in particular hosted me at Fudan University as a visiting scholar in fall, 2018 to enable both research on the book and the learning of a great deal about China by traveling through it. While I was in China, Liang Jie provided helpful guidance, and Terry Peach especially helped me by providing particularly helpful — read, pointedly critical — comments about some of my interpretations of classical Chinese texts. Carol Wang, whose office is just a few doors down from mine at Wright State University, also provided helpful and very current commentary about developments in China. None are implicated in any errors in what follows.

Joanna Andreasson made the cover and interior of the book, and Jane Shaw Stroup, through her copy editing, improved the writing considerably.

The cover photo is of the Bund in Shanghai during the city's golden age of economic liberalism, and is in the public domain via Wikimedia, and titled "Shanghai Bund seen from the French Concession." It is available at https://upload.wikimedia.org/wikipedia/commons/a/a1/Shanghai_Bund_seen_from_the_French_Concession.jpg

CHAPTER 1

Introduction

Zhou Qunfei (周群飛, 1970–) has the distinction of being named by *Forbes* magazine in 2018 as the wealthiest self-made woman in the world. Her life has been what Americans might call a Horatio Alger story, albeit in a distinctively modern Chinese way. She was born in 1970, as the worst excesses of the Cultural Revolution (CR) were winding down. Her father made and repaired household items to support his family, since he had been rendered unable to do factory work by an industrial accident. Zhou's mother died when she was five. She dropped out of school at 16, and soon got a job at a small factory that made watch parts. It closed several years later, but she started her own company making watch lenses, relying on savings she had accumulated in her previous work. The company grew and was eventually able to get orders from various mobile-telephone manufacturers, including Apple for the first iPhone.

The rest is history, though a history that would have been unimaginable when Zhou was born. Even in the new China her success is unusual, but in general the various reforms that have played out there since 1978 have borne spectacular fruit in economic achievement.

Yet China's history is long enough to include every kind of economic experience, from feudalism to cronyism to near-complete, if forced, embrace of economic liberalism in much of the country beginning in 1843, to essentially complete elimination of it after 1949 to the more recent experiences of people like Zhou. This book is about the complex and volatile history of economic liberalism in China.

Western entry into China

On June 21, 1793, a small fleet of British ships led by the flagship Lion dropped anchor off what was then known to the British as Grand Ladrone Island (today one of the Wanshan Islands (萬山群島) just off the coast of Hong Kong and Macau). The expedition, known to historians as the Macartney Embassy, had left port in Spithead, on the southern coast of England, on September 25, 1792. After traveling to Rio de Janeiro, the crew rounded the Cape of Good Hope, traveled through what is now Indonesia and dropped anchor in Chinese waters on June 20, 1793. The commander, George (later Baron and then Earl, 1737–1806) Macartney, had been charged with expanding British trade opportunities in China (opportunities which, like those of most other countries trading there, were then limited to the city of Canton). Macartney sought to acquire rights to a small island to facilitate such trade and to establish a permanent embassy.

On none of these scores was Macartney successful. Indeed, in acting on behalf of the royally chartered monopoly the British East India Company (BEIC), Macartney was advocating for sharply limiting foreign trade to the British rather than other nations, but the representatives of the Chinese system also wanted to limit trade. Both favored a dying system in which commerce, especially foreign commerce, was a thing to be tightly managed by government officials.

But a new economic philosophy was in ascendancy in western Europe and especially the United Kingdom. This doctrine, part of the newly emerging political economy, held that the conventional wisdom about the benefits of international trade was incorrect. The point of commerce was not to export products in order to accumulate monetary wealth, but to import products to obtain goods more cheaply than if resources had to be sacrificed domestically to make them. By generating more consumption opportunities for the people, including the common people, this commerce would increase their standard of living. And in this new theory it was individuals' consumption (not the nation's monetary wealth) that should dominate thinking about economic policy.

It is unlikely that the new arguments for free trade motivated the Macartney Embassy. Its primary immediate goal, like those other European commercial missions during this era, was to open markets for home-country exports, in this case primarily for the BEIC. But the Chinese government refused all the embassy's entreaties. While the mission was treated with diplomatic courtesy throughout its time in China, the Qianlong emperor (1711–1799, reigned 1735–1796) simply refused to meaningfully open his realm's markets to British traders.

The emperor listed his reasons in a diplomatically phrased letter to his British counterpart, George III (1760–1820) in 1793. Later historians emphasized what they took to be the arrogance of the letter, with perhaps the most oft-cited passage reading:

> Surveying the wide world, I have but one aim in view, namely, to maintain a perfect governance and to fulfill the duties of the State: strange and costly objects do not interest me. If I have commanded that the tribute offerings sent by you, O King, are to be accepted, this was solely in consideration for the spirit which prompted you to dispatch them from afar. Our dynasty's majestic virtue has penetrated unto every country under Heaven, and Kings of all nations have offered their costly tribute by land and sea. As your Ambassador can see for himself, we possess all things. I set no value on objects strange or ingenious, and have no use for your country's manufactures.[1]

There were also words suggesting that the emperor took Great Britain to be just another potential tributary state, and this was the interpretation subsequently made by many Western historians, partly owing to excited press coverage then and later.

More recent analysis of Chinese archives indicates that the emperor was knowledgeable about European colonial behavior in India and quite concerned about similar predation in China if British merchants were granted what were seen as special privileges. This suggests that the emperor played the game of *realpolitik* to the hilt, subsequently giving orders to local officials to boost defenses in some Chinese coastal areas—to prevent corrupt demands by local tax collectors, to make visible displays of Chinese military strength along the coast as the embassy proceeded south (without firing a shot), and to treat the

---

1. English translation taken from https://china.usc.edu/emperor-qianlong-letter-george-iii-1793.

embassy courteously in negotiations without giving up any territory or trade privileges. The interpretation of the emperor's response as contemptuous may have been a result of selective publication of Chinese records in the 1920s. At that time, officials of the Republic of China (ROC) wished to depict the final dynasty, Qing, as incompetent and isolated in order to make the new republican government, then struggling against substantial internal opposition, look better and thus facilitate its use of the state to build the nation and its economy. Other scholarship, however, depicts the emperor's response as an attempt to confirm to Han Chinese that the Qing dynasty, which had been imposed by invading Manchus in the late 17th century, was as unassailable as ever.[2]

Regardless of whether the emperor's arrogance played any role in the decision to refuse all British requests, the result was an order designed to keep the British out of China to the extent possible. But over the next century the British, and later the French, Germans, Americans, Japanese, and other foreigners, would come anyway. They would seize parts of coastal China and repeatedly wage war, usually successfully, against the imperial forces. I will refer to the onset of this period as "Western first entry." This is not strictly accurate in that Jesuit clerics and Portuguese and non-Western merchants had been in China for several centuries previously, but substantially restricted and in small numbers. Western first entry is an approximate description of China in the late eighteenth century when Western countries became a major force in China.[3]

As this process unfolded, the leadership class in the Middle Kingdom came to understand that China needed to change. To their credit, many of these officials and intellectuals eventually made remarkable efforts to try to understand what made the United Kingdom and other Western countries so strong. Many ideas were discovered and debated, and in the end some were discarded. One of the ideas that suffered this fate was one of the first encountered—economic liberalism, the belief that markets left by the state to operate

---

2. On cherry-picking historical documents to delegitimize imperial rule, see Henrietta Harrison, "The Qianlong Emperor's Letter to George III and the Early-Twentieth-Century Origins of Ideas about Traditional China's Foreign Relations," *American Historical Review* 122, no. 3 (June 2017): 680–701. On attempts by the Manchu Qing to intimidate the majority Han, see David S. Landes, "Why Europe and the West? Why Not China?," *Journal of Economic Perspectives* 20, no. 2 (Spring 2006): 3–22.

3. Unless further modified, following common modern usage terms such as "Western" and "Westerners" will refer to all of the nations that colonized parts of China in the 19th century, including European countries, the United States, and Japan.

freely in general enables greater prosperity. The extraordinary travels of this school of thought through modern Chinese history is a largely untold one. Since the forced opening of China to Westerners in 1843, after the Treaty of Nanjing that ended the first Opium War, the purportedly new idea of such economics has taken a journey very different from that in Western Europe and North America. In those countries, an economically liberal environment was either already longstanding or subsequently embraced in the 19th century, and then for the most part simply altered modestly in the name of a fairer society. But in China the journey of economic liberalism has been characterized by extremes: some knowledge of its basic principles and rising and falling acqui-escence to them, then complete acceptance, then growing rejection culminat-ing in the years between 1949 and 1978, followed by continued liberalization, and perhaps now a halt to that liberalization. This book will tell the story of that journey—why some Chinese were so entranced by economic liberalism, how and why it fell out of favor, and the path and implications of its rebirth and growth in recent decades.

1.A The neglect of economic liberalism in scholarship on China

1.A.1 The different liberalisms
The word "liberal" derives from the Latin *liber*, "free." According to Google nGrams (a tool for measuring changes over time in frequency of word or phrase use), the term "liberalism" started to continuously appear in English-language books in 1787. The variants "political liberalism," "economic liberalism," and "social liberalism" began to appear in 1798, 1871, and 1876 respectively.

In the 17th and 18th centuries, Enlightenment thinkers on political, eco-nomic, and other social questions had created a body of thought that prized individual autonomy, meaning freedom from both excessive political author-ity and the pressure of custom. This thinking was first developed most ener-getically and amply in the U.K. and France.[4] All of these liberalisms have in common a focus on the individual as the fundamental unit of social analysis, as

---

4. A similar search on Google nGrams reveals that the French word *libéralisme* first appeared continuous-ly in 1786.

opposed to social or economic classes or society as a whole. Roughly speaking, economic liberalism refers to clear property rights for individuals or voluntary associations of individuals. This right extends to the ability to create things, including ideas, that challenge the existing economic and social order. Political liberalism, which has been sometimes mistakenly conflated in the scholarship with a somewhat different concept of liberalism, will be used here to refer to protection from the arbitrary use of political power against the individual and the selection of political leaders through an open, competitive process. Social liberalism, which will deserve mention when it grows as a result of or serves to limit economic liberalism, refers to individual autonomy in the conduct of one's life beyond the economic arena. A unified theory of liberalism was a distinct creation of the Enlightenment West, as were the theoretical arguments for economic liberalism in particular. In this section I pry economic liberalism away from these other liberalisms, and then briefly sketch its development in the West.

The use of the broad term "liberalism" in politics has changed over time, especially in the United States. In American usage "liberalism" at least since the 1930s has included a measure of government assistance to the poor and broader attention to what is now called "social justice." In the American mind, government action such as providing more resources for medical care, education, etc., to the poor is a way to enable them to pursue opportunities they might be capable of taking, given their personal endowments (talents, drive, and other distinctive characteristics), but unachievable because they lack material resources. (In many countries these programs are now provided to the entire population.)

But these definitions are variations on a theme. In all of them, the individual is the key, and the difference among the definitions is how to best enable that individual to achieve his or her potential. The banning of discrimination against members of social groups historically subject to it also reflects the difference in the definitions. More traditional or self-termed classical liberals differ over whether the removal of coercive obstacles (e.g., Jim Crow laws in the post-Reconstruction American South) is enough, or whether affirmative government steps are needed. Either way, liberalism means that government should be responsive to the public while generally respecting individual autonomy, and the economy should start from the presumption of free markets, if not necessarily adhering to them religiously.

As for social liberalism, inside and outside the U.S., it has held that the individual should be free from social coercion not just by the state but by broader elements of private society, as long as the individual is merely engaging in behavior that does not harm others. Often associated with John Stuart Mill (1806–1873), social liberalism holds that the state imposing limits on individual action in such circumstances cannot be justified but also that nonpolitical social pressure can be destructive of personal dignity and social progress. (Ironically, Mill was concerned about such pressure coming from a conformist society, even as British society at the time he wrote was being increasingly dominated by Britain's rising bourgeoisie, the fruit of growing economic liberalism.[5]) Worldwide, liberalism denotes the political philosophy that centers on individuals, their welfare, and what their rights are.

1.A.2 The liberalisms in scholarship on China

Western historians have written about the Chinese discovery of broad Western liberalism. There is a significant literature on China's initial fascination with political and, in particular, social liberalism. There are numerous accounts of how a democratic political system, in which national leaders are chosen by popular vote, began to appeal to Chinese intellectuals soon after they began to meticulously study Western culture. From the time the first adventurous Chinese returned from overseas education in the late 19th century the unmodified noun democracy (民主, mínzhǔ, "rule by the people") was widely praised. Sometimes this was done by opponents outside the corridors of political power, as during the chaos of the early 20th century and during the Republic of China (ROC) rule of Chiang Kai-Shek (蔣介石, 1887–1975) and his Nationalist Party (國民黨, which I will refer to by its traditional initials KMT, for Kuomintang) in the 1920s and 1930s.[6]

Then and now, in the West "democracy" has meant various combinations

5. John Stuart Mill, *On Liberty*, ed. by David Bromwich and George Kateb (New Haven: Yale University Press, 2003).

6. See Timothy Cheek, *The Intellectual in Modern Chinese History* (Cambridge, U.K.: Cambridge University Press, 2015); Orville Schell, "China's Hidden Democratic Legacy," *Foreign Affairs* 83, no. 4 (August 2004):116–124; Andrew J. Nathan, Chinese Democracy (New York: Knopf, 1986); Jerome Greider, *Intellectuals and the State in Modern China* (New York: Free Press, 1983).

of popular sovereignty in choosing political leaders and a government subject to constitutional limitations, especially with respect to the state's power to infringe on individual liberty. Chinese democratic reforms in both of these senses were instituted at least in theory in the first post-imperial constitution, drawn up provisionally after the overthrow of the last dynasty in 1912. Even after 1949, requisite tribute was paid to the word mínzhǔ. Mao Zedong (1893–1976) himself, both before and after 1949, referred to "new-democratic government" (新民主主義, xīn mínzhǔ zhǔyì), "people's democratic dictatorship" (人民民主專政, rénmín mínzhǔ zhuān zhèng) and, borrowing from Lenin, "democratic centralism" (民主集體中製, mínzhǔ jítǐ zhōngzhì). But to the first generations of Chinese activists after Western entry, the word had primarily Western connotations. For many of them, it was clear that mínzhǔ was admirable, even essential.

With regard to social liberalism, Confucius (孔子, 551 B.C.–471 B.C) and many others before and after him emphasized the importance of distributional concerns, sometimes as a matter of basic morality and sometimes because the vast inequality in consumption and wealth threatened the stability of the state.[7] These Confucian views came under gradually harsher criticism after 1843 (when the treaties ending the first Opium War took effect) by Chinese activists of many different schools of thought. Other aspects of tradition, for example, the obligation to subordinate one's own life to the desires of one's parents, both in work and even in marriage, were criticized after first entry, and have also been the focus of extensive scholarly analysis.[8] And the story of the Chinese forced encounter with the West is often told in conjunction with Chinese adoption of more broadly liberal attitudes—toward women, toward the proper relationship among family members, and toward social change broadly speaking.[9]

---

7. See the analysis in Sungmoon Kim, "Confucianism and Acceptable Inequalities," *Philosophy and Social Criticism* 39, no. 10(December 2013): 983–1004.

8. The acceptance and even hoped-for dominance of Western social liberalism is thoroughly described in Jonathan Spence, *The Gate of Heavenly Peace: The Chinese and Their Revolution* (New York: Penguin, 1982).

9. Influential works in this genre include Jonathan Spence, *The Search for Modern China* (New York: W. W. Norton, 2012), third ed., and the papers included in Merle Goldman and Leo Ou-Fan Lee (eds.), *An Intellectual History of Modern China* (Cambridge, U.K.: Cambridge University Press, 2002).

1.A.3 Economic liberalism in particular

In contrast to this emphasis on social liberalism, little attention has been paid specifically to economic liberalism in the historical literature on post-1843 China.[10] I will take economic liberalism's political implication to be that the state should generally confine itself to enforcing property and contract rights, with a few exceptions involving major third-party effects of economic activity or substantial free-riding problems.[11] This definition is often characterized by the broader public as arguing in favor of the "free market," and to critics as "neoliberalism," with "capitalism" appropriated by both supporters and opponents of the ideology.

"Economic liberalism" is not so freighted with such meanings, and so I will generally use this less-incendiary term throughout. For supporters, its advantages include using limited resources, including labor and skill, to greater productive effect, so that both aggregate national and, over the long term, average individual wealth is greater; greater competition, assuring that prices are lower and quality is higher; greater incentive to discover socially useful knowledge, because under economic liberalism it earns the discoverer profits and thus motivates him to search for it; and less corruption, from the simple fact that the state has less power to increase some people's wealth at the expense of others, so that resources that would have been spent influencing the state are instead spent competing with other producers to try to create more value for consumers. For critics, including many in 20th-century China, economic liberalism leads to concentration of wealth, resulting in political power even-

---

10. One work does discuss economic liberalism to some degree but employs a different definition from the widely accepted one used here. Its author, William Theodore De Bary, was American, and borrowed Julius Frankel's definition of economic liberalism as "policies designed to correct imbalances of economic power." See Julius Frankel, "Intellectual Foundations of Liberalism," in *Liberalism and a Liberal Education* (New York, Columbia University Program of General Education, 1976), 3–11; William Theodore De Bary, *The Liberal Tradition in China* (Hong Kong: City University of Hong Kong Press, 1983).

11. Two landmark analyses of free-riding are Garrett Hardin, "The Tragedy of the Commons," *Science* 162, no. 3859 (December 13, 1968), 1243-1248 and Paul A. Samuelson, "The Pure Theory of Public Expenditure," *Review of Economics and Statistics* 36, no. 4 (November 1954): 386–389. Many forms of pollution are frequently characterized as free-riding on the commons of clean air and water, although people can also free-ride on the taxpayer and government-regulated commons. A telling example of robust private provision of a good that textbooks have long (and mistakenly) described as an example of free-riding can be found in Ronald Coase, "The Lighthouse in Economics," *Journal of Law and Economics* 17, no. 2 (October 1974): 357–376.

tually belonging to the wealthy, who use it for their own benefit, and cruelly.

Another aspect of economic liberalism is its acceptance of and indeed applause for economic dynamism, the idea that no contemporary economic activity should be held sacred. So when innovations (including improvements in goods or production machinery but also changes in firm organization, financing techniques, communicating with actual or potential customers, and acceptance of previously excluded classes of workers) are introduced, broad economic change can occur. Both existing firms and the institutions and customs that render existing firms less capable of satisfying individual needs must adapt or die. As long as there are few restrictions on entry, new businesses with new ideas about what to make and how to make it will ensure continuous discovery of new ways to satisfy consumer needs at lower resource cost. It will also, however, generate a significant amount of instability and economic and social change.

Dynamic economic liberalism has, according to economic liberals, over time *led to* growing social liberalism, as practices such as new business structures (e.g., the limited-liability corporation), new social freedom in the labor market (e.g., the large-scale entry of women) and so on are the results of competition for workers, requiring acceptance of social mobility and change. I will thus, following Deirdre McCloskey, sometimes emphasize the role of China's emerging new classes beginning soon after 1842—what she in general and Marie-Claire Bergère for China specifically have labeled the "bourgeoisie"—in promoting such economically driven social dynamism.[12] Thus, to merely investigate growing social liberalism without considering the growing economic liberalism that generates it is a mistake.

In sum, economic liberalism is a way of thinking about "the economy" as a whole by first thinking about the individuals who comprise it, and it recommends certain public policies— notably, free commerce through reliably enforced contract and property rights. In this, the ideology stands in contrast

---

12. McCloskey's trilogy on the role of bourgeois values and respect for the bourgeoise in what she calls the Great Enrichment of the last two-and-a-half centuries consists of: Deirdre McCloskey, *Bourgeois Equality: How Ideas, Not Capital or Institutions, Enriched the World* (Chicago: University of Chicago Press, 2017); Deirdre McCloskey, *Bourgeois Dignity: Why Economics Can't Explain the Modern World* (Chicago: University of Chicago Press, 2010); Deirdre McCloskey, *The Bourgeois Virtues: Ethics for an Age of Commerce* (Chicago: University of Chicago Press, 2006). See also Marie-Claire Bergère, *The Golden Age of the Chinese Bourgeoisie 1911–1937*, trans. by Janet Lloyd (Cambridge, UK: Cambridge University Press, 1990.

to subsequent collectivist economic thinking, which significantly influenced China to varying degrees after it encountered economic liberalism. In such collectivist thinking, society is seen either in aggregate or as the amalgamation of groups, sometimes divided into oppressors and oppressed, those with political power and those without.

1.B Why it matters

China has perhaps the world's longest continuous recorded history. Its thinkers over the centuries have explored at length questions of ethics, metaphysics, political science, and other fields. But while China also had a few thinkers who gave some consideration to economic questions, the thinking was never a part of what a good scholar had to know.

But once Western economics in the then-dominant form of economic liberalism arrived in China in the later 19th century it was seen as revolutionary, a key to Western technological and military superiority. Yet starting in the late nineteenth century, Chinese doers and thinkers began to reject economic liberalism in favor of illiberal doctrines then on the rise in the West as well, even as political and social liberalism continued for a time to have broad intellectual appeal.

The China that Westerners encountered after 1843, while subject, like other longstanding civilizations, to war and natural disasters, was in many ways economically very sophisticated. By the time of the Western Enlightenment, the Chinese had complex mercantile systems that relied on efficient transportation networks, the blood and sinews of a complex economy. At this time, some European writers were convinced of the superiority of Chinese civilization. But within several decades after first entry, many Europeans, despite inheriting this belief, developed a new image of China as an exhausted empire, with Macartney himself describing it. after his mission, as a paper tiger:

> The Empire of China is an old, crazy, first rate man-of-war, which a fortunate succession of able and vigilant officers has contrived to keep afloat these one hundred and fifty years past, and to over-awe their neighbours by her bulk and appearance, but whenever an insufficient man happens to have the command upon deck, adieu to

the discipline and safety of the ship. She may perhaps not sink outright; she may drift some time as a wreck, and will then be dashed to
pieces on the shore; but she can never be rebuilt on the old bottom.[13]

This view would be reinforced by what Westerners saw after 1843. The
Chinese soon thought so too, and both colonizers and, temporarily, some colonized thought economic liberalism was part of the cure for what ailed China. This book tells the story of its distinctive journey through modern Chinese
history. It tells the story of both ideas and of facts on the ground, of thought
on the one hand and policy and economic and social change on the other. A
primary irony of this story is that it is only now, under a government increasingly hostile to the merest hint of political liberalism, that economic liberalism
is both better understood and much more approved of. I will show that after a
promising start post-1843, the idea of economic liberalism from roughly 1927
to 1949 became progressively viewed as an obsolete, cruel, exploitive system.
In scholarship on Chinese history, the path of free markets and free-market
thinking since first entry has neither in theory nor in practice been meaningfully analyzed, nor often even defined. The initial embrace, abandonment, and
reacquaintance with economic liberalism is a neglected, yet critical, part of the
study of modern Chinese intellectual history.

This book will tell the story of the rises and falls of market economics in
China since 1843. Telling modern Chinese history this way will produce a new
way of thinking about this history and many of the events in it. Today, economic illiberalism is rising in the West and especially in the United States, in
combination with a China increasingly confident in its international position.
It is important to understand the potential appeal in China of an optimistic
economic liberalism that recommends cooperation rather than conflict, and
acceptance of social change. The now-substantial acceptance of the basics of
market competition in China should increase the Chinese public's appreciation for the decentralized source of much social progress that is such a key part
of this philosophy.

As mentioned above, some advocacy of economically liberal principles

---

13. Cited in Helen Henrietta Macartney Robbins and George Macartney, *Our First Ambassador to China:
An Account of the Life of George, Earl of Macartney, with Extracts from His Letters, and the Narrative of His
Experience* (Cambridge: Cambridge University Press, 2011), 386.

exists in the long record of Chinese scholarship, although most scholars and imperial administrators did not consistently appreciate the insights prior scholars had bequeathed them. In principle, this legacy could have coalesced to prepare Chinese for the encounter with the fully developed theory of economic liberalism that arrived in the late 19th century. Instead, it was treated as radical.

The heritage of existing ideas and the degree of competition that economic liberalism advocates are the subject of Chapter 2. Chapter 3 will discuss the initial enthusiasm for Western economic liberalism among both thinkers and commercial actors, many living outside the gilded cage of the bureaucracy. Chapter 4 will narrate the until-recently mostly neglected vibrancy of the urban middle class and the wealthy in using economic liberalism to advance the Chinese nation. This occurred even when politicians (including military leaders) and intellectuals were ensnared in struggles among each other, for territory in the first case and among competing visions of Utopia in the second; they were not up to the task of improving the life possibilities of the Chinese people. Chapter 5 will present the gradually building, violence-punctuated triumph of state direction of the economy that played out sequentially from roughly 1927 through 1949, so that economically the transition from the Kuomintang (KMT) to the Chinese Communist Party (CCP) is re-interpreted as the continuation of a trend and not a dramatic break. Chapter 6 will describe both the transition from still-extant if modest economic liberalism to essentially complete illiberalism from 1949 to 1978, and the museum-piece view of the theory of economic liberalism that was not only tolerated but officially proclaimed for 30 years after the 1949 revolution. Chapter 7 will narrate and probe the revival of economic liberalism in post-1978 China, and the changes that have been (and have yet to be) wrought there because of this school's growing triumph. The concluding chapter will test—and find wanting in some respects—the view that China is economically deliberalizing, and then explore possible futures for China. It is ironic that the government of a massive nation is committed to political illiberalism even as the people respect, and benefit from, many of the ideas of economic liberalism, and the nation confronts growing international skepticism about the role it is increasingly playing in the world.

CHAPTER 2

Initial Conditions: Chinese Economic Thought and Circumstances when Economic Liberalism Arrived

I n the roughly 150 years before first entry, numerous Enlightenment scholars in Europe had written about China, generally favorably. While some (Jean-Jacques Rousseau, [1712–1778] and the Baron de Montesquieu [1689–1755], for example), were critical and even contemptuous of what they saw as Chinese barbarism and despotism, others were not. Scholars such as Pierre Bayle (1647–1706), Gottfried Wilhelm Leibniz (1646–-1716) and Voltaire (1694–1778) received the same knowledge transmitted from Jesuits in China as did Rousseau and Montesquieu, but they admired the country's science and its ability to craft a sophisticated ethical system, even under despotism. (That China did this without monotheistic religion was appealing to some of these writers.)[14]

Yet within a few decades after the establishment of concessions—small zones inside mostly coastal Chinese cities where Chinese law could not be enforced—Western views of the Chinese people had changed substantially for the worse. Fueled by accounts of returning travelers and a newly free and opinionated Western press, the depiction of the Chinese in Great Britain and elsewhere was as a backward people, ripe for justified economic exploitation and in need of missionaries and of "civilization" more generally.

Of China's widespread poverty there could be no doubt, although it is

---

14. Simon Kow, "Enlightenment Universalism? Bayle and Montesquieu on China," *European Legacy* 19, no. 3 (2014): 347–358; Walter W. Davis, "China, the Confucian Ideal, and the European Age of Enlightenment," *Journal of the History of Ideas* 44, no. 4 (October–December 1983): 523-548.

not clear even now that it was worse than what prevailed throughout Europe on the eve of the Industrial Revolution. What is clear is that China as of 1843 had an economy that in sophistication compared favorably to Europe's. And in the long and rich history of Chinese thinking about the nature of the world, several economically liberal principles can be found, although they were never gathered together as a doctrine. This is not to argue that any of the Chinese scholars discussed below "were" economic liberals (or liberals of any kind, since at that time liberalism was a distinctively Western philosophy). Still, elements of economic liberalism were there, suggesting that the Chinese surprise upon encountering it as a package need not have been so dramatic. In this chapter, I introduce the key elements of the economically liberal society, then discuss the limited but real extent to which Chinese thinkers over the centuries had independently argued for the principles that became known in the West as economic liberalism. Finally, I look at the extent to which the Chinese economy at the time of first entry expressed these features.

2.A What does an economically liberal society look like?

The advantages of economically liberal policies depend on the existence of vigorous competition, with other firms producing substitutable products (with "products" broadly defined to include abstract ones such as ideas), using similar techniques to manufacture these products, inform consumers about them, and so on. Whether such competition truly exists is an empirical question, and what to do if it does not is a longstanding controversy. But believers in economically liberal policies leading to the best achievable outcomes assume such competition. Note that arbitrarily defining a "product" (laptop computers? laptops purchased online? computing? mobile computing? the ability to access useful information?) and observing that right now there are only a few producers of such a product, perhaps only one, is not the same as saying there is little or no competition.[15] If the product's selling price to the consumer exceeds the cost of producing it, that leaves openings for profits to be pursued by others. Those who favor economic liberalism believe that entry of other

---

15. Literally, "no competition" would imply a vertical demand curve, which is impossible as a matter of economic theory.

firms producing similar products, or better ones, will quickly compete those problems away. So competition is the key to economically liberal policies producing good social outcomes.

At the time Chinese thinkers first confronted Western political economy, the dominant work in the West by far was Adam Smith's (1723–1790) *An Inquiry into the Nature and Causes of the Wealth of Nations* (WN). Chinese attempting to understand the economic strength of the West also saw it as critically important. It was at the time a revolutionary work, and its legacy in today's economics (including as taught in China now) is substantial. Much of this legacy revolves around the social value of competition, and therefore the social cost of the state limiting it. One policy that WN took aim at was the doctrine of mercantilism, under which the goal of economic policy is to maximize exports and minimize imports, so the net inflow of gold (the primary medium of exchange in Europe and elsewhere at that time) would be maximized. In contrast, Smith advocated free international trade as preferable to state management of the flow of imports and exports between two countries. This idea, perhaps Smith's most famous, was part of a broader advocacy of the value of free competition and exchange.

There were several other contributors to the economic-liberalism (revolution France's Anne-Robert-Jacques Turgot [1727–1781] was until recently neglected in the English-speaking world), but Smith's contribution was profound, and within several decades WN was translated into numerous other European languages. As we will see in the next chapter, the book was one of only several selected for translation into Chinese by the most influential early translator of English-language books on ethics, philosophy, and political economy, who viewed it as critical for Chinese to understand why the West was so strong.

2.A.1 *Property Rights*

This is the most fundamental characteristic of an economically liberal society. Note that "property" is defined very broadly—not just tangible things, but ideas, and one's own time and skill. In addition, companies may choose to sell "services," the production of which in turn requires the use of these tangible goods. Broadly speaking, "property rights" connotes the ability to use a piece of property as one wishes, to exclude others from using it, and to transfer this authority to others.

As a practical matter, few property rights are unlimited. The ownership of a motor vehicle, for example, does not include the right to drive in ways that the state has determined endanger others. In the last half century, governments around the world have also limited the rights of property owners to use their property in ways that damage the environment.

But in general, societies that respect property rights apply exclusive rights to both resources and the things that are constructed from those resources. Note also that property rights can be vested not just in individuals but in groups or in artificial legal entities created by a group of property owners, such as the modern limited-liability corporation.

As economic liberals see it, well-defined property rights promote greater prosperity by making it easier for property to end up in the hands of people who will value it most, either through consumption or by assembling it with other property to attempt entrepreneurial ventures. Economic liberals believe that property rights are necessary, though not sufficient, to make a country as prosperous as it can be. One important vehicle through which this prosperity is built is a more fruitful division of labor. While this division was noted by other figures in other times and places (e.g., Plato in the *Republic* and Ibn Khaldun in the *Muqaddimah*[16]), Adam Smith was the first Westerner to assert it as key to what we now call economic growth.

2.A.2 Flexible pricing

As economic liberals see the world, prices will adjust in response to changes in the economic environment. If alternatives to any given product disappear, demand for that product should go up, because the substitutes are fewer. Its price should then go up, and if it does then this will elicit more quantity supplied. The opposite process plays out when a new substitute for the product is introduced—a new producer of the same good, or the introduction of a different yet competing product. When a resource is restricted in supply, it becomes scarcer and producers who desire that resource bid its price up. The price increase induces producers of the resource to incur the extra cost required to get more of it to market, raising the price of the final product. Similarly,

---

16. See Plato, *The Republic*, book 2, and Ibn Khaldun, *Muqaddimah* (مقدّمة ابن خلدون), Chapter 1.

when technological improvements (or other changes) make it possible to supply the product for less, then people who wish to sell it will compete against
one another, and the final product will sell for less.

Overall, price is a way of conveying information about how much other
people currently value a product, or the resources necessary to produce it. The
economic liberal believes that if competition is sufficient, the price conveys the
information about what we must give up in order to produce a good or to buy
this one and not that—and does so more effectively than any other information vehicle, particularly state *diktat*, can. Genuine market failures aside, prices
should thus be set by this competition among producers and consumers, rather
than controlled by the state. Given the immense amount of economic change
over time in any liberal economy, we expect prices to constantly change, so that
resources and goods are continually being moved in response to any changes
in the economic environment.

2.A.3 Information production and acquisition

Information is a key resource for producing goods when there is uncertainty
about the various uses of resources, as there always is. Information will help
a producer decide whether to install different machinery, to close a factory
(or move it elsewhere), to change the features of its products, or to make an
infinite number of other changes to the company's structure and operation. In
addition, producers must cope with changes in market circumstances beyond
their control. To acquire even some information about the existence and likely
effect of these potential changes, in other words to reduce this uncertainty, is
not free. This information must be searched for, acquired and assessed—and
even then there is no guarantee that making particular decisions based on it
will be profitable.

The cost of acquiring information depends on numerous factors. Most
obviously there is technology. Prior to Gutenberg's printing press (a process
involving block printing, not the mechanical printing mastered through a
different process in China several centuries prior), books in Europe had to
be laboriously copied by hand. Before that, information had to be carved into
stone. (Illustratively, many ancient archaeological relics of this kind involve
financial information.) The ability to transmit and consume information first
as electric signals (starting with the telegraph) and later as ones and zeros (in

computers) has dramatically lowered the cost of acquiring it. Given the role of market prices described above, financial markets and the prices that result from trading occurring in them are also a lower-cost way of generating and acquiring information, and so we have more of it to use, or, if you prefer, to cope with. In economically liberal thinking, restrictions on freedom of communication can make financially relevant information harder to acquire, and therefore are generally unwise.

2.A.4 Networks

Both to lower costs of physical transportation and of the transmission and acquisition of information, people construct networks. Examples include the long chain of people between oil drillers and gasoline buyers, or wheat farmers and people who buy and eat pasta. Final products are seldom directly plucked from the earth to be consumed as they are found; instead, they only emerge after many stages of transformation of numerous resources. Almost every product that we consume results from production and retail networks of great complexity and constant transformation, of which the consumer is almost completely ignorant. Social rules and institutions can facilitate or frustrate the construction of these transformation networks, which enable and often necessitate the construction of many more levels of intermediation between basic resources and final consumers, who often must be discovered by the final seller through another information-collection process.

2.A.5 Equality before the law; limiting corruption

In addition to emphasizing the importance of competition, WN was for its time unusually strong in its advocacy of the rights and dignity of the poor.[17] Their welfare was not Smith's only or even a central concern in WN, but he did discuss poverty, and considered it in different ways. On the one hand, he argued that in the contemporaneous United Kingdom the general standard of living was acceptable. The reason for this at that time was that the British economy was growing and had been growing for some time.[18]

---

17. Interestingly, Smith discussed the threats to Chinese national prosperity coming from what he asserted was unequal treatment of the poor there in WN I.1.8. See Smith (1976), Vol. I, 106–107.

18. See the discussion in I.1.9 and I.1.10. Smith (1976), Vol. 1, 82–100.

But what to do about the still-significant amount of poverty? The idea of the welfare state was more than a century away. Smith's remedy involved eliminating restrictions on the freedom of movement of the poor, and a more general advocacy of free competition. He was critical of government restrictions on such competition, whether it was a requirement that the poor remain in their native parish, or the British Crown handing out so many monopoly privileges, e.g., to the BEIC.[19] The idea that special interests manipulate the state for their own benefit to the detriment of the public became a key part of economic liberalism. It was popularized considerably in the 20th century through the idea of "rent-seeking," the expenditure of resources to obtain government limits on competition, a problem which goes far beyond the government-granted monopolies that Smith criticized.[20]

Smith was no anarchist or apologist for business. Among other things, for example, he worried about the dispiriting effects of factory work on workers who were doing the same mind-numbing work every day.[21] There were some things that free competition could not be trusted to do as effectively as the state, an idea that was later systematized in the twentieth century in the various forms of what came to be called market failure. But among his core ideas that might have been relevant for China in the late 19th century are these: people's consumption, and not the country's gold stocks or the balance of payments, was the measure of an economy's soundness; the importance of genuinely free competition, including free international trade; and special state privileges as an obstacle to higher standards of living.

2.A.6 Dynamism
Also important in economic liberalism is its dynamism; what is economically

---

19. Many who argue that Smith was a skeptic of big business cite a famous line from Volume I, book 1, chapter 10, "People of the same trade seldom meet together, even for merriment and diversion, but the conversation ends in a conspiracy against the public, or in some contrivance to raise prices." The subsequent sentences indicate that clearly the "conspiracies" he was referring to were efforts to get the government to limit the competition these "people of the same trade" faced, e.g., by requiring craftsmen to serve seven-year apprenticeships. Smith (1976), Vol. I, 144.

20. Krueger, Anne O., "The Political Economy of the Rent-Seeking Society," *American Economic Review* 64, no. 3 (June 1974): 291--303; Tullock, Gordon, "The Welfare Costs of Tariffs, Monopolies, and Theft," *Western Economic Journal* 5, no. 3 (June 1967): 224–232.

21. WN II.V.3. Smith (1976), Vol. II, 392–303.

important today may be obsolete tomorrow. This follows from the costly information assumption in section 2.A.3 above. When one or more firms is producing in a costly or inefficient way, others may observe that there are better ways to provide what consumers want. This can mean changing the product or the method of producing it.

To say that information is costly is to say that production decisions, especially novel ones, are fraught with uncertainty. In the end some decisions will be right, others wrong. But the right ones will ensure that costs go down, consumer satisfaction goes up, or both. In a two-steps-forward, one-step-back kind of way, old ways are abandoned, new ones adopted. Society is thus continually reshaped, sometimes gradually and sometimes quickly and radically. When economic liberalism is on full display, new companies are constantly born, old ones continuously disappear, and there is a constant flow of new products that cause the way society is structured to change, sometimes fundamentally. (Humanity's current re-organizing of itself because of ongoing breakthroughs in high technology is a vivid current example.) The dynamic, uncertain processes of free competition, whose effects on China are documented in Chapter 4, can be usefully contrasted with the radical, detailed, and comprehensive changes to Chinese economic and social structure that some Chinese intellectuals advocated in the 20th century, a process described in Chapters 5 and 6.

Competition-driven dynamism is perhaps not entirely to the good, and people will oppose it both for that reason and because their own interests are threatened. In contrast, classic conservatism argues that the reason society is structured the way it is may be lost on people currently alive, but hard lessons were learned in the past from doing things differently, and so it is important to respect tradition's tacit, accumulated knowledge. The transformations economic growth generates might therefore call for restraint. Another criticism of continuous, spontaneous transformation is the recent idea of "sustainability." In this view, buyers and sellers agreeing through decentralized, market-based exchange give insufficient account of the long-term effects of their decisions (e.g., climate change) on others, born and unborn.

While Smith acknowledged some concerns about the social effects of his "commercial society," its heedless damaging of traditional social structure or ignorance of its effects on future generations were not major themes in WN.

He did argue that one could distinguish between more and less advanced societies, and a society might be limited in the degree of prosperity it could attain because of its institutions. But what Smith in his time called the "progress of opulence" was not particularly fast, nor did it accelerate because of dramatic technological breakthroughs; such thinking was a fruit of the Industrial Revolution.[22] But this potential for continuous growth and transformation in the ways we live is a substantial part of economic liberalism today.

So an economically liberal society must have a core of people who are accepting of this sort of dynamism, this irregular but substantial long-run socioeconomic change. But it is mistaken to say that economic liberalism demands that the government be entirely divorced from the economy. In addition to the general economically liberal principles of enforcing property and contract rights, numerous economic liberals have over time advocated measures to elevate the standard of living of the poorest to some minimally acceptable level, a level that can rise in tandem with overall social wealth. The more generally these welfare-state benefits apply (through universal basic income or a minimally disruptive single-payer health-care system, for example) and the simpler and more stable the tax system used to fund them (a fixed income-tax schedule with few if any deductions or credits, for example), the more acceptable such social insurance is. But the use of public monies to elevate the poor should not limit the ability of companies, including individual entrepreneurs, to try the sorts of experiments that economic liberals believe on balance move society forward, much better in fact then centrally directed attempts to regiment society.

This dynamic argument was laid out forcefully in John Stuart Mill's *On Liberty*. Among other arguments for presuming liberty, here Mill raised the value of social experiments under conditions of incomplete information:

> It will not be denied by anybody, that originality is a valuable element in human affairs. There is always need of persons not only to

22. WN Volume I, Book 3, chapter 1 is entitled "Of the Natural Progress of Opulence." Smith (1976), Vol. 1, 401–406. Dylan Dellisanti has argued that Smith, while appreciating the relation between economic liberalism and dynamism, purposely rhetorically downplayed it to make his argument more acceptable. Dylan Dellisanti, "The Dynamism of Liberalism: An Esoteric Interpretation of Adam Smith," Journal of Economic Behavior and Organization, 184 (April 2021): 717-726.

discover new truths, and point out when what were once truths are true no longer, but also to commence new practices, and set the example of more enlightened conduct, and better taste and sense in human life. This cannot well be gainsaid by anybody who does not believe that the world has already attained perfection in all its ways and practices.[23]

That the free society will change, and generally for the better, is taken for granted. Mill also wrote a textbook on political economy, and while he was one of the first to grapple with market-failure arguments against unbridled economic liberalism (analyzed more rigorously beginning in the early 20th century), he, like Smith, appreciated the ability of economic competition not just to allocate a fixed set of resources more effectively, but to more broadly increase human possibilities. Herbert Spencer in The *Study of Sociology* also talked of the dynamism of human society when left to its own devices:

[T]ake a social appliance, as the Press, and see how from the news-letter, originally private and written, and then assuming the shape of a printed fly-leaf to a written private letter, there has slowly evolved this vast assemblage of journals and periodicals, daily, weekly, general, and local, that have, individually and as an aggregate, grown in size while growing in heterogeneity;—do this, and do the like with all other established institutions, agencies, products, and there will come naturally the conviction that now, too, there are various germs of things which will in the future develop in ways no one imagines, and take shares in profound transformations of society and of its members: transformations that are hopeless as immediate results, but certain as ultimate results.[24]

In sum, economic liberalism as Chinese thinkers confronted it in the late 19th century had the following features:

1. *Minimal political interference in market processes.* Changes in

23. Mill, *On Liberty*, 128–129.

24. Herbert Spencer, *The Study of Sociology* (New York: D. Appleton, 1904), 119.

market prices solicit the most desirable responses from buyers and sellers. Special government privileges are destructive of justice and market efficiency, and an economically
liberal society will take steps to minimize them. Advocacy
of free trade, almost literally unthinkable in China shortly before first entry, is part of this principle, but far from the
only one.[25]

2.   *Growing complexity over time.* The building of networks—e.g., the workforce within individual companies,
connections among different companies in different industries, the linking of people pursuing the same broad purpose
but perhaps with different methods, or among buyers, sellers, and intermediaries—should grow over time, and prosperity should increase accordingly. The division of labor is
constantly evolving.

3.   *Expectation, and to a substantial degree a welcoming one, of economic change—of companies and industries rising and falling.*
There is nothing special about whatever exists right now.

2.B Chinese economic thought before contact with Western economic liberalism

When Chinese travelers and scholars in the later 19th century first encountered
these ideas through European economic writings, how much of this was genuinely new to them?

With a written corpus of over 2000 years, it would be surprising if Chinese
intellectual activity never turned toward the economic arena. And, indeed,
before the discovery of European economic thought there were writings on
the relation between commercial activity and social welfare, the same matters
that had drawn significant commentary from Western thinkers even before
the development of economic liberalism.

---

25. There were intervals in Chinese history when trade over both land and sea was relatively free. But the
late Qing, just before first entry, was not among them.

However, the Chinese intellectuals most respected by subsequent generations wrote primarily on ethics, metaphysics, and history. To subsequent generations, these often took the form of collected works associated with particular scholars, but possibly written partly or even entirely by those scholars' students and other disciples. (Some ancient Greek works, especially before Plato, are similar in this regard.) But from the perspective of contemporaneous scholars consulting past works, there was little to choose from that specifically concerned "economics."

Yet a few Chinese thinkers whose influence persisted for centuries after, and since the overthrow of the Qing Dynasty persists today among specialists, anticipated by centuries some economically liberal principles, even if they did not consider them central, or united. It will be important to emphasize the European Enlightenment origins of liberalism and its focus on the individual and his (and eventually her) rights. No similar doctrine existed in China. But there were isolated strands of economically liberal thought in China, even if the people who conceived it were not in any broad sense economic liberals.

As was true in other pre-modern civilizations of any sophistication, several principles concerning the distribution of wealth were important in the history of Chinese economic thought. While the modest goods the average person used and consumed often were made purely within the family or by single artisans and thus did not require multiple-person firms, there was great wealth to be made by merchants, who would transport goods across great distances. But with great wealth came the possibility of bribing rulers from the monarch on down, bribes that might be initiated (or coerced) by the rulers themselves.

Since time immemorial, bribes to overlook breaches of the law have been offered unsolicited by those on the supply side seeking special government privileges, or demanded by rulers in the position to do someone this favor. On the latter bribe-demand side, rulers at all levels had to juggle the personal benefits of bribes with their effects on the wealth of and inequality in their realm. So in China as in most other societies, neither the political benefits nor the broader ethics of *laissez-faire* were always accepted, and never clearly stated. Again, the idea of freedom—not to mention Smith's tying it into a broader ethical system that included economic freedom—simply did not loom large in Chinese thinking. And in the traditional Chinese moral code, the possession or absence of individual wealth was at best immaterial to the individual's morality, at worst shameful; men were praised or condemned primarily to the extent that their lives were conducted in agreement with the codes for obligations to family, seniors, the poor, etc. And certainly, pursuing wealth at the expense of cultivating one's own virtue was discouraged, even more so in the writings of neo-Confucianist scholars.[26] The default view, in other words, was that being rich did society no favors, and presumptively made the rich person's moral worth suspect. But individual economically liberal ideas were there.

2.B.1 The Guanzi

While in current usage The *Guanzi* is named after a high-level official known as Guanzhong (管仲, c. 720 BC–645 BC) in the pre-unification state of Qi (齊), this work is, like many classic Chinese works, of uncertain authorship. And like other such works where economic wisdom is to be found, it was not per se about the economy or even commerce. But it had things to say about these arenas, and some of them are similar to elements of economically liberal thought as the West later defined it.[27]

The *Guanzi* did raise the idea of resource mobility continuing until its rate of return is equalized across different uses, an idea only presented centuries later, albeit in more depth, by the Europeans Turgot and Smith.[28] In China, though, the resource in question was people. The *Guanzi* did this in the form of asserting that people would migrate from farm to town when incomes were higher in the latter, and both temporary physical conditions and the burden of taxation could affect the tendency to do so.[29] Elsewhere it spoke of an inevitable tradeoff between keeping farm incomes high and keeping food prices stable in the towns. But the *Guanzi* differed from Enlightenment Western economic liberalism in seeing markets not as a means for buyers and sellers to further their interests but as a necessary evil fit only for smaller kingdoms. In

---

26. Florence Chan, "The Money Making in Ancient China: A Literature Review Journey Through Ancient Texts" *Journal of Business Ethics* 91, supplement 1 (2010: 17–35.

27. An English translation is W. Allyn Rickett, *Guanzi: Political, Economic and Philosophical Essays from Early China* (Princeton: Princeton University Press, 1998).

28. On Turgot, see Anthony Brewer, "Turgot: Founder of Classical Economics," *Economica*, New Series, 54, no. 216 (November 1987): 417–428.

29. Richard von Glahn, *The Economic History of China: From Antiquity to the Nineteenth Century* (Cambridge, UK: Cambridge University Press, 2016), 77.

fact the true king, the ruler of a peaceful and large kingdom (both measures of a successful dynasty, as to some degree was the implied definition also in Europe) did not need independent food markets cluttering up the city.[30] And commerce was valuable not because it promoted a higher standard of living but because it generated more taxes to fund the things that only the state can do.

The *Guanzi* also reveals that in some respects economic thought in China was at this point far ahead of the West. In its discussion of the role of accurate information in generating profits for those who possessed it, it included the following remarks:

> Merchants observe outbreaks of dearth and starvation, scrutinize changes in the fortunes of states, study the patterns of the four seasons, and take notice of what goods are produced in each place. With this knowledge of prices in the marketplace, they gather up their stock of goods, load them on oxcarts and horses, and circulate throughout the four directions. Having reckoned what is abundant and what is scarce and calculated what is precious and what is worthless, they exchange what they possess for what they lack, buying cheap and selling dear ... Marvelous and fantastic things arrive in timely fashion; rare and unusual goods readily gather. Day and night thus engaged, merchants tutor their sons and brothers, speaking the language of profit, teaching them the virtue of timeliness, and training them how to recognize the value of goods.[31]

The claim that merchants succeeded when they knew what was desired was not unknown in the pre-Enlightenment West, but not an influential insight. Thomas Aquinas in the *Summa Theologica* argued that up to a point it is not wrong for a merchant who knows that goods are desperately needed in a particular location and makes the effort to bring them there to charge a higher price.[32] But until the 18th century there was nothing in Western thinking

---

30. Ibid., 73.

31. Translation from Von Glahn (2016), 78.

32. See the discussion in Victor C. Klaar, "Ethics and Economics," in *21st Century Economics: A Reference Handbook*, ed. Rhona C. Free (London: Sage, 2010), 891–900.

about the economic importance of information—widely accepted today—that was as detailed as the above passage from the *Guanzi*. In fact, the first systematic treatment of the role of the entrepreneur in taking risks and searching for information that he hopes will be profitable was presented in the nineteenth century in a German-language textbook by Carl Menger.[33] Yet in *The Guanzi*, written in an era when most production was agricultural in nature, the entrepreneur almost inevitably was a merchant. In the 20th century, economists of what came to be known as the Austrian School began to emphasize the role of information that was scattered and costly to discover and accumulate, and the role of market prices in conveying it. But mainstream economics waited until the second half of that century before giving it substantial attention, even constructing precise hypotheses of how market prices could tell producers what was more valuable and consumers what was more costly.[34]

2.B.2 Sima Qian

A classic Chinese historical work is *Records of the Grand Historian* (史記), most of which was written by the imperial historian Sima Qian (司馬遷, c.145 B.C–87 B.C.). The book, which he wrote in private and was only released after his death under the authority of his grandson, is even now seen by scholars of Chinese history as one of the most important works ever written in that genre. It is a sequence of essays on important historical figures, including what he thought to be every emperor up to the then-current one.

Sima (his surname had two characters, unusual for Chinese names) was again no pure economic theorist and certainly no unalloyed economic liberal, who believed that market forces should never be restrained by the state, but there were elements of his economic thought that would have found later approval among liberal Europeans. His economic instincts emerge in book 129, a biography of 40 famous wealthy men in Chinese history. Some were merchants, others manufacturers. He specifically described these men as, like all of us, pursuing Smithian self-interest. He went on:

---

33. First published as Carl Menger, *Grundsatzē der Volkswirtschafster* (Wien: Wilhelm Braumüller, 1871) (Carl Menger, *Principles of Economics* [Vienna: Wilhelm Braumüller, 1871]).

34. George Stigler, "The Economics of Information," *Journal of Political Economy* 69, no. 3 (June 1961): 213–225; Friedrich A. Hayek, "The Uses of Knowledge in Society," *American Economic Review* 35, no. 4 (September 1945): 519–530.

Though only commoners with no special ranks or titles, they were able, without interfering with the government or hindering the activities of the people, to accrue that wealth by making the right moves at the right time. Wise men will find something to learn from them.[35]

Here he is echoing *The Guanzi* on profit flowing from possessing better information. And he continued on this theme and explicitly distinguished, as a modern economic liberal well might, between those who benefit from special privileges versus those who benefit from acquiring such information:

These, then, were examples of outstanding and unusually wealthy men. None of them enjoyed any titles or fiefs, gifts, or salaries from the government, nor did they play tricks with the law or commit any crimes to acquire their fortunes. They simply guessed which course conditions were going to take and acted accordingly, kept a sharp eye out for the opportunities of the times, and so were able to capture a fat profit.[36]

In other words, money is to be made by *knowing more than one's competitors*. Sima was arguably centuries ahead of his time on several other liberal-economic themes:

Society obviously must have farmers before it can eat; foresters, fishermen, miners, etc., before it can make use of natural resources; craftsmen before it can have manufactured goods; and merchants before they can be distributed. But once these exist, what need is there for government directives, mobilizations of labour, or periodic assemblies? Each man has only to be left to utilize his own abilities and exert his strength to obtain what he wishes. Thus, when a commodity is very cheap, it invites a rise in price; when it is very

35. Translation from Sima Qian, *Records of the Grand Historian, Vol. II: The Age of Emperor Wu 142 to circa 100 B.C.*), transl. Burton Watson (New York: Renditions-Columbia University Press, 1961), 476.

36. Ibid., 498.

expensive, it invites a reduction. When each person works away at his own business then, like water flowing downward, goods will naturally flow forth ceaselessly day and night without having been summoned, and the people will produce commodities without having been asked.[37]

This is very much an Adam Smith invisible-hand type of argument, and hints again at Smith's claim that rates of return tend to equalize through resource flows from the lower- to the higher-return industry. So reminiscent in fact are Sima's arguments to some of those of Smith's that economists have debated among themselves whether Smith learned of Sima's thinking to some degree via Turgot before writing WN; an exchange on this very question was held over several years in an economic journal.[38]

Sima also discussed the difference between wealth accrued through creating value versus through limiting competition, the latter category including robbery, grave-robbing, fraud, corruption, and bribery. Here he anticipated to some extent the idea of rent-seeking, and the point was as much an economic liberal's as an ethicist's—such efforts not only deserve opprobrium, they limit competition and distort economic activity and thus destroy productive potential.

2.B.3 Xunzi

Xunzi (荀子, c. 310 BC – c. 256 BC) was a Confucian scholar who wrote during the period in which the Eastern Zhou dynasty (770 B.C.–266 B.C.) was falling apart, to be replaced after several decades of disorder by the Qin in 256 B.C. He took the view, like many other Confucian scholars, that people were born

37. *Ibid.*, 477.

38. For the argument that Sima saw what Smith saw in WN over a millennium and a half before, and that Smith came by the arguments from Turgot during Smith's trip to France, see Leslie Young, "The Tao of Markets: Sima Qian and the Invisible Hand," *Pacific Economic Review* 2, no. 1 (September 1996): 137–45. For an argument that the documented timing of Smith's development of the arguments indicate he came by them independently, see Y. Stephen Chiu and Ryh-Song Yeh, "Adam Smith versus Sima Qian: Comment on the Tao of Markets," *Pacific Economic Review* 4, no. 1 (February 1999), 79–84; Ken McCormick, "Sima Qian and Adam Smith," *Pacific Economic Review* 4, no. 1 (February 1999): 85-87.

bad but could continuously improve through self-cultivation.[39] And in out-lining principles both of social organization and such cultivation by a king, he claimed to provide the recipe for a strong, prosperous kingdom. In *The Rule of a True King* (《王制篇》) Xunzi proposed a hypothesis for why humans, who are physically weaker than many of the animals, nonetheless came to control both them and the environment overall:

> Water and fire have substance but do not live. Plants live but are not conscious. Animals are conscious but have no virtue. People have all of these things, and are the most precious thing under heaven. They are not as powerful as the ox, and cannot run like the horse. How is it that humans can use all of these animals? Unlike these animals, they can work together. How is it that people can work together? Through the division of tasks. And how is it that this can be implemented? Because of virtue, which leads to a division of tasks and therefore harmony. Harmony makes people united. With unity, capacity is increased, and with increased capacity comes increased strength. And with strength the world can be mastered. People can thus construct buildings and inhabit them. The four seasons can then be managed, and the things of the world can be organized, doubling the usefulness of everything under heaven. There is no other cause. To achieve the division of tasks is thus its own virtue. Therefore humanity must have virtue and specialize. To work together without dividing tasks leads to conflict. Conflict leads to disorder. Disorder leads to separation. Separation leads to

---

39. Xunzi was not a comprehensive liberal; liberalism being a Western movement, no single Chinese thinker was. In "The Nature of Man is Evil" (性惡), he took a dimmer view of human nature uncorrected, arguing that "[i]t is the original nature and feelings of man to love profit and seek gain" (「夫好利而欲得者, 此人之情性也」). Here "gain" is perhaps not expressed in the essentially neutral way that Adam Smith in WN talked of the seller's "interest." Rather, Xunzi employed 利 (lì), a word with a generally more negative characterization in premodern Chinese writing. Xunzi 23.9, translation from Wing-Tsit Chan, *A Sourcebook in Chinese Philosophy* (Princeton, NJ: Princeton University Press, 1963), 130.

weakness. And if there is weakness nature cannot be organized.[40]

Xunzi did add the Confucian fillip of "virtue," but also spoke like Smith and Turgot of "harmony" (what economists today might call "equilibrium") in the division of labor. Elsewhere in *The Rule of a True King* he wrote in a way reminiscent of one of Smith's perspectives in WN:

A king should tax uniformly, should manage the people's affairs and all things in nature well, and in this way nurture the people. Taxes should be set at one-tenth of the land's produced income. At checkpoints and markets, implement the necessary inspections but levy no other taxes. The mountains, forests, bodies of water and bridges should open and close punctually, and there should be no taxes levied there. Tax land according to its productivity. Assess the necessary tributes according to the distance traveled. Let finances and grains flow freely, without obstruction. Allow free movement between places, so that the world within the four seas is like a family. In this way, those close at hand need not hide their talents, and those far away need not detest working. Even in remote and secluded countries, there are none who will not be happy to rush to such a place.[41]

In other words, taxes should be stable and low. They should not be imposed merely to increase revenue but in accordance with economic reasoning. This will encourage mobility of resources, which will improve society's functioning. In the same work, Xunzi even described how China could "use" things located or made far away by trading for them, so that specialization and trade increase

40. 「水火有氣而無生，草木有生而無知，禽獸有知而無義，人有氣、有生、有知，亦且有義，故最為天下貴也。力不若牛，走不若馬，而牛馬為用，何也？曰：人能群，彼不能群也。人何以能群？曰：分。分何以能行？曰：義。故義以分則和，和則一，一則多力，多力則彊，彊則勝物；故宮室可得而居也。故序四時，裁萬物，兼利天下，無它故焉，得之分義也。」《荀子》，王制篇第九，19-20 (Xunzi 9, *The Rule of a True King* 19-20, https://ctext.org/xunzi/wang-zhi) (author's translation).

41. 「王者之：等賦、政事、財萬物，所以養萬民也。田野什一，關市幾而不征，山林澤梁，以時禁發而不稅。相地而衰政。理道之遠近而致貢。通流財物粟米，無有滯留，使相歸移也，四海之內若一家。故近者不隱其能，遠者不疾其勞，無幽閒隱僻之國，莫不趨使而安樂之。夫是之為人師。是王者之法也。」Ibid., 16 (author's translation).

wealth not just in small villages but across great distances:

> How is it that the northern coast has wild horses and dogs, yet the center of the country is able to have livestock? How is it that the southern coast has feathers and quills, tusks and leather, but the center of the country is able to have wealth? How is it that the eastern coast has purple fabrics, and has fish and salt, yet the center of the country has food and clothes? How is it that the western coast has pelts and leather, and patterned banners, yet the center of the country can use it? Because of this, the people of the water have enough wood, those of the mountains enough fish, the farmers need not cut down their trees nor make their own pottery nor smelt their own tools to use, and merchants and craftsmen need not plow fields, yet still have enough to eat. And so, while it is the tiger and leopard who are fierce, it is the gentleman who uses these things. And so creation is transformed and used, and the ground is used to convey them all. None of their beauty is consumed, but their use results in adornments on the surface while beneath it is the nourishment and contentment of the people. As the 'Book of Poetry' has it, 'After heaven creates the mountains, the king's realm is empty. When men build, the king and his realm are at peace.' This is what is described here.[42]

And yet the match between Xunzi and Smith is far from perfect. In the first and fifth sections of Xunzi 10, *Enriching the Nation* (《富國》), whose title itself reminds one of WN, Xunzi spoke of the necessity of the division of labor in producing prosperity and avoiding conflict emanating from the inability to cooperate, but from this premise argued that social classes ought to be permanent, and that the wise king rigorously observes the necessary social reg-

---

42. 『北海則有走馬吠犬焉, 然而中國得而畜使之。南海則有羽翮、齒革、曾青、丹干焉, 然而中國得而財之。東海則有紫紶、魚鹽焉, 然而中國得而衣食之。西海則有皮革、文旄焉, 然而中國得而用之。故澤人足乎木, 山人足乎魚, 農夫不斲削、不陶冶而足械用, 工賈不耕田而足菽粟。故虎豹為猛矣, 然君子剝而用之。故天之所覆, 地之所載, 莫不盡其美, 致其用, 上以飾賢良, 下以養百姓而安樂之。夫是之謂大神。《詩》曰：「天作高山, 大王荒之；彼作矣, 文王康之。」此之謂也』*Ibid.*, 17 (author's translation).

imentation.[43]

But he waxed positively Lockean when writing in "On Nature" (《天論》, *Tiānlùn*):

> Instead of regarding all under Heaven as great and admiring it, why not foster it as a thing and regulate it? Instead of obeying Heaven and singing praise to it, why not control the Mandate of Heaven and use it? Instead of observing the seasons and waiting for them, why not respond to them and make use of them? Instead of letting things multiply by themselves, why not exercise your ability to transform [and increase] them? Instead of thinking about things as things, why not attend to them so you won't lose them? Instead of admiring how things come into being, why not do something to bring them to full development?[44]

So Xunzi, writing over 1500 years before Smith, and in a society with no tradition at that point of thinking in terms of individual liberty, saw the economic gains from the division of labor much as Adam Smith would. But unlike Smith, the idea of individuals possessing the *right* to do the work someone was willing to hire them to do did not occur to him. And of course he was nothing like an advocate of broader liberalism. But with respect to economic liberalism, key elements were there.

2.B.4 Dynamism

We saw that dynamism was not a central focus of economic theory in 18th-century Western political economy. But by the mid-19th century, with the Industrial Revolution in full flower, there was discussion in Europe inside and outside of political economy of the benefits and costs of rapid economic and therefore social change, driven from below by competing economic experiments. As we saw, John Stuart Mill viewed free competition from the bottom

---

43. See in particular 荀子, 《富國》, 第一篇和第五篇 (Xunzi 10, *Enriching the Nation*, 10.1 and 10.5).

44. 「大天而思之, 孰與物畜而制之！從天而頌之, 孰與制天命而用之！望時而待1之, 孰與應時而使之！因物而多之, 孰與騁2能而化之！思物而物之, 孰與理物而勿失之也！願於物之所以生, 孰與有物之所以成！故錯人而思天, 則失萬物之情。」荀子, 《天論》, 第十五篇 (Xunzi 17.15, "On Nature," translation from Chan, *Sourcebook*, 122).

rather than regimentation from the top as essential in sorting the good from the bad experiments (whether "economic" or not). And during his lifetime many experimental social institutions were conceived of and built in an attempt to discover something better than the existing world, seemingly deeply impoverished both materially and spiritually. These institutions were generated by what was increasingly called "capitalism."[45] Regardless of whether it was seen as desirable or lamentable, rapid social change was now the signature feature of modernity in the later 19th-century West.

What were Chinese views over the centuries about spontaneous, undirected social change? There is a default view, enunciated by Chinese themselves in the early twentieth century, that Chinese ethics, particularly in their Confucian reverence for ancient authority, were a primary obstacle to needed social reform. (Attempts to combat this attitude will be investigated in more detail in subsequent chapters.) In contrast, before the beginning of the Industrial Revolution this belief in dynamism was already instantiated in Europe. Along with Turgot, Francis Bacon (1561–1626), René Descartes (1596–1650), and Bernard Le Bovier de Fontenelle (1657–1757) were among those arguing that unpredictable, continuous progress in technology and science was desirable and in any event inevitable. The extension of this idea to "economic" progress was not completed by the time of Western first entry. But an understanding of the nature and impact of economic dynamism had begun. But Adam Smith had first acknowledged gradual progress in a society's standard of living, Mill later emphasized social improvement through decentralized, competitive experimentation, and Darwin's idea of biological change was published in 1859. These thinkers in combination indicate that the West could understand, if not always justify, the rapid socioeconomic change that started with industrialization in the late 18th century. As we will see in Chapter 5, in China a warped vision of Darwinian competition among societies would contribute to the abandonment of economic liberalism in the early 20th century.

In contrast, traditionally Chinese championed a return to the mythical past rather than creating an as-yet unknown future. There was frequent reference to the ancient kings as "sages" (聖人) and an associated idea of dynastic

---

45. Evan Osborne, *Self-Regulation and Human Progress: How Society Gains When We Govern Less* (Palo Alto, CA: Stanford University Press, 2018), esp. Chapter 5.

ethical triumphs and failures, with corresponding consequences for the dynasties' fate. The Confucian idea of an individual's potential for ethical perfectibility contrasted with traditional Western focus on the individual as carrying the burden of original sin.[46] And so China lacked an underlying social premise, which the West assumed, that society could consistently improve through trial and error.

Agreeing with the necessity of reverting to the ancient practices was not universal. Buddhism had its Ming thinkers who advocated independent thought, for example in the group of writers known as the "Left Wang School" (王學左派), including people such as Wang Gen (王艮, 1483–1541). The Tao Te Ching (《道德經》) is a work usually attributed to Laozi, a possibly fictional or composite figure about whom little is known, who is sometimes said to have lived just prior to Confucius. The work, also known as the Laozi, is often summarized as advising individuals to understand and reconcile themselves to the Way (道) rather than trying to actively bend the world to their will. Such a belief is not obviously friendly to the idea of the active entrepreneur of economic liberalism. But there is a well-known passage in section 57 of that collection that argues:

> One can use rectification to govern a country, one can use the military unconventionally, but to control the world one must avoid action and purpose. How do I know? From these: the more prohibitions there are on earth, the greater the poverty of the people; the more the people use their things to pursue their own interest, the greater will be social disorder; the craftier the people, the more strange occurrences there will be; the more the laws and orders are emphasized, the more thieves there will be. Thus, a sage has said: I will do nothing purposefully, and the people will transform themselves; I will remain motionless, and the people will rectify themselves; I will be inactive, and the people will enrich themselves; I

46. 談遠平。《中國政治思想：儒家與民主化》，台北市，揚智文化事業，2004 (Tan Yuanping, *Chinese Political Thought: Confucianism and Democratization* [Taipei: Yang-Chih Book Co., 2004]).

will have no ambitions, and the people will be content as they are.[47]

So there is modest overlap between what is preached here and economic liberalism. Thus the difficulty in admiring the agency of an entrepreneur who affirmatively acts is just as easily directed at the active minister or other official who affirmatively interferes in market ordering. So perhaps Daoism is consistent with *laissez-faire*. Even so, prior to first entry the idea of social improvement (not just mere change) was often a tough sell in Chinese scholarship. It is surely overstating matters to say, as Jean Chesneaux et al. did, that "progress" was "a notion which was almost unknown to Chinese thought."[48] There was progress, as in agricultural technology, but it was very gradual and often funded by or through political authorities.

Prosperity was in fact considered by Chinese thinkers. For example, Chen Hongmou (陳宏謀, 1696–1771), was very interested in questions of prosperity and what the government could do to promote it. But his imagination did not extend beyond, in Joel Mokyr's telling, the existing activities of "mining, commerce, and manufacturing."[49] Both the bureaucracy and business pressure groups usually did not seek change, and certainly not disruptive change but "stability and prosperity."[50] The kind of unplanned, dramatic, rapid change that by 1842 was a characteristic of some Western countries would have been almost inconceivable in this intellectual framework.

Overall, many elements of economic liberalism were found in various places in ancient Chinese thought, but there was no liberal economic doctrine, nor indeed any economic doctrine. Nonetheless, given the substantial but not complete agreement of the scattered pieces of Chinese economic thought

---

47. 「以正治國，以奇用兵，以無事取天下。吾何以知其然哉？以此：天下多忌諱，而民彌貧；民多利器，國家滋昏；人多伎巧，奇物滋起；法令滋彰，盜賊多有。故聖人云：我無為，而民自化；我好靜，而民自正；我無事，而民自富；我無欲，而民自樸。」老子，《道德經》，第五十號篇 (Laozi, Tao Te Ching, 57, author's translation).

48. Jean Chesneaux, Marianne Bastid, and Marie-Claire Bergère, *China from the Opium Wars to the 1911 Revolution*, transl. Anne Destenay (New York: Random House, 1976), 236.

49. Joel Mokyr, *A Culture of Growth: The Origins of the Modern Economy* (Princeton, NJ: Princeton University Press, 2017), 331.

50. Loren Brandt, Debin Ma, and Thomas G. Rawski, "From Divergence to Convergence: Reevaluating the History Behind China's Economic Boom," *Journal of Economic Literature* 52, no. 1 (March 2014): 45–123, 105.

with Western liberal economic principles, we might expect that the economy in 1842 would have some of the characteristics consistent with liberal policy. As is the case with economic thinking, the Chinese historical record reflects many but not all characteristics of economic liberalism. Middlemen merchants and commercial networks, yes; thoroughly free markets and complete property rights, not so much. In particular, the high political leadership was viewed as having absolute theoretical authority to control economic activity, and leaders often controlled it to the degree they could during times of disaster or to moderate price fluctuations.

Yet it is hard to deny that much of what would later be depicted as revolutionary in the economic liberalism that China encountered, notably in WN, had been argued in several core works in the extensive Chinese written record, as indicated in the following comparison with Dugald Stewart. Perhaps the single most powerful summary of Adam Smith's views on economic matters, which he would present later at length in WN, was presented in a talk Stewart gave at the Royal Society in Edinburgh over two days, which he called "Account of the Life and Writings of Adam Smith, LL.D." It was based in part on notes taken by Smith's students while Smith was a professor of moral philosophy at the University of Glasgow in the 1750s and 1760s. The record of the speech includes the following remarks:

> Little else is requisite to carry a state to the highest degree of opulence from the lowest barbarism, but peace, easy taxes, and a tolerable administration of justice; all the rest being brought about by the natural course of things. All governments which thwart this natural course, which force things into another channel, or which endeavour to arrest the progress of society at a particular point, are unnatural, and to support themselves are obliged to be oppressive and tyrannical.[51]

This compares quite favorably to the above remarks from Xunzi's *The Rule of a True King* 16. There he argued that a monarch who ruled virtuously would

---

51. Dugald Stewart, "Account of the Life and Writings of Adam Smith," in Dugald Stewart, *The Works of Dugald Stewart in Seven Volumes* Vol. 7 (Cambridge, UK: Hilliard and Brown, 1829), 64.

preside over a peaceful realm where wealth would accumulate. One passage is particularly striking:

> The gentleman [king] relies on ethics, and the common people on strength. Those who rely on strength serve the king. For those with strength, wait for a time and later they will succeed, their collective will be peaceful, their wealth will gather together, their potential will be actualized, their skills will be secure, their means will increase.[52]

This is not an invisible-hand argument, but it is an argument that growth is natural given only certain conditions. Here the emphasis is on the virtue of the ruler, rather than the more Smithian model of good governance, but in combination Xunzi, writing many centuries earlier and thousands of miles away, offered a reasonable facsimile of parts of 18th-century European economic liberalism. Smith emphasized the tyrannical nature of government direction of the economy, and this element was missing in Chinese thinking before first entry, but the wisdom of low, stable taxes, and elements of Smith's invisible hand in guiding resource use can be found.

Why was Western liberal political economy so much more influential than similar previous thinking in China? There are several reasons. First, as noted above, scholars in China when writing preferred to focus on political, metaphysical, historical and ethical questions. When touching upon economic matters it was usually in the service of these larger purposes. Sima Qian, for example, was urging a rethinking of the *ethics* of profit-seeking when he had his insights about decentralized information. And by 1842, "political economy" was a specific field of inquiry in Europe and North America, while in China it was not. Works such as WN and Turgot's *Reflections* were already following earlier writers (the physiocrats, for example) in trying to explain economic outcomes in a scientific way. Given the widespread growth of scientific inquiry at the same time in Enlightenment Europe, this is not surprising. Finally, Europe

---

52. Xunzi, *Enriching the Nation* 6 (《富國》6: 「君子以德, 小人以力；力者, 德之役也。百姓之力, 待之而後功；百姓之群, 待之而後和；百姓之財, 待之而後聚；百姓之埶, 待之而後安；百姓之壽, 待之而後長。」) (author's translation). In section 8 Xunzi went on to describe the present era as one in which unethical officials were using taxes to plunder the people.

already had a dense network of correspondents who discussed scientific and later social-scientific matters, often across national borders. As we will see in Chapter 3, the Chinese network was considerably sparser. Chinese scholarship accumulated to a much greater degree vertically over time and not horizontally, based on exchanges among scholars alive at any particular moment, as was the case to an unprecedented degree in Europe.

2.C The Chinese economy at first entry

What turned out to be the final Chinese dynasty, the Qing, took power in Beijing in 1644, and the 18th century in China was one of significant stability, prosperity, and technological innovation in agriculture. Von Glahn cites the increased liquidity of the economy caused by the flow of New World silver as well as a policy that gave peasants unusually reliable property rights, including transfer rights, in contrast to much of the time during the Ming Dynasty (明朝, 1368–1644. The details differed depending on the location, as one might expect given the absence of a comprehensive nationwide legal code. But it was common for peasant families to choose to switch crops and to engage in commercial handicraft production. The introduction of crops from the New World in the Columbian exchange further contributed to specialization and innovation. Substantial fractions of agricultural output were sold through markets, mediated by sophisticated contracts. Individual farmers would sell their grain to middleman merchants, who would store it en masse, with markets in places like Suzhou and Guangdong mediating the trade. The silk industry, including factories to convert silk into consumer goods, were also well developed. Firms operating both as merchants and as financiers grew in sophistication and by the late 18th century they were driving the thickening of commerce throughout much of the nation. Firms were either family-dominated or took various forms of limited partnership, and were growing substantially during this time.[53]

2.C.1 Commercial networks and division of labor
We have seen that the Guanzi and Sima Qian both discussed the importance of merchants, many of whom historically presided over large firms and net-

---

53. Von Glahn, *Economic History of China*, 322–346.

works. *The Travels of Marco Polo* attests to the complexity of Chinese society and of commerce and technology in particular. By 1843, Shanghai already had a population of between one-third and half a million people. Its economy had a substantial cotton-processing industry and a division of labor scattered throughout the city among shipping, storing, spinning, and weaving, among other activities. The city also had a large shipbuilding industry.[54]

And like the long, global supply chains of today, these networks were constantly if more slowly evolving. The availability of grains, fuels, handicrafts, and more complex goods were clearly signs of a sophisticated division of labor not just in the production but the transportation and selling of these goods. Lee Ou-Fan Lee and Andrew J. Nathan described this era as having "active local and long-distance trade, cosmopolitan cities, frequent travel, and extensive communication across regions and among social groups," a highly integrated society by contemporaneous standards.[55]

In terms of complexity, examples from the late Ming and Qing compare favorably with what prevailed in Europe at the time. Writing in 1996, Ming-Te Pan described the discovery and evolution of patterns of specialization in silk via the sale and purchase of mulberry leaves from trees grown in several counties south of Lake Tai (太湖), where irrigation had been introduced in the seventh century and continuously improved since. The growth of towns that sold different kinds of mulberry saplings, silkworm eggs, and other inputs, with individual towns sometimes specializing in particular inputs such as charcoal, preserved a warm growing environment for cocoons.[56] Beyond silk, Kenneth Pomeranz has noted that many consumption products, in particular sugar, tea and tobacco, were generally not produced and sold personally but often produced in specific places and then distributed through complex market networks.[57]

---

54. Jeffrey N. Wasserstrom, *Global Shanghai, 1850–2010: A History in Fragments* (London: Routledge, 2009), 28–30.

55. Leo Ou-Fan Lee and Andrew J Nathan, "The Beginning of Mass Culture: Journalism and Fiction in the late Ch'ing," in David Johnson, Andrew J. Nathan and Evelyn S Rawski (eds.), *Popular Culture in Late Imperial China* (Berkeley: University of California Press, 1985), 360–395, 360.

56. Ming-Te Pan, "Rural Credit in Ming-Qing Jiangnan and the Concept of Peasant Petit Commodity Production," *Journal of Asian Studies* 55, no. 1 (February 1996): 94–117.

57. Kenneth Pomeranz, *The Great Divergence: Europe, China, and the Making of the Modern World Economy* (Princeton: Princeton University Press, 2000), 124.

Pan focused on specialized financing that allowed farmers who grew silk in addition to food crops to borrow money both to expand production and to smooth personal consumption. Such credit arrangements were merely one example of a much larger extension of the increasing division of labor in finance over time in Chinese history.[58] Von Glahn's evidence indicates that urban Song China "boasted a broad array of specialists in financial and credit services, including goldsmiths and silversmiths, moneychangers, pawnbrokers, and dealers in bills of exchange and commercial paper such as salt and tea certificates. By the late eleventh century merchants commonly settled accounts through assignment transfers on bank deposits. Merchants also negotiated consignment contracts (賒, *shē*) to obtain goods on credit."[59] Chen Zhengping has said that going back at least to the northern (960–1127 A.D.) and southern (1127–1278 A.D.) Song dynasties, some firms called *dàngpù* (當鋪) engaged in secured lending. Other firms with a variety of Chinese terms developed later and exchanged different paper currencies and metal coins, and by the time of the Ming, *qiánzhuō* (錢桌) were also transporting currency. During the reign of the Qianlong emperor in the late 18th century bills of exchange (錢票, *qiánpiāo*) are known to have been in use.[60]

So by the time of first entry, Chinese finance was already very sophisticated, and in some ways more advanced than in Europe before the financial revolution there. Having said that, innovations created in Europe included life insurance in early Renaissance Italy, fractional reserve banking governed by a central bank in Sweden in 1688, and over several decades in the 17th century futures and options contracts in Dutch Republic and the creation of the limited-liability joint-stock company in Dutch Republic and Britain. All of these were first created in Europe, although risk management and supply of investment funds were common in China. China also had a sort of corporate personhood in the form of what von Glahn called "lineages," which by Ming times were intergenerational financial firms exempt from many of the ordi-

---

58. Pan, "Rural Credit Markets."

59. Von Glahn, *Economic History of China*, 267.

60. Chen Zhengping, *A Brief History of Finance in China*, trans. Qian Suqin (Beijing: Social Sciences Academic Press, 2014).

nary inheritance rules for family heads.[61] In China and then independently in Europe, roughly similar institutions developed to address several problems inherent in larger organizations anywhere—e.g., the profitability of adherence to longer time horizons and effective risk management, including financing of investment.

Particular mention should be made of Chinese guilds. These were different from European guilds in critical ways. Whereas the latter functioned significantly to limit entry into particular trades (a goal their mandatory long apprenticeships facilitated), the Chinese *háng* (行) were frequently authorized by the state and had numerous other functions. Entry into them was not limited nearly to the extent that it was in European countries. Instead, being willing and able to do the job rather than enduring a long process of accreditation was the primary requirement. In the case of merchant guilds, their work involved things like managing infrastructure and facilitating communication about conditions at the location of commodity production (mines or farming areas) or along transportation routes. Many guilds in China were based on the place of family origin rather than, as in Europe, a common trade. With the consent of the state, these guilds would often have large buildings in a city that would accommodate both businessmen with origins in various regions and visitors/ migrants to the city from those regions. Unlike European guilds, these organizations facilitated migration and (apart from sharing information on production innovations, which European guilds also did) producing and sharing other economically relevant information. This trend would expand dramatically in the treaty ports after 1843. Overall, these Chinese-style guilds, notably of merchants, were sufficiently active and complex that Tang Lixing has referred to a Chinese "capitalism" well before Western entry.[62]

What about the overall level of commodity-market integration, which we would expect to engender increased division of labor? Carol H. Shiue and Wolfgang Keller have tested the dispersal of prices for the same grains in markets across great distances in China. They found that prices differed more in Western Europe than in China in the 18th century, indicating markets were more

---

61. "Boasted": Von Glahn, *Economic History of China*, 267. "Lineages": Ibid., 301–302.

62. Tang Lixing, *Merchants and Society in Modern China: From Guild to Chamber of Commerce* (London: Routledge, 2017). He used this term throughout.

closely integrated in China.[63] This suggests a greater ability to rely on networks and the information they can produce to transport goods more economically.

2.C.2 The climate for technological innovation

A particular driver of dynamism is technological progress. By contemporaneous standards the Chinese had no shortage of consequential mechanical and social improvements during the long imperial era, stretching all the way to the Qing. Innovations were numerous if not closely spaced in time, sometimes well-documented, and found in a variety of economic activities. Writing in the 17th century, Francis Bacon (1561–1626) listed in his *Novum Organum* the Chinese inventions of paper, the compass, and gunpowder as the three most consequential innovations worldwide to his time. He did not mention that they were created in China.

Broadly defined, of course, innovation goes beyond mere material goods. The financial and institutional changes listed above certainly qualify. And the right to buy and sell agricultural land in China, while limited by the rule of preserving patrilineal property holdings, was not as limited as it was in primogeniture-restricted Britain (although in China as in most of Europe, inheritance was limited to males). What was permitted changed over time in response to economic need. For example, when certain types of arrangements short of outright transfer of the land itself—usufruct rights, for example—evolved, market prices for these different sales reflected these differences, a sign that prices could adjust reasonably freely, and sensibly. Song dynasty courts relied heavily on precedent in their decisions, as Richard Posner has argued judge-made rules about property rights should.[64] Chinese created and used many innovations broadly defined, many of them specific to Chinese environmental circumstances. For example, polders were created during the Song to make more land suitable for crops in the vicinity of parts of the Yangzi, including the delta. These polders were subdivided during the Ming because harvest productivity had increased. This era also saw the expansion of extractive-cum-refining industries such as silk, tea, sugar, timber, and iron. A more complex division of labor also emerged in such manufacturing activities as porcelain, so here too

63. Carol H. Shiue and Wolfgang Keller, "Markets in China and Europe on the Eve of the Industrial Revolution," *American Economic Review* 97, no. 4 (September 2007): 1189–1216.

64. Von Glahn, *Economic History of China*, 276. Richard A. Posner, *Economic Analysis of Law*, 8th edition (New York: Wolters Kluwer, 2011), Chapter 19.

division of labor was not just sophisticated but becoming more so over time.[65] There were innovations in shipbuilding, which operated to the benefit of trade on both of China's great rivers and the oceans. During the Qing era such broad-spectrum innovation continued, now more spontaneously discovered and less state-instigated.[66]

Not all of these innovations were the fruits of economically liberal policy, let alone of economically liberal ideology. Nor did they proceed at the rate innovation did in Europe, starting in the 18th century. But they were frequent enough to disabuse us of any notion that the Chinese state was hostile to innovation per se. If an innovation was seen as productive, especially in the agricultural sphere, there was not only tolerance but active encouragement by the authorities for the spread of such innovation. And yet therein was the problem.

2.D Networks and industrialization, China and Europe

By the death of the Qianlong emperor, often considered the greatest of the Qing rulers, in 1799, China compared well to Western Europe, broadly speaking, in both the extent of economically liberal policy (remember that Adam Smith in WN offered many criticisms of existing economic illiberalism in Europe) and in economic complexity. In addition, the standard of living in the two places in roughly 1750 was about the same, although of course there were significant regional differences in each place. There was at least rough equality between coastal China and northwest Europe (northwest Europe being the most prosperous part of Europe). The claim that longstanding cultural hostility to commerce or desire for stability was an obstacle to economic development in China is hard to reconcile with the evidence of comparable living standards.

In spite of this relative comparability, a sense of crisis took hold after the forced opening to China for Western firms and the institutions and technology that followed it. That sense of crisis was strengthened by internal disorder and then war with France and Britain from 1856 to 1860, with France from 1884 to 1885, and with Japan in 1894–95. Of course, Chinese defeats in these wars had a clear proximate military cause—Chinese weapons, strategy, and

---

65. Von Glahn, *Economic History of China*, 242.

66. Von Glahn, Ibid., 346

tactics were simply no match for those of the Europeans, Americans, and then the Japanese.

But lurking behind this large and growing military imbalance was a liberal spontaneous re-ordering already well underway in the West, but one that had eluded China: industrialization. The changes in 19th-century Europe properly bear the name of a revolution. Whereas someone born in the Egypt of the pharaohs in 2500 BC and transported 1000 years into the future might well recognize the social contours, someone living in London in 1820 transported suddenly into 1870 would be stupefied by much of what he saw. In contrast, someone transported in China from 1750 to 1843 would see more that was familiar.

To oversimplify somewhat, humans' standard of living improves by rearranging matter through human labor to better suit human purposes. The creation and continuous improvement of steam power in the late 18th and early 19th centuries made machinery possible, which made it much more profitable and productive to collect humans in one place—factories—and have them work with such machinery, substantially increasing productivity. Steam and other new sources of power also enabled more rapid transportation, and together these things enabled the division of labor to evolve continuously and more quickly.

Science had a role, too. While science (as opposed to atheoretical experimentation by businesses) played only part of Europe's role in these expansions of human possibilities, the growing specialization among scientists themselves caused scientific knowledge to expand from the base laid down during the scientific revolution of the late 17th and the 18th centuries. With the discovery and refining of the principles of the interaction between electricity and magnetism, starting with the 1875 publication of James Clark Maxwell's *A Treatise on Electricity and Magnetism*, ladled on top of Newtonian mechanics and the principles of chemistry, the science to literally further power the Industrial Revolution was now substantial.

Deirdre McCloskey in her bourgeois trilogy has provided a handy summary of the ways the Industrial Revolution suddenly and dramatically transformed human life for first a few and then ever more members of the human race. It allowed people to live longer in better health, travel more, and learn more—all of these a result of the fact that people could produce more. (In addition, as time passed workers themselves could even gain fulfillment and not just a paycheck from the work they did.)[67]

Identifying the proximate causes, however, just begins to unravel the mystery. Why did these things happen in Europe and not elsewhere, notably in the ancient, complex civilization of China? Joel Mokyr has summarized attempts by both Western and Chinese economic historians to answer this question.[68] First, scholars have acknowledged that like other social trends, technological progress sped up and slowed down in China at various points in its history. Over a long career of researching Chinese scientific history, Joseph Needham (1900–1965) argued that a slowdown in innovation began with the Ming.[69] Several hypotheses have been proposed and disputed to explain this slowdown in spite of a roughly equivalent technology base and the social infrastructure necessary to innovate. Was innovation in China deterred by lower real wages there, thus lessening the urgency of inventing machines to replace workers? Was there a weaker capacity to apply scientific knowledge to production, an ability accelerated dramatically in 18th-century Europe? Did China lack the cultural willingness to challenge the established intellectual order (perhaps because of excessive reverence for the ancients), thus wasting or never discovering new commercial or scientific ideas? Was the country's vast area an obstacle? In China one sovereign typically ruled a vast region, while in Europe there was usually another jurisdiction to escape to if one said unconventional things that a government might seek to repress. This was particularly important after the Reformation.

Among 20th-century economists, a common way of thinking about technological progress was to suppose that output is mathematically related to the amount of inputs efficiently applied. Thus attempts were made to measure the three most easily conglomerated inputs—labor, capital (often interpreted as physical input to the rearrangement of matter, such as plows or water wheels)

67. Deirdre N. McCloskey, *Bourgeois Equality*, esp. Ch, 1; McCloskey, *The Bourgeois Virtues*, 14–21; McCloskey, *Bourgeois Dignity*, 48–59.

68. Joel Mokyr, *The Lever of Riches: Technological Creativity and Economic Progress* (New York: Oxford University Press, 1992), esp. Ch. 9.

69. Joseph Needham, *Science and Civilisation in China*, Vols. 1-7 (Cambridge, UK: Cambridge University Press, 1954–2007).

and skill (human capital).[70] Additionally, they view the legal protection of property rights as essential if production that is profitable in theory is to be profitable in fact.

And yet none of these explanations, in Mokyr's telling, are persuasive. China was by no means poorly endowed with physical and finance capital, its people had at least comparable literacy to Europe, and there was a vibrant trade in books by the 18th century—a mix of a backward-looking reverence for the classics among credentialed scholars and books emphasizing artisanship.[71]

Mokyr instead emphasized a factor that is consistent with the facts as we know them so far. In his account, the reason for the commencement of the Industrial Revolution in Britain at that time was not inputs, or merely protection of property rights, or other institutional considerations (although these may have been necessary conditions). Instead, there were tremendous opportunities to overcome the decentralized, costly information problem mentioned in section 2.A.3. Suppose A has knowledge that will help B earn profits. In modern economies it often happens that B pays A for that knowledge, or is

---

70. Joel Mokyr, *The Enlightened Economy: An Economic History of Great Britain*, 1700–1859 (New Haven: Yale University Press, 2009). It must be noted that human capital is often highly task-specific, so that measures of literacy, for example, are very crude measures at best for how much relevant skill a population actually possesses. This is a weakness of the literature cited in the next footnote.

71. Slowdown in scientific progress: Joseph Needham, *The Grand Titration: Science and Society in East and West* (Abingdon, UK: Routledge, 2013); low real wages, pro: Robert C. Alan, *The British Industrial Revolution in Global Perspective* (Cambridge, UK: Cambridge University Press, 2009); low real wages, con: Morgan Kelly, Joel Mokyr, and Cormac Ó Gráda, "Precocious Albion: A New Interpretation of the British Industrial Revolution," *Annual Review of Economics* 6 (2014): 363–391; science and production, pro: Justin Yifu Lin, "The Needham Puzzle: Why the Industrial Revolution Did not Originate in China," *Economic Development and Cultural Change* 43, no. 2 (January 1995):269–292; cultural hostility, pro (including accounts of Westerners such as John Dewey who thought Confucianism in particular made Chinese excessively conservative): Greider, *Intellectuals and the State in Modern China*; cultural hostility, con: Ma Tao, "Confucian Thought on the Free Economy," in Chang Lin, Terry Peach, and Wang Fang (eds.), *The History of Ancient Chinese Economic Thought* (London, Routledge, 2014), 153–165; human capital, confined to books printed and amount of education, pro: Jan Luiten van Zanden, "Explaining the Global Distribution of Book Production before 1800," in Maarten Prak and Jan Luiten von Zanden (eds.), *Technology, Skills in the Pre-Modern Economy in the East and West* (Leiden: Brill, 2013), 321–340; Jorg Baten and Jan Luiten van Zanden, "Book Production and the Onset of Modern Economic Growth," *Journal of Economic Growth* 13, no. 3 (2008): 217–235; human capital, confined to books printed and the amount of education, con: Kai-Wing Chow, *Publishing, Culture, and Power in Early Modern China* (Palo Alto: Stanford University Press, 2004). On the book market in China over the centuries, see Joseph P. McDermott, *A Social History of the Chinese Book: Books and Literati Culture in Late Imperial China* (Hong Kong: Hong Kong University Press, 2006).

already paying him to go discover it. When A has chosen not to hire personnel but has a sudden need for them, it may hire A permanently or temporarily to engage in research, enable a major business deal, make a major repair or install new equipment in its factory, etc. In 18th-century Britain, numerous opportunities were created to share the new scientific and industrial knowledge with others—through, for example, societies organized for that purpose and newly introduced journals. Such means of getting the knowledge out spread rapidly during those times, in ways that had no parallel elsewhere. And the relative openness of British society meant that if people from different circles each knew different things that in combination created potential profit opportunities, there were over time fewer social barriers to those two getting together and sharing what they knew as the Industrial Revolution unfolded.

Indeed, the use of the word "invention" often misstates the steady, trial-and-error process of improving our ability to rearrange matter, as mentioned above. It is a continuous process, not a discrete movement from one great breakthrough to another. Of course, some new ways of thinking do qualify as dramatic shifts, especially in science—one thinks of Newton's *Principia*. (Other acclaimed scientific works, for example Darwin's *Origin of Species*, while still qualifying as revolutionary, especially in hindsight, did build on earlier, more problematic work on the same questions.) But with respect to industry, even great successes seldom come from nowhere, and instead are enabled by the record of unsuccessful or imperfect attempts before them. Innovation, in other words, is a process often characterized by many small steps among a few larger ones, with many missteps along the way; a key function of competition is to discover the missteps. Thus, we may refer to the social conductivity of information. The greater such conductivity is, the greater is market competition (other legal and institutional features held equal), and the more quickly competitive mistakes are purged of mistakes and the more rapidly technology advances.

And Britain at the onset of the Industrial Revolution, Mokyr claimed, was friendly to the spread of both scientific and industrial information. There was substantial public interest in both, and this generated two-way feedback between the two communities. Industrialists were interested in the new science, and scientists were interested in the operation of the new machinery, sometimes created without much science. Both scientific hypotheses and practical inventions in fact proceeded in the same trial-and-error way.

The steam engine, one of the touchstones of the early Industrial Revolution, is a classic example. Ancient Greeks at least conceived of using steam to move matter, and Robert Temple has cited Chinese examples described in the sixth century B.C. of the use of water power to drive a piston to sift flour, and later to power bellows for blast furnaces in Chinese metallurgy.[72] As was the case later in Europe, the main purpose of these earlier devices was to produce more work using fewer resources by having power generated by a mechanical process (here, the motion of a piston) replace power generated by human or animal muscles.

So not only were Chinese flexible enough to imagine generation of power by a piston, there was (slow) improvement over time in the operation of such devices. But the steam engine should not be thought of as a single invention at a single moment in time. In an attempt to improve the ability to evacuate water from mines, Italy's Evangelista Torricelli (1608–1647) had in 1643 hypothesized the existence of air pressure and subsequently invented the first barometer. It was soon realized that the creation of a vacuum, which had been an effect of Torricelli's experiment, could generate power to do work. Subsequently France's Denis Papin (1687–1713) and England's Thomas Savery (1650–1715), Thomas Newcomen (1664–1729), Scotland's James Watt (1736–1818) and England's Matthew Boulton (1728–1809), almost certainly among others lost to history, tried new ways of constructing and financing the construction of machinery to generate power more effectively. They ended up with a workable and inexpensive way to repeatedly inject steam and then push it out of the chamber so that the piston on top would rise and fall. Because of the still-small number of participants in the growing scientific/industrial network, and because of communication and transportation limits (which steam-based power would soon relax), there was roughly a half century between Newcomen's engine and Watt's. So while it is not clear that any one step was decisive, the process collectively raised human capacities substantially. Only by serially altering others' ideas that one has learned about, and by having a number of ways to pitch the altered idea to raise funds, could we get from Torricelli to

---

72. Robert Temple, *The Genius of China: 3000 Years of Science, Discovery and Invention* (New York: Simon and Schuster, 1986), 64–66.

Watt and Boulton.[73] This fact, that progress often comes from *many* trials and some errors, was central to the industrialization process.

In northwestern Europe—especially the United Kingdom, France, the Netherlands, and Germany—scientists were sharing information about hypotheses and experiments by 1700. (Indeed, one early scientific break-through was the design of the scientific method itself.[74]) In China in contrast, while living scholars would sometimes communicate about rather traditional concerns, it was confined to the fields mentioned earlier, such as philosophy and history. For much of Chinese history, the information contained in books was also found mainly in large libraries in the hands of private collectors or the imperial authorities. (These authorities, as in Europe, sometimes sought to censor books containing what they saw as dangerous information.[75])

By failing to develop the kinds of networks that emerged in Europe, Chinese also failed to develop the immensely useful machines, and the institutions to most effectively use them, that could now be constructed and improved using these networks. One critical innovation was factory-based mass production, which people could learn about and imitate even when they wanted to make different products. This development played out over perhaps a century, first in the United Kingdom from the mid-1700s. For some time, it had been common in the UK for business owners to oversee workers who produced, say, clothing in their own homes and were paid by the piece. The initial factories brought such workers together in one place. Because they could use the existing machines, coordination and supervisory costs could fall. However, there were additional gains from division of labor within a building, for example, moving fabric or cleaning up, and better monitoring workers. Adam Smith's pin factory (introduced in the first chapter of the first volume of WN) is the classic example of such a smaller-scale factory.[76] Profit-maximizing scale of production began to increase. The spread of this new institution, the factory

---

73. When steam power arrived on foreign ships in China, the Chinese were unfamiliar with it. For the story of the almost 20-year process by which they came to understand it see Hsien-Chun Wang, "Discovering Steam Power in China, 1840s-1860s," *Technology and Culture* 51, no. 1 (January 2010): 31–54.

74. Osborne, *Self-Regulation and Human Progress*, Chapter 3.

75. McDermott, *A Social History of the Chinese Book*.

76. The example is used at the outset of WN I.1.1 to illustrate how productivity can go up when tasks are divided up among numerous workers. Smith (1976), Vol. I, 7–8.

with a very sophisticated division of labor and soon the application of large amounts of mechanical equipment, resulted in products becoming less expensive, more reliable, and much more varied. In addition, because skilled workers, scientists and engineers, and senior managers could be in one place, new products could be designed and initial versions built much more quickly. Thus, progress was now much faster.

Before European movement into China began, only the Smithian effects—more complex division of labor given existing technology—had been there for the taking. A few factories existed in China in the late Ming—von Glahn argued that the demise of labor-market rigidities imposed in the early part of that dynasty led to the consolidation of many silk factories into a few larger ones, with 300 looms found in one case.[77] Benjamin A. Elman noted large porcelain factories dating to the eleventh century, whose output was destined for the elite or for export.[78] But the other benefits mentioned above derived from constant change generated by vigorous competitive pressure, given the base of available finance (which to a great degree existed in China) and substantial mechanical power (which did not).

Military examples serve to illustrate both the contemporaneous benefits of mass production and its continuous improvement in the 19th century in the West. The first shots of the first Opium War were fired in the area of Amoy (now Xiamen, 厦門), after several Chinese refused to take possession of a letter that the British fleet commander demanded be presented to the emperor's local representative. Shots were fired from the shore at the ship containing the Chinese-speaking representative of the British fleet. Literal gunboat diplomacy immediately commenced, with British naval guns firing on Chinese junks and a fort. After being fired on after sending another message that was not accepted, the British fleet proceeded to the island of Zhoushan (舟山島) near the mouth of the Yangzi River. The imbalance in weaponry was dramatic—on one side, bags of grain as defensive barriers, muskets, and junks, and on the other, the state-of-the-art British Navy, with its increasingly mass-produced weapons. Here the British fired the first shot, and one shot from a Chinese

77. Von Glahn, *Economic History of China*, 298.

78. Benjamin A. Elman, *A Cultural History of Modern Science in China* (Cambridge, MA: Harvard University Press, 2009), 75–76.

junk came in reply, whereupon the order was given to every British ship available to shell, and the shelling continued for about eight minutes. Several of the
junks, the only defensive tower on the entire island, and a wall that had been
built to protect against the sea were destroyed.[79] The continuous firing of the
mass-produced shells demonstrated how easily they could be acquired, and
how indiscriminately used. And the dynamism generated by modern industry
was on display as well. This is the case even though China did have some useful weaponry. In the words of the military historian Bruce A. Elleman, "con-
trary to popular belief, China's war junks, cannon, and military organization
were not all equally backward. In fact, at the beginning of the conflict, Cap-
tain Charles Elliott (1801–1875) was extraordinarily concerned that the vast
size of the Chinese fleet might simply overwhelm his own forces. However,
the British rapidly pulled ahead of the Chinese during the course of the war."
Elleman cited improvements shortly before or during the war in ship-mount-
ed guns and in "mobile artillery."[80]

It would not be the last time modern, mass-produced weapons would
play a role in Chinese military defeat. By the time the first Sino-Japanese war
started in 1894, the dynamism of Western industrial technology in its military manifestation, as modified by the Japanese, was apparent. What was to
contemporary observers the shocking defeat of China had many causes, but
some blame can be placed on the empire's failure, despite continuing efforts,
to master military mass production and to understand the speed of modern
industrial change.

In sum then, the relevant networks in China compared unfavorably to
those prevailing in Europe just before first entry. Thus the essential economic
characteristic of the Industrial Revolution, mass production and continuous
introduction of new and more useful products, combined with the tremendous social changes generated by these products, was not there. Within a few
decades (fast enough by the standards of the long flow of Chinese history) many
Chinese decided that they had to understand it. And private individuals, notably businessmen, did so even more quickly. The next chapter focuses on this
process, and what was learned about economic liberalism during this time.

---

79. Peter Ward Fay, *The Opium War: 1840-1842*, 2nd ed. (Chapel Hill: University of North Carolina
Press, 1997), 219–223.

80. Bruce A. Elleman, *Modern Chinese Warfare, 1795–1989* (London: Routledge, 2001), 26.

CHAPTER 3

Enthusiasm: Initial Reaction to Economic Liberalism

Toward the end of the fighting in the first Opium War, in June 1842, the British military took Shanghai. The Treaty of Nanjing, combined with the supplementary Treaty of the Bogue in 1843, established British sovereignty over Hong Kong Island (a colony that eventually expanded onto the mainland), and in 1844 Shanghai was, along with Canton, Ningpo, Xiamen, and Fuzhou, made one of five so-called treaty ports. Each of these cities was opened to foreign commerce. The subsequent sequence of events in many of these and later treaty ports would then be characterized by at least one of these features: extraterritorial concessions (where foreigners could buy and sell land and were not subject to Chinese sovereignty), the near-elimination of taxation of imports, and the elimination of interior taxation beyond transport fees as foreign goods moved inland. In these cities almost complete freedom was given to foreign merchants and manufacturers to make what they liked, to charge any price and pay any wage the market would bear, and even to hire child labor at a time when the Factory Acts in the U.K. were already limiting it. Shanghai would prove the most transformatively influential of these ports. Chinese tariffs in Shanghai, which had under the Treaty of Nanjing been subject to negotiation between the Qing and foreign representatives, were limited to 5 percent. (Soon after, foreigners distrustful of Chinese corruption were collecting and administering the customs duties at the ports as well.)

The number of treaty ports, and the number of countries that possessed them, grew over the next several decades as the government of China came under increasing duress from Western countries. While some treaty ports, including Shanghai, had had significant populations before extraterritoriality, almost all of them also saw large increases in population and economic activity after its advent. Foreigners brought their different business methods, technology, and culture. Because of the limited size of the foreign concessions and the large amount of migration to the surrounding area, the culture was not so much imposed at colonial gunpoint as sought out and absorbed by the Chinese themselves. Spontaneous re-ordering of many of these cities, in which both Chinese and foreign culture mingled to create something new, was extensive. This process—the construction of a modern economically liberal society by the Chinese people themselves and why it unfolded the way it did—will be discussed in detail in Chapter 4. This chapter emphasizes the economic ideas introduced after first entry, how Chinese thinkers and officials reacted to the challenges presented by the sudden and large-scale entry of Westerners and these ideas, and the role economic liberalism played in their debate about how to respond to the growing Western challenge to China's traditional way of doing things.

3.A Initial contempt, indifference, and eagerness to learn

In the next three chapters, it will help to know the key political events affecting the story to be told here. They are listed in Table 3.1. The number of treaty ports expanded after the second Opium War (also known as the Arrow War) from 1856 to 1860. After several decades of shifting Chinese responses to military defeats and lost territory, war with Japan broke out in 1894, and a treaty ending it was signed after the Chinese defeat in 1895. The treaty ending this first Sino-Japanese war, plus its aftermath, meant that foreign companies could construct factories themselves.

In 1898, the Guangxu emperor (光緒, 1871–1908) oversaw attempts to reform China socially and politically, a period known as the 100 Days (戊戌變法), a brief and unsuccessful attempt to quickly implement substantial economic and political reforms. From 1899 to 1901 there was an uprising against the foreign and especially missionary presence in China by a movement known in English as the Boxers, and now known to Chinese history as the Society for Righteousness and Peace (義和團). While the Dowager Empress Cixi (慈禧太后, 1835–1908) supported it, the Boxer Rebellion ended in disastrous defeat for the Chinese and the imposition of yet another round of reparations. In 1911, the Qing dynasty was removed from power through the Xinhai Revolution (辛亥革命), and on January 1, 1912, the Republic of China began. (The formal removal of the last emperor occurred on February 12, 1912.) The first president of the republic was Sun Yat-Sen (孫中山, 1866–1925), who had been elected by an assembly of revolutionaries prior to overthrowing the emperor in late 1911, but only after the revolutionaries agreed that the commander of the strongest military force, the military leader Yuan Shikai (袁世凱, 1859–1916), would take power in March, to be followed in due course by democratic elections. After the KMT won the elections in 1913, one of their major parliamentarians and a rising political figure, Song Jiaoren (宋教仁, 1882-1913), was assassinated, almost certainly by Yuan, who then consolidated power. After a brief and unsuccessful attempt to name himself the new emperor in 1915, Yuan died on June 6, 1916. His death was followed by roughly a decade of disintegration of national political authority amid military struggles around the country. After Sun's death in 1925 the KMT), the successor to Sun's pre-revolutionary organization, the Tóngménghuì (同盟會), led by its army under Chiang Kai-Shek, launched the so-called Northern Expeditions (北伐). This military campaign defeated most of the opposition regional military leaders and also struck an initial blow against a growing communist movement, the Chinese Communist Party (CCP). Civil war continued between the KMT and the CCP until late 1936, just before Japan, which had captured Manchuria in 1931, began its invasion of the rest of China in July 1937. After Japan surrendered to the Allies in August 1945, the bloody war between the KMT and CCP resumed, and it continued till the CCP triumphed in 1949. These events form the political backdrop of the story—how economic liberalism came to China—to be told in the next two chapters.

The story begins with the arrival of modern war, and defeat. By the time of first entry the Qing had for some time fought the production and consumption of opium in China. Foreign and especially British commercial activity increased the severity of the problem starting in the second half of the 18th century.

British smuggling of opium had begun out of the country's mercantilist policies. Since the 17th century, China had run a significant trade surplus with Britain, mainly driven by the porcelain trade. To counter Britain's corresponding deficit and protect its gold reserves, in 1773 the Crown extended the monopoly trade privileges of the BEIC to include the export of opium to

China from India, even though this violated Chinese law. By the late 1830s, the Chinese government was exerting every effort to fight opium smuggling, but in 1833 the British government revoked the BEIC's monopoly privileges while continuing to allow the trade in opium overall. As usually happens in such circumstances, private entrepreneurs saw the opportunity to compete away the BEIC's monopoly profits, and their competitive energies served to increase the availability of the drug in coastal China, notably Canton. In June 1839 China seized the opium on British ships in the Canton area, imposed an overall embargo on the foreign section of Canton, and war soon followed. It is a historical irony that the war that brought the idea of Western economic liberalism was arguably waged by Britain for mercantilist reasons less than 75 years after the publication of WN.

While the research cited in Chapter 1 supports the possibility that the Qianlong emperor, whose rule was characterized by unparalleled heights of prosperity (as we would expect with slow liberal progress under the Qing up to that point) was concerned enough about European military power to refuse the request of the Macartney Embassy discussed in the first chapter, it may be that the Chinese were relatively unconcerned about their defeat by the British. At that point at least one major disaster was unfolding in China, with another soon to come. The first was the Daoguang depression, generally held to have taken place from 1820 to 1850. The second was the Taiping rebellion, lasting from 1850 to 1864. And piled on top of this catastrophic southeastern Chinese war was the second Opium War, fought primarily against the U.K. and France from 1856 to 1860. The Treaty of Tianjin that ended it allowed foreigners to travel freely throughout the country, increased the number of treaty ports, forced the Chinese government to pay significant reparations, and gave Western powers the right to establish embassies in Beijing, the latter right without precedent under the Qing. In light of these events, perhaps there is room for Fay's contention regarding the first Opium War that "for many years [after the war], indeed, the Chinese did not perceive that anything fundamental had been altered by the war and by the treaty. If anyone had told them that an irreversible active penetration had occurred, they would have looked incredulous."[81] By the early 1860s, however, there was a cohesive sense that

---

81. Fay, *Opium War*, 363.

there was a new threat afoot as the treaty ports multiplied, opium continued to surge in, and Western government demands for more economic openness and diplomatic representation grew.

Economic thinking in the West of course was far from the only aspect of Western entry that drew attention. Foremost at first was advanced technology (first military, then industry more generally) that Chinese officials and intellectuals sought to explain. The scholar Feng Guifen (馮桂芬, 1809–1874) in 1860 arrived in Shanghai and lived for a time very near the foreign concessions.[82] While there he composed a short book, essentially a series of essays. The book title is translated into English as "Dissenting Views from a Hut Near Bin," a classical-Chinese allusion to a situation in which foreigners threatened China. In the work Feng said little that constituted economic thinking per se. But in one portion of the book he coined the phrase "self-strengthening" (自強), later to become the designation for the initial era of less-frantic Chinese government reaction to the new circumstances.[83] And he did partly see a key reason for Western success: their machines economized tremendously on labor, thus lowering production costs. He said about China that "[i]t is too common to use hundreds of millions supporting themselves, and there is too little of using one person to support thousands."[84] Thus, there was nothing sacrosanct about the Chinese way of production, although Feng asserted the country's ethical values were superior. And to his credit, Feng considered where the machines came from. While making a standard Confucian lament about the decline of traditional mores, especially among officials, he noted that Western countries (none of which Feng—and hardly any other Chinese—had seen to this point) had more practical education, did not have such a vast material distance between rich and poor, and lacked such different perspectives between the tiny elite class and the vast impoverished countryside. And it did have governments who were closer and therefore more responsive to the people (and whose officials were not as pointlessly idle as those in China). He also recognized the dynamic nature of military technology, warning that it was urgent for China to learn

---

82. The British, French and Americans had all established their own concessions quickly, but the British and American ones merged into the so-called international concession in1863.

83. 馮桂芬,《校邠廬抗議》 (Feng Guifen, *Dissenting Views from a Hut Near Bin*), https://ctext.org/wiki.pl?if=gb&chapter=916939,152, 155, 156, 157, 159, 164.

84. Ibid., 47. (「以億萬人自養則有餘, 以一人養千百人則不足。」).

how to make modern Western combat ships quickly, or else the West's disadvantage in military technology would grow.[85] Lacking any European-style concept of political economy, he did not make specific economic policy recommendations. He represented an era in which those who were active in the economically liberal world, whether as businessmen or bureaucrats or because they traveled abroad, were more aware of the benefits of economic competition than someone who watched from inside China.

A few scholars such as Liang Tingnan (梁廷枏, 1796–1861) and Xu Jishe ((徐繼畬, 1795–1873) did explicitly recognize the importance of commerce for prosperity and more importantly for national strength in Europe. But there was disagreement over even the need to reform. The contemporaneous official Wei Yuan (魏源, 1794–1857) reflects—or at least is seen that way by scholars—Confucian skepticism of merchants, providing a sort of proto-Leninist interpretation of British and French military aggression. He said that their aggression derived from commercial imperatives, which he saw as in contrast to an old, more moral rule by the pope of the Roman Empire. This vanished empire was seen as analogous to the Chinese empire, requiring that the emperor must preserve social order, with the merchant in turn needing to sublimate his greed to this higher purpose. As Wei saw it, the papal empire had collapsed in the face of this insatiable greed.[86] In his collection known as *Illustrated Treatise on the Maritime Kingdoms* (《海國圖志》), he described Western expansion as driven by the insatiable thirst for profit but, among other things, he recommended that the government adopt the liberal policy of allowing any Chinese to build factories to manufacture machinery and weapons.[87]

And outside the literal walls in which the bureaucracy was confined, it was easier to recognize the importance of commerce. An example is the prolific

85. Ibid., 158 (「目前古無隙，故可暫也；日後豈能必無隙。」).

86. On Liang, see 梁廷枏,《海國四說》, 北京, 中華書局, 1993 (Liang Tingnan, *Four accounts from the Maritime Countries* (Beijing: Zhonghua Publishing, 1993)). On Xu, see 徐繼畬,《瀛寰志略》, 第四卷, 駱驛和劉曉編輯, 上海上海書店, 2001 年, 115頁 (Xu Jishe, *Summary of the Maritime Realms*, volume 4, eds. Luo Yi and Liu Shao (Shanghai: Shanghai Bookstore Publishing House, 2001)), 115. On Wei, see Kate Leonard, *Wei Yuan and China's Rediscovery of the Maritime World* (Cambridge, MA: Harvard University Press, 1984; Shinzo Suzuki, *Civilization and Empire: China and Japan's Encounter with European International Society* (London: Routledge, 2009)), 59–60.

87. Yunzhi Geng, *Evolution in Ideology and Culture After the Opium Wars and Up To the Westernization Movement* (Berlin: Springer-Verlag, 2015), 33.

writer Cheng Kuan-Ying (鄭觀應, 1842–c. 1922). The track of his life was the very example of the social dynamism that much of China traversed over the course of it. He failed an imperial exam, but then found work as a comprador, a job whose importance will be discussed in section 4.2, notably for the British firm Butterfield & Swire (巴特菲爾德和太古). Later, he found employment in buying and selling tea, and wrote numerous works advocating economic and political reform. For example, he advocated repeal of the *lǐjīn* (釐金), a tax on domestic trade imposed during the Taiping rebellion, and he clearly saw dynamic commerce as contributing to both higher standards of living and national strength. He also argued that Western strength had not emerged suddenly but was a function of the gradual, dynamic building of their civilization. Continual change was inevitable, and the primary task facing China after the unequal treaties (a term widely used now by both Chinese and foreigners to describe the accommodations a weak China had to make) was to make institutional reforms so that China's potential progress could be encouraged.[88]

Another case was Xue Fucheng (薛福成, 1838–1894), who served as a diplomat in several European countries during the early 1890s. (He was struck down by an infection acquired in China after he returned home.) In his travel diaries he commented on what he viewed as the exalted role of the businessman in several European societies, whose dynamism he also remarked on.[89] The wandering scholar and serial entrepreneur Tan Sitong (譚嗣同, 1865–1898) took an almost Hegelian view of humanity as always in motion, and forward, because of the contradictory forces within it. To oppose change was thus wrong, and a view of imperial dominance and the status quo as being the will of heaven were thus mistaken, and costly. Finally and tellingly, the failed scholar, later merchant and comprador, Zheng Guanying (鄭觀應, 1842–c. 1922) advocated the ending of government supervision of commerce and appreciated its dynamic function.[90] And Xu Jiyu (徐繼畬, 1795–1873) was a

---

88. Y'en-Ping Hao, "Cheng Kuang-Ying: The Comprador as Reformer," *Journal of Asian Studies* 29, no. 1 (November 1969): 15–22.

89. Tang, *Merchants and Society in Modern China*, 156. On enthusiasm for the role of business activity in Western strength, see 李澤厚, 《中國近代思想史論, 》北京, 人民出版社, 1982 (Li Zehou, *A History of Modern Chinese Historical Debates* (Beijing: People's Publishing House, 1982)).

90. See Hao, Yan-Ping, "The Comprador as Reformer," *Journal of Asian Studies* 29, no. (November 1969): 15-2

traditional scholar who worked in Guangxi and Fujian and thus met numerous Western missionaries and consular officials. In a geographic survey of the known world, he drew attention to the importance of commerce as part of European strength.[91] This was a notable contrast to the rarity of the attention paid to dynamism before first entry.

In the decades after 1843, many were not shy about diagnosing Chinese difficulties. And while comprehensive embrace of the dynamism deriving from commercial liberalism was clearly common among Chinese who now had contact with the West, it was not universal. In diagnosing Chinese deficiencies, Feng Goufen and other self-strengthening thinkers, perhaps by diagnosing a disease and giving a prescription that allowed minimal disruption to the deeply rooted social structure of China, set the template for the next quarter-century of Qing reform efforts. And the template was, in Feng's own now well-known words, "Western (thought) for practical purposes, but our essence must be Chinese" (「中學為體，西學為用」, *zhōngxué wéi tǐ, xīxué wéi yòng*). At the government level Feng's approach was to copy the machines, reform the bureaucracy, and become more open to foreign ideas, while preserving Chinese norms. Thus, the task was how to bring about this "self-strengthening." That the Chinese government thought to go no farther than this may have been because the contending school of thought inside the imperial walls at that time was major resistance to any Westernization at all.

And, despite Wei Yuan's entreaties for practical actions, the government's default position, much as with many newly decolonized countries after the end of World War II, was to have the state engineer the needed catch-up, in this case through outright ownership of production facilities to achieve self-strengthening's goal of mastering Western technology. A noted manifestation of the belief that the imperial government should direct this catch-up process was the various "arsenals" (sometimes known as 機器製造總局) that were set up to manufacture the goods that Feng Guifen and his acolytes believed needed to be manufactured.

The highly influential modernization-oriented official Li Hongzhang (李鴻章, 1822–1901) first recruited the British diplomat Samuel Halliday Macartney (1833–1906), a relative of George Macartney, to supervise the pro-

---

91. See Tang, *Merchants and Society in Modern China*, 49.

duction of guns in Suzhou, near Shanghai, in 1863. The other main arsenals were constructed between 1865 and 1867 in Jiangnan, Nanjing, Fuzhou, and Tianjin. The Jiangnan Arsenal, located in Chinese Shanghai, was one of the most comprehensive. In addition to producing weaponry, it had educational facilities where experts, at first Western, taught Chinese students the essentials of European languages, as well as science, engineering, and modern mass production.

But the results in terms of production were less than stellar. While through these arsenals and direct purchases from Westerners the Chinese government accumulated significant amounts of seemingly modern weaponry, when push came to shove the performance of the Chinese military in combat with modern nations was mixed. While they acquitted themselves well enough both tactically and strategically in the war with France from 1884 to 1885, they were routed by the Japanese in the first Sino-Japanese war a decade later. While beyond the battlefields the arsenals did help to introduce Western technology to the Chinese more generally, Jean Chesnaux et al. have contended that the ready availability of cheap Chinese labor discouraged the use of machinery outside battlefields, thus limiting the use of the most advanced production techniques.[92] (The failure in war was of course not just a matter of technology; strategic and tactical limitations, especially in the former case due to the unwillingness to use all of the weapons the Chinese military had acquired, also hurt.)

In light of this record, two contrasts generated by the self-strengthening movement deserve attention. The first is the fate of state-directed manufacturing versus traditional Chinese merchants and financiers who were left to fend for themselves when Western competitors were allowed unlimited access via the foreign concessions after first entry. (This may have been due, to some degree, to traditional contempt for them and to some degree to a lack of appreciation of their importance.) Many of these native merchant firms and networks had become somewhat dependent on their management of government monopolies, e.g., the monopoly on salt. But the much greater scale of commercial activity along the coast put these old merchants with their old arrangements under severe competitive threat once foreign firms set up shop. Left to

92. Jean Chesnaux, Marianne Bastide, and Marie-Claire Bergère, *China from the Opium Wars*, 211–212.

fend for themselves, the merchants and financiers either adapted or their businesses died. As we will see in Chapter 4, new economic networks, sometimes involving those outside the traditional merchant class, displaced the old ones, so that the financial structure changed substantially, sometimes but not always involving the new Western businesses and their methods.

The second contrast is more ambiguous with respect to the value of unalloyed economic liberalism. That is the difference between the performance after Western entry of China and Japan. Japan's experience after the forced entry of Commodore Perry in 1853 and the Meiji Restoration in 1868 was in some (but only some) ways similar to that of China. Under the unequal treaties (forced on both), Westerners got small extraterritorial concessions while imposing nearly free trade—and unilateral free trade to boot.[93] From the perspective of national sovereignty, these treaties are outrageous. Yet liberal economic theory predicts that they should have been good for consumers, most of them very poor, and should have resulted in Chinese and Japanese resources being used to more productive ends. This seems to have been the case. (The elimination of most of the restrictions on foreigners establishing and operating businesses in China by the 1895 Treaty of Shimonoseki substantially increased the independence of Chinese entrepreneurs.[94] Whether that was good or not depends on whether one evaluates it from the perspective of entrepreneurs and consumers then and in the future, or from that of nationalism and/or pre-entry indigenous businesses.)

The Chinese and Japanese treaty experiences were also different. While Japan was forcibly opened under threat of bombardment, it did not fight wars with Western nations, and thus paid no reparations (which China did repeatedly from 1842 to 1901), nor did it face escalating demands for more territorial cession. Initially, both nations saw their governments create, own, and operate factories to make mass-produced goods. In Japan financial losses soon induced

---

93. The Treaty of Nanjing sharply limited the ability of the Chinese emperor to tax British exports either at the border or in the interior, and made no pretense of giving similar privileges to any Chinese exports to the United Kingdom that Chinese entrepreneurs might contemplate. The later move by Britain to near-free trade (minimal tariffs) with respect to imports from China, excepting only a small number of goods with very inelastic demand to preserve U.K. government revenue, took place after the repeal of the Corn Laws in 1848 and was not a gesture of goodwill specifically directed at China.

94. Parks M. Coble, Jr., *The Shanghai Capitalists and the Nationalist Government* 1927–1937 (Cambridge, MA: Harvard University Press, 1980), 76.

the government to sell the factories and, instead, sometimes strategically sub-
sidize desired production. In China, in contrast, production at the state arsenals lasted longer even though military output frequently turned out to be of
low quality. State production in the "Western" (洋務) industries also deterred
private investment by increasing the risk of having to compete against state
industry. And even if private Chinese companies considered entering such
activities, they had to be licensed by the state. Companies were reluctant to
apply for fear of facing demands for bribes, the existence of which is a standard
prediction of liberal economic theory: when the state has such control, the
need to get a government license, as with any required government permission, generates opportunities for officials to exercise their monopoly power and
demand them.[95] After a financial crash in 1883 the Qing became less trusting
of private joint-stock companies, some of which had been established in the
preceding years but had been subject to extensive political manipulation.[96] The
dynasty engineered instead the creation of government-managed companies
(官督上辦). Although these were allowed to raise private funds, the aggressive establishment of standardized joint-stock companies by foreigners who
held treaty rights provided far superior alternatives for Chinese investors, and
the government companies suffered from the usual deficiencies of state-run
industries (present even today, especially in developing countries).[97] The tilt
toward private and away from public production was thus more pronounced
and faster in Japan than in China.

3.B Leading the charge to understand economic liberalism — Yan Fu and his influence

After defeat in 1895 by a Japan with both military matériel and a command
structure far superior to those of China, the Treaty of Shimonoseki granted
liberties to citizens of Japan. They received the right "to engage in all kinds of
manufacturing industries in all the open cities, towns, and ports of China, and
shall be at liberty to import into China all kinds of machinery, paying only the
stipulated import duties thereon," and the Chinese government could impose

---

95. Chesnaux et al., *China from the Opium Wars*, 233.

96. Coble, *The Shanghai Capitalists*, 19.

97. Von Glahn, *Economic History of China*, 379.

no internal taxes or fees on the Japanese that it did not also impose on their Chinese equivalents.[98] The freedom to operate factories was soon extended to the other Western treaty powers.

After almost three decades of "self-strengthening," China had been revealed to be so militarily weak relative to the West that Chinese intellectuals and political leaders now treated its condition as a catastrophe. That the defeat came at the hands of China's smaller neighbor Japan made the situation especially more alarming. As the previous section noted, there was a strain of thought during self-strengthening that advocated the free play of economic forces. Because orthodox British economic liberalism ruled the day in the West, a handful of Chinese intellectuals relied on both translated Western texts and their own works to transmit the ideas underpinning that liberalism. A Beijing institution of higher learning founded in 1862, a forerunner of Beijing University, then known as 京師同文館 (Beijing School of Combined Learning), began to offer a course in political economy in 1867. From 1880 it was taught using a translated textbook by the Englishman Henry Fawcett (1833–1884), *Manual of Political Economy* (《富國策》, roughly *Policies to Make Countries Wealthy*). A short 1852 book by the Scotsman John Hill Burton (1809–1881), *Political Economy for Use in Schools and for Private Instruction* (《佐治芻言》, roughly *Helpful Remarks for Good Governance*) was translated in 1885. It discussed the history of laws, rights, duties, and equality in various countries. It also specifically raised the standard liberal-economic idea of the importance of property rights and competition and circulated its commentaries among Chinese intellectuals.[99]

But the most influential person to take up his pen in the name of national salvation through economic liberalism between 1895 and the end of imperial rule in 1911 was Yan Fu (嚴復, 1854–1921). Born in Fuzhou into a family familiar with both scholarship and commerce, Yan was trained in his youth to be a scholar, but the early death of his father closed off this path and pushed him to the Fuzhou Naval Yard School, part of one of the aforementioned arsenals established during the self-strengthening period. There he studied

---

98. "Treaty of Peace" (Treaty of Shimonoseki), http://taiwandocuments.org/shimonoseki01.htm.

99. Paul B. Trescott, *Jingji Xue: The History of the Introduction of Western Economic Ideas into China, 1850–1950* (Hong Kong: The Chinese University Press, 2007), 24.

English and what we would now call STEM fields. After graduating with distinction, he spent several years on military ships, before being able in 1877 to go to the U.K. and study at London's Royal Naval College. He returned to China two years later and spent some time as, first, a teacher at the Fuzhou school and then as a teacher at and later the leader of a similar school in Tianjin, where he remained through 1895.

Yan Fu also wrote foundational work on how to translate foreign works into Chinese and was the first Chinese person to translate British works without retranslating them from an initial Japanese translation.[100] Like others, he was convinced that the defeat by Japan was a signal that China needed fundamental transformation. He wrote a series of essays in the newspaper 直報 (*Zhíbào*, roughly "Frank Talk") in the treaty port of Tianjin, many of which drew on his exposure to European ideas while in Britain. They proved influential in China over the next several decades. They explained both the ideas and their relevance for China's predicament, and Yan sometimes personally created Chinese words for them. His readers became familiar with such terms as evolution, progress, freedom, democracy, rights, and national strength. Yan also explained and advocated what he thought to be the Western attachment to the search for new knowledge—as opposed to mastery of past knowledge—and the respect for talent wherever it was found. These essays and their reception spurred him to translate several books he had become acquainted with in Britain. He sometimes changed the title to reflect his view of the central point : Smith's WN (《原富》), Herbert Spencer's (1820–1903) *The Study of Sociology* (《羣學肄言》), Mill's *On Liberty* (titled《群己權界論》, *On the Boundary Between the Self and the Group*) and *A System of Logic: Ratiocinative and Inductive* (《穆勒名學》, translated as *Mill's Logic*), William Stanley Jevons' (1835–1882) *Primer of Logic* (《名學淺說》), the Baron de Montesquieu's (1689–1755) *The Spirit of the Laws* (《法意》), Edward Jenks's *A History of Politics* (《社會通詮》), and Thomas Huxley's *Evolution and Ethics* (《天演論》, translated as *On Evolution*).

Collectively, these writings indicate that Yan Fu attached the most importance to three ideas in explaining the West's strength—liberalism (political and economic), social evolution, and epistemology. There are several interpre-

100. 韓承樺,《斯賓塞到中國--一個翻譯史的討論,〈編譯論叢,〉2010年, 第3卷第2期。33頁至, 60頁 (Han Cheng-Hua, "Spencer Comes to China—A Discussion of Translation History," *Compilation and Translation Review* 3, no. 2 ((2010): 3--60).

tations of how he saw the relation between and the significance of these ideas. For our purposes economic liberalism and social Darwinism are the most important. His translation of the ideas of social Darwinism go back at least to an influential 1895 essay he wrote in *Zhíbào* in which he discussed constant Western social change as deriving from the search for knowledge and truth. He also argued that social Darwinism (in the sense of evolutionary struggle among societies rather than the 20th century meaning that individuals struggled against one another in society and deserved whatever happened to them) was inevitable, and that China needed to adapt or die. In this he clearly accepted that dynamism was an unavoidable result of a free society, although rather than seeing it primarily as generating human progress he saw it in terms of the threat it posed to a China with inadequate social institutions.[101] This view would become considerably more important in China in subsequent decades, although the view of what qualified as "adequate" would change dramatically.

In a classic analysis of Yan Fu's effect on Chinese reaction to Western ideas, the historian Benjamin Schwartz proposed that he started from the premise of needing to explain not the West's prosperity or its ethical framework, but its strength.[102] If true, he was using the same framework as Feng Guifen. But Yan's understanding of at least the United Kingdom was much deeper than that of most of the self-strengtheners. In Schwartz's view, while Yan understood the idea of political liberalism in the sense of individual rights, given China's ongoing trauma and his own background in traditional literary culture he believed and made clear in his various writings that such freedom should be granted merely to build a strong nation. As Schwartz put it at one point, Yan believed that "the value of individual liberty lies in its power to advance the wealth and power of the nation-state."[103] In so doing, Schwartz argued, Yan to some degree missed the centrality of individual rights in the Western tradition.

It is not disputed that in the end Yan Fu shared with the self-strengthening advocates a belief in the value of traditional Chinese thought and ethics. In his translation of *On Liberty*, beginning with the title he chose, *On the Boundary*

101. 嚴復,《論世變之極》, 直報, 1985年2月4日至5日 (Yan Fu, "On the Speed of World Change," *Frank Talk*, Feb. 4-5, 1895).

102. Benjamin Schwartz, *In Search of Wealth and Power: Yen Fu and the West* (Cambridge, MA: Harvard University Press, 1964).

103. Ibid., 73.

Between the Self and the Group, this is clear. However, unlike the self-strength-eners, he argued that China should not merely copy Western machines but adopt Western institutions, to remake the Chinese political system and economy root and branch along Western lines. It was the West's institutions, especially liberal ones, that generated its power; the machines were a product of the system. As we will see, in this he is a bridge from a generation of intellectuals who thought it sufficient to copy the machines and give no thought to the system, and those later on who would argue for embracing the system, i.e., Western civilization, top to bottom. But from the end of the self-strengthening period on, Chinese advocates of change were divided into two groups which came be known as the reform camp (改革派) and the revolutionary camp (革命派). Because of his belief that unbridled freedom led to socially destructive selfishness, Yan on balance belonged to the former camp.

Whether Yan Fu misunderstood Western liberalism in the way Schwartz contended has come into dispute. Max Ko-Wu Huang has argued that Yan did see the ethical value of liberty, which meant that the state should respect each person as unique, leaving him free to attain his potential.[104] Indeed, to translate "freedom" or "liberty" Yan sometimes did not use the then already common 自由 (*zìyóu,* "emanating from the self"), which had been used rarely in the past—and with a negative meaning when it was used. (This translation is now the standard one in Chinese.) Instead, he often used 自繇 (*zìyáo*), with the meaning of the second character, phonetically almost identical, being "method," "reason" or "process." Huang interpreted these two characters in combination as meaning "self-realization."[105]

But Huang also asserted that in translating Mill and his arguments for freedom, especially freedom of speech, Yan Fu failed to take account what Huang called Mill's "epistemological pessimism," i.e., the idea, now much more widely accepted, that all human knowledge is tentative and is subject to revision as new ideas emerge and compete. This idea became quite important in economic liberalism in the 20th century because of the work of Friedrich Hayek, George Stigler, and others cited in Chapter 2. As noted there, infor-

---

104. Max Ko-Wu Huang, *The Meaning of Freedom: Yan Fu and the Origins of Chinese Liberalism* (Hong Kong: Chinese University Press, 2008).

105. Ibid., 94–5.

mation is costly and distributed so widely that each economic actor can only know a minuscule fraction of the whole. But individuals who uniquely possess particular pieces of information can, based on that information. perceive unexploited profit opportunities, and in an economically liberal system can act on them. In Huang's judgment Yan failed to substantially grasp this. If these individuals are right, they make money, and if they are wrong their experiments fail, people notice and avoid doing things precisely this way again, and resources are released for other economic experiments.

The other essential elements in liberalism that had been lacking in pre-1843 China were an appreciation for free competition (as against domestic government monopoly, restraining of merchants' prerogatives, and restricting or banning imports), and for the unending dynamism generated by economic competition, whatever its underlying theoretical basis. It is likely that Yan Fu understood this. This is not so apparent in his notes or in his translation of WN but it is revealed in his essays and his translations of *The Study of Sociology* and *Evolution and Ethics*, where Herbert Spencer's idea of social evolution (with its unplanned nature) loomed large. It has been more recently argued that Yan believed voluntary, individual-driven progress to be the essence of economic liberalism. In this way, the overall framework of Yan's thinking was that in combination, the evolutionary results of willful human competition lead to unending progress. In particular, Yan's translation of *Evolution and Ethics* suggested that he saw a difference between Spencer's belief in the ironclad link between human competition and social improvement and the soulless biological evolution in Darwin. In an essay known in English as "Learning from the West," Yan argued that, given good governance, progress can be endless, and economic setbacks only temporary, a combination of Smithian and Spencerian perspectives.[106] So Yan understood the importance and source of dynamism.

Overall, while Yan Fu did express alarm over the more ruthless aspects of economic competition and thought the Chinese should retain traditional values to shield against these excesses, he was as much of an economic liberal

---

106. Yan Fu, "Learning from the West." In *China's Response to the West: A Documentary Survey, 1839–1923* (Cambridge: Harvard University Press, 1979), ed. Ssu-yü Teng and John K. Fairbank, 150–15. See also 韓承樺,《斯賓塞到中國——一個翻譯史的討論 1》,《編譯論叢》, 第三卷 第二期, 2010 年 9 月, 33–60 (Cheng-Hua Han, "Herbert Spencer Came to China: A Discussion of Translation History," *Compilation and Translation Review* 3, no. 2 (September 2010): 33–60).

as it was possible to be at that time. It is fair to say that from the beginning of China's era of openness after the first unequal treaties until the consolidation of power and control by the KMT in the 1920s (to be discussed in Chapter 5), he was one of the two pillars of economic liberalism in China. In his own words, from his annotations to WN, "We cannot hurt other people without hurting ourselves. Conversely, we cannot benefit other people without benefiting ourselves. This is the most important principle in human affairs...Alas! If the idea that the public good coincides with private interests were not true, human beings would have disappeared a long time ago, and the theory that natural evolution leads to perfect rule would be untenable. Smith's views surely do not apply to trade and business only."[107] Until a number of years after Chinese economic reform began in 1978, Yan probably understood economic liberalism's benefits as thoroughly as any Chinese ever had.

3.C Resisting the retreat — Hu Shi

Yan Fu died in 1923 after a rich life and varied career. By this time another voice had taken his place as the standard-bearer of liberalism, both economic and political, and his understanding was equally deep. Hu Shi (胡適, 1891-1962, sometimes romanized as Hu Shih) was born and raised in Shanghai, then as now the most cosmopolitan of Chinese cities. From a young age he acquired both a modern and a traditional Chinese education. In 1910, using funds made available by the government of the United States from the reparations it received after the Boxer Rebellion, he went to study at Cornell University, where he changed his major from agriculture to philosophy. Upon graduating in 1914, he then studied philosophy as a doctoral student at Columbia, studying under the great American pragmatist philosopher John Dewey (1859–1952), which almost surely played a role in his later liberal thinking about the nature of human progress and Chinese progress in particular.[108]

Hu believed that social change was valuable, but he was profoundly skeptical of radical visions imposed by force, preferring competition through exper-

---

107. Translation in Huang, *The Meaning of Freedom*, 216.

108. He actually never achieved the degree, although he was commonly referred to with the title of 博士 (*bóshì*, Ph.D.) among Chinese.

imentation to determine the best, rather than reasoning out the best and then being appalled or outraged or vindictively violent when it failed to unfold as predicted. Dewey's view was similar to John Stuart Mill's, in that much social activity was trial and error, mediated by competition. (John Stuart Mill thought so in much of the economic sphere as well.) Truth was not an absolute, but a thing to be approached (but never reached) through learning. Hu carried this view with him throughout his professional life.

One of Hu's earliest efforts at social reform was an attempt to make written Chinese conform to the way people actually spoke, so that ideas would no longer have to be expressed in classical Chinese (古文, or 文言文), which Yan Fu had used in translating WN. In a famous piece entitled "The Debate Over Literary Reform" (《文學改良爭議》), drawing on already visible trends in written Chinese, Hu argued that, given the tremendous amount of change and new knowledge in the air in China at the time, the written language should closely resemble the modern spoken language. While a movement already existed to abandon the use of obsolete, arcane forms of written Chinese, his essay gave it a substantial boost, and its implied premise was the need for evolution in social institutions to adapt to new circumstances.[109]

Hu came to think that most social improvement was gradual; many mistakes were made on the way, and so humanity could live better, but in a two-steps-forward, one-step-back sort of way. Science and technology, politics, standard of living, they were all like this. And this was a theme that he propounded in various arenas throughout his intellectual career. While today's Americans would not necessarily consider John Dewey an economic liberal, among his main contributions was the idea of pragmatic philosophy itself—that our knowledge is limited, and all we can do is experiment and see if things get better, and, if not, try something else. One of the reasons modern economic liberals are suspicious of this philosophy is that Dewey extended it to the political arena as well, believing that politics was a system perfectly capable of

---

109. 胡適,《文學改良爭議》,《新青年》, 2 券 5號, 1917年一月 (Hu Shi, "The Debate Over Literary Reform," *New Youth* 2, no. 5 (January 1917)). The Chinese written language by the time this article appeared was not as rigidly divided into "classical" and "spoken." But there were many old grammatical patterns that persisted in written Chinese, and by the 19th and into the 20th century written Chinese more closely resembled, although was still different from, the Chinese people spoke in daily life. This essay was ironically written in language that contained many more traditional usage patterns. Despite this, it caused a huge sensation among Chinese intellectuals.

conducting and evaluating its own trial-and-error experiments. Modern economic liberals find this a dubious proposition for the informational reasons outlined in Section 2.B.4. But it was perfectly reasonable at the time for this to be part of Hu Shi's liberalism. Hu was evaluating pragmatic philosophy against the backdrop of China's experience, where ethical absolutism was combined with a new recognition that progress in science and technology had occurred in societies without such rigid, ancient ethical codes.

He sketched his thoroughly liberal view of social progress in a Chinese-language essay called "Our Attitude Toward Modern Western Civilization." In it, he wrote:

> The Industrial Revolution followed [other European social changes], manufacturing techniques fundamentally changed, and productivity increased substantially. In the subsequent two to three hundred years, material bounty has gradually increased, and human sympathy has correspondingly gradually broadened. This broadening sympathy is the foundation of a new religion, a new ethics. The individual wants to strive for his freedom, and at the same time thinks of the freedom of others. So, not only is one's freedom limited by the equal freedom of others; it also requires the freedom of the vast majority of other people.[110]

This thoroughly Millsian way of thinking shared features with an argument Hu Shi made in English at a talk at a conference in Chicago in 1931:

> When we talk about a cultural conflict it always means a graded absorption of the various elements of cultural impact; some are more readily accepted, some are accepted after hesitation, and some are

---

110. 「工業革命接著起來，生產的方法根本改變了，生產的能力更發達了。二三百年間，物質上的享受逐漸增加，人類的同情心也逐漸擴大。這種擴大的同情心便是心宗教新道德的基礎。自己要爭自由，同時便想到別人的自由，所以不但自由需以不侵犯他人的自由為界線，並且還進一步要要求絕大多數人的自由。」 (The English in the text is the author's translation.) 胡適，《我們對於西洋近代文明的態度》，《現代評論》，第四券第八十三期，1926年7月10日 (Hu Shi, "Our Attitude Toward Modern Western Civilization," *Contemporary Review* 4 no. 83 (July 10, 1926)). Chinese version reprinted in Sharon Shih-jiuan Hou and Chih-p'ing Chou, *The Hu Shi Reader* (New Haven: Far Eastern Publications, 1990), 19–74, 58.

never accepted. Cultural change or growth is the natural result of a contact of peoples. When nations come together it is the most natural thing for one to take from the other those elements that are most advantageous to its own culture.[111]

To put it simply, little is known, and nothing is best forever. We can do better, but there are no sure things. In "Our Attitude Toward Western Civilization" he did criticize unbridled "capitalism" (資本主義) for being an obstacle to full freedom, equality, and love and therefore in need of restraint through activism and politics. But he was an admirer of the market process. In the same essay he lauded its spontaneous, evolutionary nature, which he thought was essential to creating the new technology that helped create new human possibilities, and a greater amount of profound, Aristotelian happiness (幸福). Human choice and its possibilities were paramount. In a different context, a discussion about how to write the new laws of the Republic of China on extramarital sex, Hu argued that the draft document was unethical, since it was proposed that the punishment for females be worse than for males, and argued that adultery was a question of individual rights.[112] Other contemporary Chinese intellectuals such as Chen Duxiu (陳獨秀, 1879–1942) and the author Lu Xun (魯迅, 1881–1936), both of whom we will get to know more thoroughly in Chapter 5, opposed the punishment of females who remarried or engaged in sex outside of marriage primarily because it was an archaic relic of feudal times, not consistent with the modern world, and a "wedge issue" opportunistically used by those who wanted to return to traditional values. Hu, in other words, took a liberal perspective and argued that these were fundamental ethical issues, while Chen and Lu viewed the debate in terms of political tactics and hostility to tradition for its own sake.[113]

Other remarks beyond those in "Our Attitude Toward Western Civilization" indicate that Hu Shi was not a supporter of untrammeled capitalism. He

111. Hu Shi, "Conflict of Cultures," in Hu Shih, *English Writings of Hu Shih*, ed. Chih-Ping Chou, Chinese Philosophical and Intellectual Writings (Berlin: Springer, 2013 [1932]), 46–56, 51.

112. Hu Shih, "Our Attitude Toward Modern Western Civilization."

113. 周麗卿，《探索現代中國的政治轉型：<新青年>與民初政治, 社會思潮》, 台北: 台灣學生書局, 2016 年, 106–107 (Zhou Liqing, *Exploring Modern China's Political Transformation: "New Youth," Democratic Politics, and Trends in Social Thought* (Taipei: Students Press, 2016), 106–107).

opposed both the excessive wealth and immoral tactics, as he saw them, of late 19th-century plutocrats in the West, and during the time he was studying in the U.S. he saw, and to some extent came to agree with, growing enthusiasm for increased antitrust regulation. Initially he also saw value in what he saw as the Soviet experiment, although soon he dismissed its totalitarian nature and, according to his diaries, by the late 1930s was being persuaded by the claims of such economic liberals as Hayek and Ludwig von Mises (1881–1973)[114] But having observed what he thought to be growing dictatorial government in China in the 1930s, he returned to preferring economic liberalism overall. And throughout his career he was in favor of decentralized social and economic experimentation, and the technology and social improvement it brought. As he traveled through life as a professor and administrator at Beijing University in the second and third decades of the 20th century, he continued to advocate for dynamic social progress in China. He did the same from the United States, where he served as ambassador from 1938 to 1942, and briefly back in China after the Japanese surrender until he fled to Taiwan. He and Yan Fu carried the banner for dynamic economic liberalism for much of their lives.

Overall, while Chapter 2 demonstrated that at the time of first contact China already had a complex market economy, with much in it that economic liberals could admire, there were in 1843 three clear deficiencies that newly minted Chinese economic liberals could target. First, there was an extensive strain of the equivalent of British or Dutch chartered monopolies of the East India Company type. While the details differed, many Chinese firms were protected from competition by having exclusive contracts with the state at the central or local level. Second, for centuries there had been strong resistance to anything beyond a minimal presence for international trade. Third, as we saw, before 1843 there was little presence in Chinese thinking of the idea of the aforementioned unpredictable, unplanned, continuous progress. In fact, there were strains of thoughts that pointed in the opposite direction—a desire

---

114. 潘光哲,《胡適與近代中國的理想追尋—紀念胡適先生120歲誕辰國際學術研討會論文集》, 秀威資訊出版社, 2013年, 270頁至281頁 (Pan Kang-Che, *Hu Shi and Modern China's Pursuit of Ideals: Proceedings of the International Symposium to Commemorate the 120th Birthday of Mr. Hu Shi* (Taipei: Showwe Information Co., 2013), 270-281). On his earlier attention to the Soviet experiment, see also Jerome Greider, *Hu Shih and the Chinese Renaissance: Liberalism in the Chinese Revolution, 1917-1937* (Cambridge MA: Harvard University Press, 1962), 232–233.

to return to a past near-Utopia, and a belief that ethical and social perfection was possible (often through a return to this mythical past). But the forced opening of the Chinese coast from 1843 meant that whether they liked it or not, the Chinese were forced to overcome the first two problems, in reality if not intellectually. And Hu Shi was for a time a tremendously influential intellectual voice for broad reliance on and appreciation for unguided but continuous progress. As we will see in Chapter 5, Western utopians would eventually come to exert a powerful hold on the mind of Chinese thinkers. But, first, the next chapter investigates the fruits of true economic liberalism, how several decades of dramatic change after Western contact played out more or less as economic liberals would have predicted—unpredictably, but moving forward.

TABLE 3.1 — KEY EPISODES IN CHINESE HISTORY, 1843–1949.

Date	Event
1843	Treaty of Nanjing, ending First Opium War
1860	Treaty of Tianjin, ending second Opium War
1895	Treaty of Shimonoseki
1898	100 Days Reform
1898–1901	Boxer Rebellion
1911	Xinhai Revolution
1912–1916	Yuan Shikai dictatorship
1926–1928	Northern Expeditions
1927–1937	First KMT-CCP civil war
1945–1949	Second KMT civil war

CHAPTER 4

Dynamism the First Time: Economic Liberalism Starts to Remake China

Between 1839 and 1949, China lost (usually militarily, and unquestionably diplomatically) four wars with world powers and won just one against Japan only after fighting for more than a decade in alliance with other powers. It surrendered sovereignty over parts of many coastal cities to these same foreign powers. It also suffered the devastation of the Taiping rebellion, the civil war between the KMT and the Communist Party of China (CCP), and other lesser internal conflicts. It was largely ungovernable from the center from 1912 to 1927. It is perhaps no wonder then that some Chinese, including political leaders, believe that one benefit of China's immense economic transformation in the last forty years is the ability to eliminate its "century of national shame" (百年國恥, *bǎinián guóchǐ*).

But in fact there was a period, straddling both the late Qing and the early years after its toppling, where much of China, despite continuing political catastrophe, was economically on the move. This chapter describes that interlude, which took place between 1843 and 1927. In so doing, I will rely among other things on McCloskey's argument raised in the first chapter emphasizing the importance of the bourgeoisie, and the role of that class in facilitating economic and broader social experimentation to move society forward, one attempt at a time. (Strictly speaking, some of those considered "bourgeoisie" during this time were wealthy, but the term "bourgeoisie" has stuck, in McCloskey's work and elsewhere.) From 1843 to 1927, decentralized, economically liberal trial and error were given the freest rein in Chinese history. While paying attention to government affairs as much as private ones, Jonathan D. Spence is sweeping in his description of the kinds of change that occurred in some places:

"Steamboats plied the lower Yangzi, huge new banks lined the waterfront in Shanghai, military academies were training young officers in Western tactics, scientific textbooks were rolling off the presses, and memorials flashed by telegraph from the provinces to the Grand Council. Victorious in a series of wars, the Western powers had imposed their presence on China and were now beginning to invest heavily in the country, especially in mines, modern communications, and heavy industry."[115]

In this chapter the focus is not so much on politics but businesses, their creators, and the changes they promoted beyond "mere" business. This change, while somewhat limited in geographic scope, surely merits the adjective "revolutionary." It was among the most dramatic episodes in China's long history, as a longstanding, politically cohesive society with deep traditions and economic arrangements suddenly confronted something radically different. That the "bourgeoisie" carried out this revolutionary role at a time of near-continual political failure is all the more striking.

As already noted, free trade, both with the rest of the country and (more gradually) with the rest of the world, was fairly quickly imposed in the concessions and their surrounding environs. In theory, foreign powers could limit their exports into the concessions, but few such limits were imposed. Over time, the number of concessions grew to 75, along either the coast or the Yangzi River. Foreigners handled provision of public goods, including law enforcement, within the concessions, and, as noted above, sometimes took over collection of import duties as well. The international, i.e. Anglo/American concession in Shanghai was run by a municipal council that almost from the beginning was elected by commercial and other elites among the foreign community. (Elite Chinese got the right to vote in municipal elections, and limited representation on the concession council, in the 1920s.) As a result, commercial figures dominated governance there. They tended to establish night-watchman states, whose officials saw their job as controlling crime, enforcing contract and property rights, and providing (often world-class by contemporary standards) municipal infrastructure and services. Some of the treaty ports were barely answerable to foreign ministries or colonial commissioners. (The French concession in Shanghai, however, was governed by French diplomats.)

---

115. Spence, *Search for Modern China*, 215–216.

So we may say that for many decades many of the treaty ports, especially on the coast, were a close approximation of pure economic liberalism. Qing political weakness meant that its writ did not meaningfully extend even to the areas around the concessions. A growing number of Chinese pushed by domestic chaos and pulled by economic opportunity moved in not just to the settlements but to the areas that were growing around them. Much of what motivated governance friendly to economic liberalism was a genuine belief in its virtues held by some foreigners, especially the British and Americans. (Recall that the United Kingdom's Corn Laws were repealed in 1848, very soon after the signing of the Treaty of Nanjing.) And part of the motivation for economic liberalism was certainly European politicians acting on behalf of powerful home-country businesses, who could leverage their competitive strengths into profits in a liberal environment, and in turn benefited from colonial control over political decisions, especially in and around the settlements.

Conventional history, including Chinese historiography that recognizes a "century of national shame," depicts this period as tragic because the Qing Dynasty and later the Republic of China lost sovereignty over what had long been Chinese territory. But many sovereigns throughout history have inflicted tremendous hardship on the people subject to their sovereignty, and the focus in this chapter is on how economic liberalism led to dramatic changes, mostly for the better, in some parts of China. The direct economic effects, reflected in both the data and the new products and technology, are investigated first. Then the chapter explores how Chinese society was transformed by the operation of liberal forces beyond mere economics, and how the new middle class and rich took on responsibilities that the Chinese government was unable to shoulder after 1912, when political liberalism failed to take hold. This part draws heavily on McCloskey's argument that the "bourgeoisie" both have special values that need to receive extensive respect before modern economic growth can happen and that their role in society is to continually remake it. The emphasis is thus particularly on the dynamic aspects of economic liberalism.

4.A Economic growth in and around the treaty ports

That a tremendous amount of wealth was created from the forcible opening of the various treaty ports is undisputed, if we define (as economic liberals often do) wealth creation as the total gains to producers and consumers from the existence of a market. For many years, both in and out of China, many—not least the supporters of the CCP—have seen the wealth created in this period as the fruits of exploitation, with most of the gains going to foreign and later native capitalists, while workers lived in filthy and humiliating conditions. Photographic and written documentation of the state of the poor in the treaty ports from the late 19th century, along with the country's perceived overall weakness, contributed to the self-assessment of China as a "sick man" (病夫); the term was originally drawn from a similar English-language description of the Ottoman Empire and soon used by reformist Chinese intellectuals themselves, including Yan Fu and Liang Qichao (梁啟超, 1873–1929). This image of poverty and weakness was shared by many foreigners and persisted over the decades.

But what was the truth of the matter? While generally a stable polity and a cultural giant for centuries prior to 1843, the China found by Westerners was by then quite poor compared to the parts of the West that were already rapidly industrializing. Research on real wages in five cities starting in 1738 estimates that those in Amsterdam and London were already over twice as high as those in Beijing, the political capital of the Qing at the time. However, they were also twice as high as in Leipzig, and even more compared to Milan. These gaps grew during the rest of the century with respect to Beijing and Milan (whose wages closely tracked Beijing's throughout the study period), and before Leipzig's wages finally began to take off around 1813. By just before the first Opium War in 1836, wages in London, the center of the Industrial Revolution, were roughly four times those in Beijing and Milan, while they were twice as high as those of Leipzig and not quite three times the wages of Amsterdam. Absolute real wages in Beijing bottomed out in 1857 during the Taiping Rebellion and rose steadily but not spectacularly until shortly after the turn of the century.[116]

Beijing, the capital, suffered continually from political instability, sometimes violent, during this period. The major treaty ports, in contrast, suffered remarkably little political instability of the sort routine elsewhere in China.

---

116. Robert C. Allen, Jean-Pascal Bassino, Debin Ma, Christine Moll-Murata and Jan Luiten Van Zanden, "Wages, Prices, and Living Standards in China, 1738–1925: In Comparison with Europe, Japan, and India," *Economic History Review* 64 (Series 1) (February 2011): 8–38.

Warfare in these ports was not unknown but much rarer, even during periods of extensive civil war in much of the rest of China.

What was the effect of being designated a treaty port? First, the population exploded, both inside and outside the concessions, particularly in the Yangzi valley. Overall, Shanghai's population is estimated to have been between a quarter million in 1843, roughly a million in 1880 and four million in 1935.[117]

Why? There are several contributing factors. But greater economic opportunity must loom large in any tenable explanation. Ruixue Jia compared treaty ports with other Chinese ports, similar in many respects but not ceded to foreign countries. She found that the treaty ports grew faster economically and had resident populations that grew significantly faster than in otherwise comparable cities. The main contributors to the former were commerce and services, but manufacturing and agriculture, forestry, and fishing also contributed to the treaty ports' better performance. Migration was a major contributor to the growth of commerce.[118]

And why was there was so much economic and population growth in and around the treaty ports? First, their rulers had designed legal systems similar to those they knew from home, and these were much more liberal than those that existed elsewhere in China. Business activities were thus drawn there. Thomas Sowell has argued that large numbers of migrants were drawn from China (and India) to Malaysia and Singapore, despite their utter lack of any right to participate in governance there. They were drawn by the much stronger commitment to property and contract rights and the rule of law (in the Hayekian sense of people being free to pursue their goals through mutually beneficial agreements with others, and all government rules being equally applied to all).[119] A similar arrangement of strongly uniform and thorough enforcement of contract and property rights in the concession cities certainly appealed to Chinese, would-be workers and would-be entrepreneurs alike.

Second, the rapid construction of superior modern infrastructure, enabling

117. Lei Shi, "Moving to Shanghai: The Massive Internal Migration to the First Chinese Megacity (1927–1937)," working paper, Spanish Association of Economic History, July 2015, https://www.aehe.es/wp-content/uploads/2015/04/dt-aehe-1510.pdf.

118. Ruixue Jia, "The Legacies of Forced Freedom: China's Treaty Ports," *Review of Economics and Statistics* 96, no. 4 (October 2014): 596–608.

119. Thomas Sowell, *Race and Culture: A World View* (New York: Basic Books, 1994), 121.

greater mobility, among other things, and the introduction of modern public-health practices had significant and beneficial effects on public-health outcomes. Until the Japanese invasion of the city proper in 1937 the Shanghai area also saw substantially less war than much of the rest of China—partly because of the power of foreign nations and partly because the residents and people fleeing turmoil elsewhere in the country wanted to get along to preserve the opportunity to make money. Turmoil was kept well enough away until the 1925 "May 30th" incident, in which British municipal police shot Chinese protesting against the death of a Chinese worker at a Japanese-owned factory. The shooting was followed by several days of rioting in Shanghai and protests against foreign-owned factories nationwide. In Shanghai at least several dozen people were killed. In 1927, KMT forces cemented control over the country and killed or arrested thousands of actual or accused communists and pro-labor radicals; the estimated deaths range from several hundred to several thousand. However, Shanghai itself, while subject to much labor agitation, was, along with the other concessions, comparatively free from the larger-scale war between the KMT and CCP. It was for the most part (literally) business as usual.

In combination, what were the effects of this economically liberal environment? We can learn from data on male height, which demonstrate a consistent trend for different Chinese birth cohorts in different population samples of adult migrants to Australia and the U.S. Most of these migrants came from the southern, coastal regions where the most active treaty ports were. After declining from the time the samples began with the 1850 birth cohorts, male height figures began rising in 1890 and rose substantially through the last cohorts in either (depending on the sample) 1910 or 1920, with the total increase roughly one centimeter.[120] Elsewhere, Debin Ma reported that from 1900 to 1929 average male railroad-worker height increased by over 2 centimeters in the Yangzi delta (Shanghai and two provinces immediately north and south of it, Jiangsu and Zhejiang respectively), while it was flat or declin-

---

120. Joerg Baten, Debin Ma, Stephen Morgan, and Qing Wang, "Evolution of Living Standards and Human Capital in China in the 18–20th Centuries: Evidences from Real Wages, Age-Heaping, and Anthropometrics," *Explorations in Economic History* 47, no. 3 (July 2010), 347–359.

ing in the rest of the country.[121] Stephen L. Morgan found in Chinese government records a slow but steady increase in male heights over a longer period, 1880–1930.[122] Poor nutrition is correlated with lower heights, and so growth in average height is often used as a proxy for better nutrition.

As for economic output directly measured, Debin Ma has also documented that from 1840 until roughly 1937, Shanghai's growth exceeded even overall Chinese growth in output, trade, and foreign investment. He reported that between 1912 and 1936, China itself reported a national annual growth rate of "modern" industrial output of 8.4 percent (other estimates are higher), while Shanghai itself grew at 9.6 percent. These are sustained rates that had never been seen before and would not be seen again anywhere in the world until the emergence of economic miracles in east Asian nations after the Second World War.

In 1933, combined "net national product" in Shanghai and the Yangzi delta was more than 50 percent above that of the country as a whole. Debin Ma also notes that the two centimeters-plus height increase in the delta was accompanied by flat or declining levels in the rest of the country.[123] Meanwhile, as people, especially business people, traveled from Shanghai, knowledge spread to other parts of the country. And financial capital, almost all of it owned by Chinese who had made their fortunes in greater Shanghai, began to build other flourishing commercial centers in the nearby cities of Wuxi and Nantong. (Another major hub of modern economic activity developed in Manchuria, based on Japanese investment before the 1931 takeover, although its modern legacy is more modest than those in Shanghai and Canton.)

Wages too were competitive. While they were low compared to the U.S. or U.K., labor markets indicated workers had choices. Their wages reflected the underlying economic conditions, rising and falling over the business cycle but with an overall rising trend. While the economy at any moment might be in boom or bust, the trend in wages was much more like 19th-century London and Berlin than pre-1842 China, and these wages were soon generally suffi-

121. Debin Ma, "Economic Growth in the Lower Yangzi Region of China in 1911–1937: A Quantitative and Historical Analysis," *Journal of Economic History* 68, no. 2 (June 2008):355–392, 369.

122. Stephen L. Morgan, "Economic Growth and the Biological Standard of Living in China, 1880–1930," *Economics & Human Biology* 2, no. 2(June 2004): 197–2018.

123. Ma, "Economic Growth in the Lower Yangzi Valley," 262.

cient to provide basic sustenance for families.[124]

4.B Economic dynamism

The above descriptions are data-based. When the data indicate so strongly improvement for the better, they can be trusted to tell such a story. But sometimes the details of social change are informative as well. Several such changes are described in this section.

4.B.1 The leading wedge—merchants and compradors

We know China at first contact already had an extensive economic structure that changed over the centuries at an approximately pre-Industrial Revolution European pace. But 1843 brought rapid, genuinely dramatic changes in how Chinese in and around the treaty ports did business.

In the early years after the entry of Western businesses, it became apparent that those who wanted to buy from or sell to the Chinese needed assistance from locals. The legacy of the Canton system, in which foreigners, starting from 1757, could do business with imperial permission, but transact and live only in a small section of the city, is important here. This tradition enabled some Chinese, after first entry, to learn enough of (perhaps several) European languages to communicate with ship personnel from, say, the British and Dutch East India companies and facilitate the limited trade there. They became valuable middlemen.

Middlemen produce the service of intermediation, the linking of producers and consumers by specializing in information about who the two (or more) sides of a mutually beneficial exchange are and what each desires or can offer. In modern societies these chains of intermediation can be highly complex and ingenious, whether they involve getting cassava from farmers in Africa to buyers elsewhere in the continent or crabs from the waters of Bangladesh

---

124. 張忠民，《近代上海工人階層的工資與生活——以20世紀30年代調查為中心的分析》，《中國經濟史研究》，2卷2期，1頁至16頁 (Zhang Zhongmin, "The Life and Wages of Shanghai Workers—An Analysis of 1930s Survey Data," *Researches in Chinese History* 2011 (2), 1-16).

to restaurants in wealthy countries.[125] While such networks had long existed in China, the new ones that had to be built after 1843 in China were equally complex, and the need for them expanded dramatically as the rules for commercial interaction and in particular for engagement with foreigners changed from "whatever the Qing permitted" to "whatever individual foreigners and Chinese in combination thought worth trying."

Initially, because of limited knowledge on each side (language and culture on the Western side, technology and business structure on the Chinese), it was common for Western firms to directly hire many Chinese, and those who held the highest positions in these intermediation structures were called (from Portuguese) compradors (買辦, mǎibàn). (After 1949, the label became a term of derision in Maoist-era writing.[126])

These compradors arranged for the provision of food, fuel, ship repair, and other services, speaking with crews in English, Portuguese and pidgin languages as needed.[127] Between 1844 and roughly 1895, the role of compradors, along with merchants both traditional and newly created, helped the treaty ports and other parts of China travel along the modernization road. Because initially they had exclusive knowledge of the Chinese side of Chinese-Western exchange, their responsibilities were great. They worked primarily in financial institutions and trading companies. There they handled all the money coming from and going out to Chinese producers, learned about and advised Western firms on various local market conditions, kept track of political developments, and recommended and then supervised other Chinese staff. Soon they began supervising short-term loans to smaller but numerous traditional Chinese financial firms, and then began guaranteeing such loans themselves.[128] By

125. On the former, see A .A. Anete, "Middleman and Smallholder Farmers in Cassava Marketing in Africa," *Tropicultura* 27 (2009): 40-44. On the latter, see Zannatul Ferdoushi, Zhang Xiang-Guo and Mohammed Rajiv Husan, "Mud Crab (*Scylla* esp.) Marketing System in Bangladesh," *Asian Journal of Food and Agro-Industry*" 3 , no. 2 (2010): 248-265.

126. The term "comprador class" (買辦階級 , mǎibàn jiējí, or 買辦階層, mǎibàn jiēcéng) in post-1949 propaganda and historical scholarship came to denote anyone who sold out Chinese interests for personal gain. Among the people so designated was Hu Shi.

127. Paul A. Van Dyke, *The Canton Trade: Life and Enterprise on the China Coast*, 1700–1845 (Hong Kong: Hong Kong University Press, 2005).

128. Zhaojin Ji, *A History of Modern Shanghai Banking* (Armonk, NY: M.E. Sharpe, 2003), 55–56.

1900 there may have been over 10,000 compradors across all the treaty ports.[129]

Along with officials with imperial-exam credentials who chose to move into first middleman-mercantile and later modern economic activity more broadly, they were the first of China's new bourgeoisie. Again, the difference between the skeptical reaction of officials and the embracing attitude by those Chinese actually involved in commerce is important.

Helped at least modestly by the Qing's retention until 1895 of the policy of not allowing foreigners to buy or sell land outside the treaty-port settlements, these compradors soon moved into much larger-scale middleman activity, either within the firms that hired them or breaking out on their own. Away from the cities Chinese had long produced commodities such as silk, tea leaves, or coal. Compradors were increasingly hired, first as individuals and later as heads of teams working for the foreign firms, to seek out and purchase commodities directly from producers, and then sell it to these firms.

4.B.2 Structural commercial change

And soon, as people with specialized skills in high demand are wont to do, these compradors formed their own firms, and worked with Qing authorities during the early self-strengthening period. This was the first stage of the broader *domestic*, market-driven remaking of the Chinese economy, the doers equivalent to (and sometimes the same as) the thinkers of section 3.B who wanted to learn from foreigners. Compradors were among the first part of the larger Chinese bourgeoisie, the key stronghold of reformist sentiment. Their ranks included all manner of modern jobs— industrial entrepreneurs, doctors, lawyers, and others. So too they were key sources of funds for both economic and social entrepreneurship. One such agent of Chinese change was Tong Kingsing (唐景星 , 1832–1892). He was educated at a missionary school, became fluent in English, and after some time as a comprador at the British trading firm Jardine Matheson (怡和輪船公司), he worked under Li Hongzhang, the reformist Qing official.[130] Two other agents of Chinese change were Ho Kai (何啟, 1859–1914) and Hu Liyuan (胡禮垣, 1847–1916) The former was not a

---

129. Tang, *Merchants and Society*, 61.

130. 歐陽躍峰,《唐廷樞：中國第一位近代企業家》,《安徽師範大學學報 (人文社會科學版)》, 2004 年第3期, 5頁至11頁 (Ou-Yang, Yue-Feng "Tang Tingshu: The first Modern Entrepreneur of China," *Journal of Anhui Normal University* (Philosophy and Social Sciences), 2004 (3), 5-11).

comprador but the son of a Christian clergyman and a barrister trained in the UK, but with a brother fitting the classic mold of businessman. The latter was a comprador, who with his son worked for a time for Butterfield and Swire. Both strongly believed in British-style economic and political liberalization and advocated for reform in the last decade of the Qing, yet simultaneously were nationalists who wanted China to be governed by the Chinese—but more effectively. Their publications after the Sino-French war of 1884–5 have been described as a key moment in the end of self-strengthening. Both saw a weak China as needing further foreign intervention to oust the Qing and to enable the installation of a modern government.[131]

Collectively the new Chinese commercial elite in the treaty ports, especially in Shanghai, changed the commercial structure of the surrounding area substantially. Sometimes they would do this by adapting Western business practices to the local commercial structure, as Coble argues was the case for the Ningbo Guild, whose economic network later evolved to dominate banking in Shanghai.[132]

While China before 1843 had also had its own very sophisticated financial network, the arrival of new firms with new products and new technology provided an incentive to think about better ways to organize financial activities and to *discover* new ways of doing business. Both Western firms and traditional Chinese financial institutions benefited from the process, with foreign firms bringing capital and modern accounting methods, while Chinese firms provided more immediate access to local markets and knowledge of traditional financial networks. Suggestive evidence of learning in the new economic environment can be found in Shanghai's first major financial crisis after the rise of post-1843 finance, in 1883. Set off by the bankruptcy of a major silk merchant, almost 90 percent of native Chinese banks operating in Shanghai failed in response. But there were additional panics in 1897 and 1911, and better-capitalized, modern banks established by Chinese in Shanghai in the interim survived this time around. This is because the people who started them had learned from what they had seen in 1883. In addition, banks

131. Tsai, Jung-Fang, "The Predicament of the Comprador Ideologists: He Qi (Ho Kai, 1859–1914) and Hu Liyuan (1847–1916)," *Modern China* 7, no. 2 (April 1981): 191-225..

132. Coble, *Shanghai Capitalists*, 23–24.

of a traditional style native to the Jiangnan area, *qiánzhuāng* (錢莊), served as loan intermediaries for Western financial institutions in the first decades after 1843 and also took part in building new commercial networks to move crops across greater distances, a development whose importance is discussed in Section 4.C.1 below. At the consumer level, the introduction of banks with individual accounts gave individual savers a sense of control and possibility.[133]

Later, after the Treaty of Shimonoseki ended all Qing prohibitions on the transfer of the most advanced production technology, compradors created their own firms, involving steamship transportation of merchandise, mining, and factories producing such goods as flour, textiles and factory machinery, which soon had the latest Western tools and management methods. Xu Run (徐潤, 1838–1911), after migrating to Shanghai from Zhuhai, spent seven years (1861–1868) rising in the comprador ranks, following other family members who had also entered this work, at the British firm Dent & Co. (上海寶順洋 行, *Bǎoshùn Yánghǎng*), following other family members who had also entered this work. After leaving, and while building his own network, Xu went on to found or co-found companies specializing in, among other things, textiles, real estate, insurance and printing. His printing firm became the second firm in Shanghai, and the first owned by non-Chinese, to use lithography.[134]

On the other hand, traditional qualifications could matter too. Zhang Jian (張謇, 1853–1926) actually achieved the highest score nationwide in the highest-level imperial examinations (省試) in 1894. Even so, after the Sino-Japanese War he founded numerous firms (possibly assisted greatly by his bureaucratic status), beginning with cotton spinning, establishing a firm that lasted until it was nationalized in 1953. He soon branched into activities that included flour and other food products, printing, salt, iron mining and river transport. Such activity expanded dramatically after the economic liberalization due to the Treaty of Shimonoseki. Roughly 110 new factories opened in Shanghai, Suzhou, and further down the coast to Canton between 1895 and 1900 alone.[135]

---

133. Weipin Tsai, Reading Shenbao: *Nationalism, Consumerism and Individuality in China* 1919–37 (London: Palgrave Macmillan, 2009), Ch. 2.

134. 沈俊平,《晚清同文書局的興衰起落與經營方略》,《漢學研究》第33卷第1期, 2015年3月, 261 頁至294頁 (Shen Junping, "The Development and Business Strategies of the Tongwen Press in the Late Qing Dynasty," *Chinese Studies*, 33, no. 1 (March 2015): 261294).

135. Chesnaux et al., *China from the Opium Wars*, 302.

4.B.3 Financial and business-structure change

Western structural innovations such as contract law and joint-stock companies with limited liability made their way into China through the entrepreneurship of onetime compradors.[136] A formal commercial legal code that defined these institutions did not even exist until the Qing promulgated one in 1904. But Chinese entrepreneurs even before this would sometimes employ these tools on their own. Then after the introduction of the official code, they would use the new laws to preserve family dominance of their firms. With or without such controls, Western firms would sometimes contentedly work with compradors with only a thin layer of foreigners at the top, and sometimes try to transplant the structure and style of the new, massive Western hierarchical corporation.[137] Here it is important to remember that modern factories themselves were new to the Chinese in 1843. Gathering several hundred people together to produce things had happened before, but the factories now introduced were unlike those under the Qing during early self-strengthening, let alone like the imperial silk and porcelain factories before first entry: they consistently faced competitive pressure, and thus collectively were forced to either become more efficient or die. So from the point of view of production technology, it was now also a different world.

Unsurprisingly, being constructed according to market strictures rather than political decisions, successful manufacturing firms were strongly driven by comparative advantage, which at that time on China's coast was mostly in labor-intensive production. But after 1895, Chinese entrepreneurial activity quickly rose up the product-lifecycle ladder, with machines replacing increasingly expensive workers. Products evolved from labor-intensive goods such as yarn to more capital-intensive ones such as machinery, with the displaced workers or their children sometimes able to move from rapidly declining industries to rapidly emerging new ones. Chinese production along the coast became more capital-intensive over time, with Chinese entrepreneurs moving into shipbuilding, machine and machine-tool manufacturing, and even automobile

---

136. Yen-p'ing Hao, "A 'New Class' in China's Treaty Ports: The Rise of the Comprador-Merchants," *Business History Review* 44, no. 4 (Winter 1970): 446–459.

137. For case studies of the various organizational forms attempted, see Sherman Cochran, *Encountering Chinese Networks: Western, Japanese, and Chinese Corporations in China*, 1880–1937 (Berkeley: University of California Press, 2000).

production by the 1920s, although the latter relied extensively on imported parts.[138] This pattern had already played out in Japan and would do so again in the East Asian miracle nations after World War II. More broadly, firms beyond the treaty ports in the Yangzi delta combined domestic capital provided by early market creators to remake the economic activity that had existed before first entry. Chinese imports of labor-intensive yarn and textiles initially grew dramatically after 1844. But soon, as free trade comparative advantage asserted itself and domestic production in both industries spread to Fujian and Zhejiang, both coastal provinces built overseas contacts through emigration to Southeast Asia and, soon, the Western Hemisphere. In and around the major treaty ports, in other words, China was developing.

In any economy information conductivity, the speed with which knowledge about opportunities and tradeoffs can be learned, is important. In the post-1843 Chinese economy, new technology also improved the ability of entrepreneurs to find out where opportunity existed. The revolutionary invention of the telegraph, the first machine that allowed information to be transmitted at the speed of light, allowed traders in financial assets and commodities to react (and sometimes overreact) to information more quickly. Tellingly, the first telegraph lines in China were built by the Danish Great Northern Telegraph Company, and hence (clandestinely and illegally) gradually connected Hong Kong and Shanghai in 1870 and 1871. The illegal nature of both the early telegraph and, similarly, railroad lines led to opposition by local residents, who found them culturally disruptive and often destroyed portions of them.[139] (Jardine Matheson had illegally built a rail line from Shanghai to Wusong in 1876, but the Qing forcibly removed it after a year.) Finally, in a demonstrative example of both foreign-local cooperation and bourgeois initiative, the former comprador Tong King-Sing (唐景星, 1832–1892) conceived of the idea for a standard railway and arranged financing for it, hiring British engineers

---

138. On autos, see 關雲平, 《中國汽車工業的早期發展》（1920–1978年）》, 上海人民出版社, 2015年 (Guan Yunping, *The Early Development of the Chinese Auto Industry (1920–1978)* (Shanghai People's Publishing House, 2015)). The term "product lifecycle" in development economics refers to the path whereby as countries develop they first exploit their comparative advantage in unskilled labor, then as skill and experience are acquired, production in these industries falls and shifts to first capital-intensive and later skill-intensive production.

139. Dwayne R. Winseck and Robert M. Pike, *Communication and Empire: Media, Markets, and Globalization*, 1860–1930 (Durham, NC: Duke University Press, 2007), 129–136.

to supervise its construction. It was built in stages between 1879 and 1888, with a need to get government approval at every stage. It ran from Tongshan in Hebei to Tianjin.

Summarizing the dilatory if not obstructive nature of Qing authorities during this challenging time, the expatriate then-Qing official Robert Hart (1835–1911) wrote in a letter to the former official James Duncan Campbell (1833–1907) dated August 26, 1873:

> The policy of the central Government in China is not to guide, but to follow events. Its duty seems to be to keep records of past occurrences, legalize *faits accomplis*, and— strangle whatever comes before it in embryo. It recognizes the grand truth that eyes have two uses,—to see, and not to see; and it, as a rule, pins its faith to not seeing. This way of looking at things has given unnatural strength to its sense of smell; the moment you force it to see a thing, it "smells a rat" and whips its head off! In plainer language, the government wishes the Provincial Authorities, and the Provincial Authorities, in turn, wish the people to take the lead: what the people wish for— so long as it does not mean resistance to authority—the government in the end sanctions. To come to the Government *first* and ask for its written permission to do anything, is simply to elicit an answer in the negative and to weight a scheme, at the very start, with an official prohibition.[140]

The tactic of doing first and asking for permission later gave first movers the room to take the initiative. Such dynamism, the essence of the treaty-port economy for decades after 1843, would decrease nationwide as political control increased after 1927.

4.B.4 *The unique blending role of overseas Chinese*
While communities of overseas Chinese (華僑, *huáqiáo*) had been growing in nearby parts of East Asia for centuries, the growth accelerated substantially in

140. Robert Hart and James Duncan Campbell, *The I.G. in Peking: Letters of Robert Hart, Chinese Maritime Customs, 1868–1907*, ed. John King Fairbank and Katherine F. Bruner (Cambridge: Harvard University Press, 1975), letter 62, 118.

the 19th century because of the establishment of European colonies in Southeast Asia, which like the treaty ports were seen by many Chinese as a migratory destination worth the gamble of moving to, especially given the devastation of the Taiping rebellion. Such migration received the blessing of the Qing through its ending of a ban on emigration, in the belief that emigration could be an asset to the empire. Most migrants went to places such as the Philippines, Singapore, Malaysia, and Indonesia, although a significant number went to the Western Hemisphere. Some lived the rest of their lives and built families in all these places, others returned after working for a time. Prior to 1911 the nationalist movement in China (to be explored in Chapter 5) received significant financial and moral support from these communities, driven both by a shared belief that China was desperately behind and by racism encountered overseas. Political ideas, some of them more in agreement with economic liberalism than others, came with the return of those who had spent time overseas as well; Hu Shi, as we saw, spent time in the United States, and Sun Yat-Sen spent his teenage years in Honolulu. In addition, both Zhou Enlai (周恩來, 1898–1976) and Deng Xiaoping (鄧小平, 1904–1997) learned of Marxism while spending time working in France in the early 1920s.

In terms of facilitating economic transformation, returning *huáqiáo* founded firms at least as far back as 1862, and their entrepreneurial adventures spanned textiles, importing and exporting, mechanized silk production, and later finance and department stores. Frequently they relied on production or finance techniques that they had learned abroad. Even when they did not operate in the treaty ports, they played an important role in blending foreign and domestic economic knowledge. Returning Chinese also made a major contribution to the evolutionary change in Chinese culture, bringing knowledge of how foreign societies and their economies operated.

4.C Freedom-induced broader social change

One of Deirdre McCloskey's claims is that bourgeois society, built on the premise that you can pursue your goals through voluntary exchange as long as you respect my right to do the same, is associated with growing tolerance. People learn to accept social behavior and norms that were intolerable before, a change usually accompanied or generated by the elimination of historical and legal barriers to these new attitudes. This growing freedom to choose among different life options creates social innovations (very broadly defined) at a faster rate than before as people network more and ideas are created and recombine at faster rates. And so, for example, while formal schooling in China outside the home was rare (although not unknown) before 1842, in coastal Fujian province in 1923 "one third of all elementary education in the province was being provided in Protestant schools," with Protestantism itself almost unknown before 1842. Sixty percent of middle schools there were also private.[141] The collective schools were social innovations, as were the education they provided and the educated students who emerged. Beyond education, at the height of the Chinese openness that prevailed from 1844 to 1927, this social transformation played out in several major ways.

4.C.1 New products

In the modern consumer-good-besotted developed world of today, it is possible to feel that overconsumption is a serious problem, whether for environmental reasons or on the grounds that there are better ways to live a life genuinely worth living. But the impact of new products on human life and its possibilities of course far exceeds adding one more brand or style of toothpaste to the several dozen that already exist. New products, including things like toothpaste, poured into China soon after foreign businessmen arrived, with the new imports and entrepreneurship giving Chinese new, life-altering choices.

One example is that most mundane of commodities, food. China is certainly large enough that dietary staples differ from place to place. But the opening of substantial contact with the wider world meant that, first and foremost, in regions sufficiently close to the coast, foodstuffs became more diverse, with obvious nutritional advantages. Manuel Pérez Garcia has gone so far as to describe the "the introduction of American cereal crops as probably one of the most important events in China's agricultural history." Here he is referring to the entire Western Hemisphere, as crops from there entered China through the Spanish colonization of the Philippines. But growing wealth and com-

---

141. Ryan Dunch, "Mission Schools and Modernity: The Anglo-Chinese College, Fuzhou," in Glen Peterson, Ruth Hayhoe, and Yongling Lu (eds.), *Education, Culture, and Identity in Twentieth-Century China* (Ann Arbor: University of Michigan Press, 2004), 109–146, 112.

mercial complexity in China after 1843 accelerated this process.[142] The tomato is a striking example. Tomatoes and scrambled eggs make up a common
dish in many Chinese households today, but the scrambling technique was
known but seldom employed before modern China, and tomatoes came from
overseas. They first arrived during late Ming times, as part of the Columbian
exchange. For several centuries after, few Chinese consumed them, but beginning in roughly the 1880s, and expanding throughout the Republic of China
era, Chinese consumption grew, albeit never to dominant levels.[143]

In addition, improved production techniques increased the availability of
a number of crops that had also been known in China at least since they were
introduced via the Philippines if not sooner. Frank Dikötter listed corn (some
of it animal feed, and a crop that may have already come into western China
by land) and sweet potatoes, along with cotton and rapeseed (used to produce
cooking oils).[144] More comprehensively, Ma Junya collected numerous sur-
veys of residents of the Jiangnan region, and in combination with historical
testimony and scholarly assessment of the changing quality of life in booming
Shanghai and other nearby cities, established that the diet eaten by residents
of this region both improved nutritionally over time and compared favorably to
that of residents of Beijing after 1842. Meat in particular was soon consumed
much more frequently than just on traditional holidays, previously the dominant custom of the poor. It was frequently urban Chinese entrepreneurs from
Shanghai who went into rural areas and introduced new crops, and at the same
time introduced new technology and built trading networks for crops already
grown there, increasing rural incomes and the availability of both old and new

142. Manuel Pérez Garcia, "Challenging National Narratives: On the Origins of Sweet Potato in China
as Global Commodity During the Early Modern Period," in Manuel Perez Garcia and Lucio De Sousa (eds.), *Global History and New Polycentric Approaches. Palgrave Studies in Comparative Global History:
Europe, Asia and America in a World Network System* (Singapore: Palgrave Macmillan, 2017), 53–80, 53.

143. Alvin (Jun Young) Choi, "History of the Tomato in Italy and China: Tracing the Role of Tomatoes
in Italian and Chinese Cooking," https://scholarblogs.emory.edu/noodles/2018/07/03/history-of-the-to-
mato-in-italy-and-china-tracing-the-role-of-tomatoes-in-italian-and-chinese-cooking/. Even today the
two most common translations for "tomato" in Chinese invoke the foreign, 番茄 (fānqié, "foreign egg-
plant") and 西紅柿 (xīhóngshì, "Western red persimmon").

144. Frank Dikötter, *The Age of Openness: China before Mao* (Berkeley: University of California Press,
2008), 87.

crops.[145] This presumably was a significant reason for the height increases of Chinese men documented in section 4.A.

Ma Junya also documented other improvements in and around Jiangnan. Families there, in addition to higher real income, had the things higher income buys: bigger houses with more rooms (hence more privacy), more access to daily health-related goods beyond toothpaste, taken for granted now but major innovations in their time, and more access to medical treatments and thus had better self-reported health. Fabrics such as wool, cotton and even silk became more widely available, so that families could have more sets of clothing.[146] Kerosene lamps became much more widely available, thus allowing people to make much better use of the time after the sun went down, whether for study or social activities. (During the Great Leap Forward (GLF, 1958–1962), the communes still used kerosene and not electricity for street lighting, which had since become standard in developed countries. That has been viewed as a sign of Chinese poverty.[147]) In Shanghai, even shopping, particularly along Nanjing Road, which after the late 1970s once again became the retail center of a revitalized city, ceased being a chore and became something enjoyable.[148]

Beyond this, entrepreneurs in the countryside, whether working through the traditional land-ownership system or buying land personally, changed that countryside. They invested in maintaining old and constructing new traditional-style temples (often centers of social activity) and built schools. Increased income for peasants, through bigger markets for what they grew and for their handmade tools and other goods, and greater opportunities for family members to earn money from second jobs in the countryside and through rural migration to Shanghai and elsewhere, raised their standard of living and helped them during still-frequent personal financial crises.[149] This served to lower

---

145. 馬俊亞，《混合與發展：江南地區傳統社會經濟的現代演變》，北京，社會科學文獻出版社，2003年），第5章 (Ma Junya, *Blending and Development: The Gradual Evolution of Traditional Society and the Economy in the Jiangnan Region* (Beijing: Social Sciences Academic Press, 2003)), Chapter 5.

146. *Ibid.*

147. Duanfang Lu, "Third World Modernism: Utopia, Modernity, and the People's Commune in China," *Journal of Architectural Education* 60, no. 3,(February 2007): 40–48, 43.

148. Wen-Hsin Yeh, "Shanghai Modernity: Commerce and Culture in a Republican City," *The China Quarterly* 150 (June 1997): 375–394, 385.

149. On the effect of second jobs and income earners on family income, see *Ma, Blending and Development*, table 5.8, 307.

longstanding urban/rural income differences. Working through traditional institutions (later characterized as feudal, especially by the CCP) certainly retarded social change relative to the often-different changes the Party would later impose. However, Debin Ma argued that at a time of weak governance and widespread military clashes it "preserved social stability and therefore contributed to lowering the potential for violence."[150] This is classic dynamic social liberalism: introducing new ideas and replacing or merging them with existing ideas and institutions as the (social, often) entrepreneur sees fit.

We should not exaggerate here. While the combination of vastly improved transportation and entrepreneurial network-building and creativity made new goods more widely available, especially in regions closer to the major treaty ports, China in 1927 at the end of Bergère's "golden age of the bourgeoisie" was a poor country, especially in the countryside. But during this era, parts of China were undergoing social change in ways that mere aggregate statistics on economic growth significantly understate. All of this change was dynamically liberal in nature, with Chinese people experimenting individually or in groups, causing their society, especially in the regions where the foreign presence was the greatest, to be in constant churn, as Japan, North America, and Western Europe were already. And the consequences of the innovations went well beyond the personal utility of the products themselves.

4.C.2 Liberalism in ideas

In Scandinavian and Anglo-American society, the late 18th century saw governments make binding commitments to protect freedom of speech. (In the U.K. clear traces of this idea go back to the mid-17th century.) One argument in favor of such policies is that if ideas compete freely, just as with any other product, the new ideas "produced" will overall be better, specifically with respect to social improvement. The original version of this market-for-ideas argument dates back to the Scientific Revolution.[151] So as the market for ideas in China became more competitive and advanced, many more ideas were generated, partly because of the importation of foreign ideas and partly because of what Chinese thinkers and doers did with them.

---

150. Ibid., 82.

151. Osborne, *Self-Regulation and Human Progress*, chapter 3.

Such changes in what people thought about and how they thought about them were initially resisted by some of those conservatives discussed in Chapter 3 who thought the essence of Chinese culture had to be protected from corrupt, predatory or mercenary Westerners. In the 1870s school-age boys were sent to the U.S. to study, accompanied by credentialed Chinese scholars, who soon were bemoaning the "Americanization" of their students.[152]

Yet foreigners continued to come to China, even to the interior of the country, and young Chinese went abroad. And this exchange led some Chinese to look for and find new examples of how to organize and/or run their lives, their businesses, and their societies.

4.C.2. A new media

As noted earlier, China by 1843 had a long history of both idea creation and assessment. Generation after generation of scholars commented on ancient works from the Four Books and Five Classics (四書五經), texts written and compiled before Chinese unification under the Qin Dynasty (秦朝, 221 B.C.–206 B.C.), and whose commentaries sometimes were themselves added to the roster of Chinese classics. But this was a process that played out over centuries, owing to technological limits (the speed of information transmission) and the tendency of scholars to also have public-administration functions. But Western colonialists arrived with the ability to produce many more ideas much more quickly. (The periodical, eventually including the daily newspaper, had spread in Western Europe and North America during the eighteenth century.)

And so almost immediately after the establishment of British Hong Kong and the foreign concessions, several papers that had served British working for the trading firms in Canton before 1843 decamped to Hong Kong. In addition, one of the most influential new newspapers, the weekly English-language publication *North China Herald*, began in Shanghai in 1850, and was published until Pearl Harbor. (Its sister daily newspaper, *The North China Daily News*, was published from 1864 until 1951.) With the waning of the self-strengthening ideology, Chinese-language papers began to be published. The first may have been *The Shanghai News* (《申報》), founded in 1872 in the international

---

152. Chesnaux, Bastid and Bergère, *China from the Opium Wars*, 230. "Americanization" is their word. This particular program was brought to a halt after the U.S. banned Chinese immigration in 1880.

settlement in Shanghai by Ernest Major (1841–1908). The next year the daily *Xúnhuán rìbào* (《循環日報》, no standard English translation), was founded in Hong Kong using printing equipment from the London Missionary Society and funded by members of the society and by Wang Tao (王韜, 1828–1897). Both papers, along with many that would follow, operated in places where the Qing Empire's (and later the Republic of China's) jurisdiction did not reach, allowing them substantial liberty to publish whatever suited them.

During the period of thorough introspection that followed the loss to Japan in 1895, the rate at which newspapers were created grew. Twenty-five dailies, weeklies, and monthlies were created between 1896 and 1898, including different ones by Yan Fu and admirers of Kang Youwei (康有為, 1858–1927), who will play a role in the early stages of the drama in Chapter 5. Both general chambers of commerce and specific industry associations gradually brought out their own journals, and generally spoke of the necessity of growth and change, something the journals founded earlier seldom had done.[153] According to various estimates, by the turn of the century, the total periodical audience in China may have been between two and four million. By 1907, there were over 100 newspapers, and over a thousand periodicals appeared after 1911, many published in the concessions.[154] Taken as a whole, the new Chinese press was sometimes scholarly, sometimes vulgar, sometimes of general interest, but it was all new, and the novel media served to introduce literate Chinese to a kaleidoscope of new ideas, which they would soon recombine and add to. The number of literate Chinese was growing rapidly (although from a small base), especially in Hong Kong and Shanghai. Economic, political, and broader social ideas—economic liberalism, feminism, various forms of socialism, and ultimately communism—were discussed, as were more mundane concerns of the new bourgeoisie such as gardening, architecture, cooking, music, and literature.

And while history has given famous intellectuals such as Kang Youwei and Liang Qichao much of the credit for persuading urban, educated Chinese of the need to adopt new ideas, there were many others. Xiong Yuezhi has compiled a list of idea propagators in Shanghai—-those involved in formal

---

153. Bergère, *Golden Age of the Bourgeoisie*, 134.

154. Total periodical audience: Lee and Nathan, "The Beginning of Mass Culture," 373. 1907 newspapers, 1911 periodicals: Dikötter, *Age of Openness*, 23.

education, journalism and publishing, those in Western-influenced law and medicine, and those working for or with Western firms. The number of such people is estimated to have grown from 1200 at the time of the Hundred Day's Reform in 1898 to 4000 by 1909.[155] Such growth could not help but dramatically increase ideological churn. And such cultural entrepreneurs were certainly not limited to the treaty ports; while foreign-dominated Shanghai was where many major Chinese-language publishing houses were located initially, these presses had national distribution networks, and many purely local publications flourished along with the spread of local presses.[156] Commercial and cultural growth were thus partners and not antagonists.

4.C.2.b Science

Especially after 1895, Chinese familiar with science and technology studied what modern science was and how it worked. As in so many other arenas during this time, they spontaneously formed groups to discover and transform foreign institutions and practices, in this case via organizations like the Jiangsu Provincial Educational Association (江蘇省教育會). In the first decade of the 20th century, driven by the interest and the funds of merchants, this group gathered together Western-trained doctors, Chinese philologists, and missionaries to figure out how best to translate modern medical and scientific terms for the benefit of Chinese learners. Modern universities began to be constructed as well, first by the central government in 1896 in the form of what became Beijing University (the successor to a school that already existed), and later by religiously motivated people, both Western and Chinese.[157] Chinese students studying at Cornell formed the China Scientific Society (

---

155. 熊月之，《略論晚清上海新型文化人的產生與匯聚》，《近代史研究》，1997年04期， 257頁至 271頁 (Xiong Yuezhi. "On the Emergence and Convergence of the People of Shanghai's New Culture in the late Qing Dynasty," *Research in Modern History* 4 (1997): 257–271).

156. Robert Culp, "Local Entrepreneurs, Transnational Networks: Publishing Markets in the Cantonese Communities Within and Across National Borders," in *The Business of Culture: Cultural Entrepreneurs in China and Southeast Asia*, 1900–1965, Christopher Rea and Nicolai Volland, eds. (Vancouver: UBC Press, 2015), 181–206.

157. Fudan University (復旦大學), located in Shanghai and now one of China's nine elite universities, was one of several universities founded by the extraordinarily active Jesuit priest Ma Xiangbo (1840–1939). He had founded Aurora University (震旦大學) two years prior, an explicitly religious school whose functions were scattered among several Shanghai schools after 1949. In 1925 he founded Furen Catholic University (天主教輔仁大學) in Beijing, which still operates in Taiwan.

中國科學社) in 1915, and the domestic version was soon founded in Nanjing. Modeled after the American Association for the Advancement of Science, in China it supervised research and scientific education. And by the mid-1920s Chinese had gone beyond merely absorbing modern scientific knowledge and were actively contributing to it, science being the classic dynamic, continuously evolving activity. Again note the similarity, this time more immediate, to the societies for popularization and transmission of scientific knowledge in the U.K. that Joel Mokyr described, referred to in Section 2.D. Note also that a similar pattern, carried out more dramatically, began once again when Chinese students began returning to Western universities in large numbers in the early 1980s, increasingly returning home to add to what scientists had learned in the rest of the world.

4.C.2.c Other aspects of culture

This synthesis played out too with respect to art, broadly defined. With regard to literature, there were numerous Western forms that had no parallel in classical Chinese fiction and poetry. And Chinese fiction changed tremendously in the decades after 1843. Few Chinese anthologies of twentieth-century essays contain pieces in the classical idiom, even though vernacular literary essays were virtually unknown at the beginning of the century. China has its own acclaimed classical works of literature. But the culture of the Western colonial powers was vastly different.

And so, unsurprisingly, the dominant feature of late Qing and republican literature was its diversity. The combination of modern printing technology, the successful efforts to popularize vernacular *báihuà* as a medium for literature, the significant increase in literacy and formal education and even the introduction of various European languages, going well beyond English and French, helped make the literature of this period multifaceted and always in motion. While much attention has been paid over the years to gifted writers seen later as part of the revolutionary trek toward communism (the author Lu Xun most notably), at the time there was an extraordinary variety of literary societies and (often evanescent, admittedly) literary journals. Some literature was political. Others, e.g., the so-called "ducks and butterflies" variety (鴛鴦蝴蝶派) of popular novels centered on romance and what we might now call soap-opera elements, appealed to a broader audience. At the same time, some Chinese argued that literature and poetry ought to serve the politics of Chinese reform. This process arguably began with the young writer and later a founder of the CCP Chen Duxiu, in his essay "On Literary Revolution" (《文學革命論》).[158] This line of thinking would culminate in the Yan'an Forum on Art and Literature (延安文藝座談會) in the CCP refuge of Yan'an in 1942, in which Mao Zedong argued that art should *only* serve revolutionary politics.

Cinema was an art form invented during the time period encompassed by this chapter, and movies were produced in great abundance in China during the 1930s and even into the 1940s, albeit for part of this time under, first, KMT censorship and then Japanese occupation. Between 1928 and 1932, roughly 400 films were produced in Shanghai alone, often invoking what Dikötter called "[c]lassical costume, knight errants, martial arts and magic spirit."[159] For such popular films, Hollywood-style story-making was often placed within a blended framework that appealed to Chinese audiences, again a form of cultural reshaping.

While leftist works were an important part of China's cultural dynamism before 1937, China's idea market was far broader than that. As with economic dynamism, the combination of an influx of new ways of looking at the world combined with the freedom to pursue them made this stretch of history perhaps China's most innovative and dynamic. But it was not to last. The writer Eileen Chang (張愛玲, 1920–1995) became famous writing essays, movie scripts, and novels in occupied wartime Shanghai, and was later judged in 1961 by noted literary scholar C.T. Hsia (夏志清, 1921-2013) to be, perhaps, China's greatest 20th-century writer to that point.[160] After 1949, she attended one Shanghai meeting of artists organized by the CCP to plot the role of art in the new China. She sat in the back of the room, and as famous as she was nonetheless asked no questions. Within two years she had sneaked across the border to Hong Kong under an assumed name, never to return. All of China's intellectual spontaneity during this time seemed to cross the border with her, not to return until after Mao's death.

---

158. 陳獨秀,《文學革命論》, 新青年第二券第五期, 1917年二月 (Chen Duxiu, "On Literary Revolution," *New Youth* 2 no. 5 (February 1917)).

159. Dikötter, *Age of Openness*, 75.

160. C.T. Hsia, *A History of Modern Chinese Fiction*, 3rd edition (New York: Columbia University Press, 2016 [1961]), 389.

4.C.2.d Women in society

A characteristic trait of modernizing societies, whether modernization is driven by economically liberal forces or by dictatorial attempts to transform society, is that the role of women changes dramatically. Claudia Goldin has summarized the relationship between economic development and the role of women this way: first, women are traditionally actively involved in peasant agriculture (even if as part of the family), then as economic development advances women spend most of their time engaging in what labor economists refer to as household production, then re-emerge into the broader economy when economic development progresses sufficiently far.[161] In China before 1843, Goldin's first stage prevailed in the peasant-agricultural economy outside the cities; rural and urban elite women could participate in some kinds of charity work with other women, but they were expected to largely remain apart from the male society around them.

This of course was not unique to China; most complex ancient civilizations sharply limited the ability of women to participate in public society, to the extent such a thing even existed. In Europe this consensus began to break down in the decades before the Enlightenment. In Britain the Leveller faction during the English Civil War had made demands that in modern terms can be seen as the protection of liberties, equality before the law, and parliamentary authority. Several times during this period groups of women also petitioned Parliament to ask that they too have these rights. In the 18th century there was a rising tide of arguments for female equality. In 1792, Mary Wollstonecraft's (1759–1797) *A Vindication of the Rights of Women* was well-received in certain British circles. To a modern believer in women's equality what was being requested seems like thin gruel, but such women set in motion a wellspring of ideas about women's rights that continue to flow even now.

It is true that in the mid-18th century the percentage of women regularly participating in the labor market was small in all of the nations with a colonial presence in China, and in the U.S. (at the federal level) and the U.K. they did not get the vote until the early 20th century, and in France not until 1944 (and initially for literate women only). But at the time of first entry, women's rights

---

161. Claudia Goldin. "The U-Shaped Female Labor Force Function in Economic Development and Economic History," in T. Paul Schultz (ed.), *Investment in Women's Human Capital and Economic Development* (Chicago: University of Chicago Press, 1995), 61–90.

in the modern sense were significantly more advanced in these countries than in China itself, and they continued to advance back home.

And many Chinese, both male and female, beginning in the late 19th century sensed that Chinese social attitudes toward women needed to change. Chinese thinkers before first entry had included some explicit advocates of equality between the sexes (e.g., the Ming writer Li Zhi (李贄, [1527–1602]). But what was essentially polygyny was widespread (although Chinese did have different words for, and social distinctions between, "wife" (妻, qì) and "concubine" (妾, qiè)). Also, the idea prevailed, as it did in much of the world, that women and men had different social roles to play, often to the detriment of women. The first proposed national education system put forth under the Qing in 1904 purposely did not include girls' education, which for reasons of propriety was recommended to be done at home. In 1907, however, girls were by law included in the final national educational blueprint, although initially under a curriculum stressing household management.[162]

As often happens, under economic liberalism and the social liberalism that accompanied it, commerce outraced politics in recognizing the costs of systematically neglecting or explicitly excluding, in the name of some normative purpose, members of some groups, women in this case. Private schools for girls began to be opened soon after the British takeover of Hong Kong, and the first Chinese female students started attending American institutions of higher education in 1881.[163] By the time the Qing educational system was extended to girls in 1907 there were many modern girls' schools in the major treaty ports, especially Shanghai. From roughly 1890, a growing number of thinkers and activists, some of them foreign, campaigned against foot binding and in favor of girls' education, and these views rapidly became a bourgeois consensus. (Separate schools for boys and girls had been opened in the major treaty ports soon after 1843, and women-only colleges were later constructed there from the 1870s.)

162. Paul Bailey, "Active Citizen or Efficient Housewife? The Debate over Women's Education in Early-Twentieth-Century China," in Glen Peterson, Ruth Hayhoe and Yongling Lu (eds.), *Education, Culture, and Identity In Twentieth-Century China* (Ann Arbor: University of Michigan Press, 2004), 318–347, 319.

163. Huping Ling, "A History of Chinese Female Students in the United States, 1880s–1990s," *Journal of American Ethnic History* 16, no. 3 (Spring 1997), 8_1-109.

Meanwhile, by the 1910s women, even without formal schooling, were attending science lectures promoted by the types of societies described in Section 4.C.2.c above, and as the Qing changed to the ROC, there was a growing acceptance of women having the same chances to participate in society as men did. Factories in Shanghai and other treaty ports, particularly those making labor-intensive goods such as textiles, hired large numbers of women workers. While there is undoubtedly much truth to the argument that this was because women could be hired more cheaply, the ability to earn income independently of husbands gave women more autonomy within the home— the ability to stand up to oppression by the husband's family, for example. Women working in factories, themselves not from elite backgrounds, sometimes out-earned husbands who were doing traditional work, and engaged in and even led strikes. On the other hand, the ability of women to move beyond factory work and professional employment was not matched with respect to the high-executive ranks in Shanghai businesses. Chinese firms still generally stuck to family ownership, and by long-standing custom running these businesses was men's work. In addition, custom and law defined property rights patrilineally. However, behind the scenes women in the family were able to exercise considerable influence even while seldom having official titles.[164]

It is true that many of the most visible advocates for women's rights were men (Liang Qichao, for example), although a conspicuous exception was Qiu Jin (秋瑾, 1875-1907). Seen even now in Communist history, like Lu Xun and Sun Yat-Sen, as an incompletely formed revolutionary, Qiu in her 1904 essay "An Address to My Two Hundred Million Women Compatriots in China" (《警告中國二萬萬女同胞》), written while she was a student and budding revolutionary in Japan, criticized foot-binding, the system of arranged marriages (to which she herself had been subjected in 1896) and other obstacles to women's equality. While there she became involved with Sun Yat-Sen's *Tóngménghuì*, and in 1907 was executed by the Qing government for plotting an uprising. (Qiu, considered a hero by both the KMT and later the CCP, was born and raised in the treaty port of Xiamen.)

After his first return from the U.S., Hu Shi argued in a 1918 lecture at Beijing Women's Normal School (北京女子師範大學) that Chinese women

---

164. Bergère, *Golden Age of the Chinese Bourgeoisie*, 154.

should take after the independence of American women, which while sometimes extreme (「極端」), was also admirable. (「獨立」). Hu also has been credited as the first Chinese intellectual to explicitly raise the idea of China's "new woman" (various contemporaneous translations).[165] Henrik Ibsen's play *A Doll House* took intellectual China by storm in the 1920s, and the Chinese ideology later known as "Nora-ism" (娜拉主義, *Nàlā zhǔyì*) itself took inspiration from the woman who walked away from the burdens of traditional obligations.[166]

The need for female equality, and a strict definition of marriage as a lifelong, monogamous commitment, played a big role in the May 4 movement, an overall embrace of social reform that began in 1919 and will be discussed in more detail in the next chapter. Indeed, Lynn Pan has contended that the introduction of Western culture that gradually played out in the late Qing and early Republic of China caused educated Chinese, both male and female, to explore and embrace the very idea of love itself for the first time.[167] And the CCP in its literature strongly promoted female equality, both before and after 1949. But all of this was made possible both by the original *idea* of equality, the facts of its partial realization in Western countries and among Westerners who went to China, and the flexibility of post-1843 Chinese society, in which a single believer could further equality, one experiment at a time. Change with regard to women's equality was already underway, spontaneously, in at least the cities of the liberal China of the late 19th and early 20th centuries.

4.D.2.e Movement

The final cultural category deserving elaboration is the improved mobility of Chinese after 1843. Historical China is justly praised for being a relative meritocracy, but mainly in one sense: since the 11th century, the exam system for

---

165. A transcript of the lecture, originally published in the 1920s, is available as 《美國的婦人》("American Women"), at https://zh.m.wikisource.org/zh-hant/美國的婦人.

166. Shu Yang, "I Am Nora, Hear Me Roar: The Rehabilitation of the Shrew in Modern Chinese Theater," *Nan Nü* 18 (2016), 291-325. Lu Xun, in another talk on December 16, 1923, at the same university called "What Happens After Nora Walks Out?" (《娜拉走後怎樣》), argued that in the face of a society as oppressive as China's, individual acts of rebellion were not sufficient, and systemic change was required. As we will see in the next chapter, this theme would grow in importance in the coming years, and not just with respect to women's rights.

167. Lynn Pan, *When True Love Came to China* (Hong Kong: Hong Kong University Press, 2015).

becoming a bureaucrat had meant that any male from any background had an equal legal opportunity to become a scholar and hence part of the elite. But after 1843, the level of openness was far broader. There were now many more ways in which people with skills beyond merely mastering the Chinese classics could do good and do well. Their new mobility played out both geographically and socially.

Before the modern era and across many dynasties slavery in China had existed, although it was not as extensive in scope nor as cruel as in many other places over the centuries. It was common practice for Chinese leaders who had conquered territories to forcibly move people either from or to those jurisdictions to secure control.[168] Von Glahn also cites examples of smaller numbers of people being transferred with the land title when land was sold.[169] That people might choose what to do and where to live was as rare in China as it had been in most pre-modern civilizations.

With respect to geographical mobility, there was some tradition of southern, coastal Chinese merchant diasporas doing business in Southeast Asia, with trading caravans extending as far as the Arabian Peninsula and east Africa. Foreign trade was essentially terminated by the Hongxi emperor (洪熙, 1378–1425, reigned 1424–1425), primarily for cost reasons. Recall that under the Qing emigration was banned in the early 18th century. And as was true in most empires, for the majority of the population it was "born a peasant, die a peasant." It was common for people to spend their entire lives in the vicinity of where they were born.

In short, China was not a society where it was common for people to move, to start over, or to try new paths in life. But this changed almost immediately after China's forced opening, based on the space provided by the new economic liberalism that had had similar effects elsewhere. Limits on internal migration, at least for free whites, had never been part of the American tradition. In Britain, at the height of economic liberalism's political triumph, advocates of free movement could draw on Adam Smith's attack on a portion of the Poor Laws requiring aid recipients to remain in their native parish, thus preventing

---

168. Examples of this practice are found in Patricia Buckley Ebrey, "State-Forced Relocations in Imperial China, 900-1300" in Patricia Buckley Ebrey and Paul Jakov Smith (eds.), *State Power in China*, 900–1325 (Seattle: University of Washington Press, 2016), 307–340.

169. Von Glahn, *Economic History of China*, 33–34.

them from seeking better opportunities.[170] In short, such freedom was a key part of the economic liberal framework. And Chinese had it to a much greater degree soon after the extraterritorial jurisdictions were established. People moved to the vicinity of many of the concessions in large numbers, and people inside them were somewhat mobile with respect to social class as well; one case, a survey of factory owners in 1913, indicated that 80 percent had started off as factory supervisors or owners of small workshops.[171]

In addition, in the extraterritorial jurisdictions and the space around them, once factories began to be constructed their owners desired competition among workers and hence supported the freedom of poor Chinese to migrate to work in these factories. In 1905, during the very late Qing, the walls erected centuries before throughout old Shanghai, once meant to keep dangerous outsiders out, began to be torn down under the initiative of Chinese businessmen. In 1912, shortly after the deposing of the last emperor, known now as the child Puyi (溥儀, 1906–1967), the ROC government tore down the primary wall. Note that in this Shanghai resembled many cities in Europe, where many medieval walls were torn down in the 19th century, as the benefits of free movement replaced fear of siege warfare as a primary fact of urban life. In the modern world, letting people in yielded more than keeping them out.

And as Shanghai's dramatic population growth attests, those who governed the colonial jurisdictions, frequently not diplomats but businessmen, were not particularly concerned about migration. As noted above, while in Shanghai huge numbers of people moved from elsewhere to spaces outside the borders of the concessions, the Chinese population inside them grew dramatically as well. These were often people who could afford to live there, paying higher home prices because of the greater security and better public services available there. This massive migration was liberating for people whose families had been trapped in rural poverty for generations. Many of them found that difficult lives faced them when they arrived in or near these foreign-governed jurisdictions, but as noted above there were many ways in which new possibilities presented themselves. Extraterritoriality overall generated the kind of

170. WN I.1.10, Smith (1976), 151–158.

171. Tang, *Merchants and Society in Modern China*, 73, quoting (上海民族機器工業第1卷), 北京, 中華書局, 1979年, 197頁 (Survey of Shanghai Machine Industry, Vol. 1 [Beijing: Zhonghua Publishing, 1979]), 197.

social mobility that had not been common before.

The newly wealthy in the Yangzi delta and elsewhere took over traditional functions of traditional merchants (for example, providing assistance to new migrants or for disaster relief), and added functions already significantly state-provided in the West, but still unknown in China. As noted above, they provided a significant amount of education for the broader masses, male and female, funding schools on top of those first provided by foreigners. Education was often provided in foreign tongues, producing elite Chinese who disproportionately brought foreign perspectives to domestic problems as businessmen and political leaders, and who, as we saw, often studied overseas themselves. Before the Qing introduced commercial laws at the end of their rule, merchants' associations also built their own schools for their members.[172] In Shanghai outside the settlements, the rising class of Chinese businessman also invested in surface rail lines and road construction, with the effect of increasing the ability to build commercial networks by allowing people to travel more easily within the metropolitan area itself, and adding to the intercity rail lines described in Section 4.B.3.[173]

Shanghai in particular had a tolerant and even welcoming attitude toward refugees, first domestic and later foreign. Outside the foreign concessions, Shanghai suffered violence—from the Small Swords Society (小刀會) in the 1850s, from KMT/CCP conflict in the second half of the 1920s, and from organized crime throughout much of its history between 1843 and 1949. But it took in even more of those fleeing violence elsewhere. Michael Marmé has noted that "up to 500,000 refugees [from the Taiping Rebellion of 1850–1864] crowded into the International Settlement and the French Concession at Shanghai," although most had moved to greater Shanghai or back home by 1870.[174] After the November Revolution in Russia, White Russian refugees fled in large numbers first to the regions of China bordering Siberia (especially near Vladivostok, the location of the last stand of the White Russians) in 1921, and then, having become stateless when the ROC recognized the Soviet Union

172. William C. Kirby, "China Unincorporated: Company Law and Business Enterprise in Twentieth-Century China," *Journal of Asian Studies* 54, no 1 (February 1995): 43–63.

173. Coble, *Shanghai Capitalists*, 5.

174. Michael Marmé, "From Suzhou to Shanghai: A Tale of Two Systems," *Journal of Chinese History* 2 (2018), 79–107, 89, 90.

in 1924, moving to Hong Kong and the treaty ports.[175] In the 1930s and early 1940s thousands of Jewish refugees flooded into the city, many of them thanks to the heroic action of the Japanese diplomat in Lithuania Chiune Sugihara (1901–1986), acting against his country's wartime national interests, and by the less well-known ROC diplomat in Vienna Ho Feng-Shan (何鳳山, 1901–1997). These latter refugees, even in wartime Shanghai, integrated as smoothly as could be expected before mostly emigrating between 1945 and 1949.

Even apart from these specific episodes, Shanghai, like much of China, between 1842 and 1949 saw an unprecedented freedom of movement, accepting the energy, initiative, and ideas of a large number of people, whether foreign or native. Such massive, peaceful, permanent migration to the coastal extraterritorial areas and their vicinities was, like other phenomena in this chapter, nearly unprecedented in Chinese history. As we will see in Chapters 6 and 7, while restrictions on internal migration were imposed after 1949, they have in the reform era been significantly rolled back. In much of the country Chinese people during the treaty-port era were more free to do what they wished, where they wished, than ever before.

4.D Governing, when no one else could

The first Opium War (1839–1842) can be seen as one episode, although subsequently a very consequential one, in the process of dynastic collapse. Earlier, when a Chinese dynasty was healthy, major businessmen in China had long had to take some direction from its officials as they produced and managed the flow of goods. But the foreign challenge was different—it was a threat to the existence of traditional commerce itself. It was adapt or die. Unsurprisingly, businessmen were the leading edge of contact with foreigners until after 1911, and foreign advantages and Chinese weaknesses were increasingly obvious to the businessmen most directly affected by it, even as cloistered high government officials initially largely minimized the importance of the new challenges. The commercial class, Chinese and foreign, thus took it upon itself to do

---

175. Stuart Heaver, "How the White Russian Refugee Crisis Unfolded a Century Ago, and the Lucky Ones Who Made it to Hong Kong," *South China Morning Post*, May 7, 2017, https://www.scmp.com/magazines/post-magazine/long-reads/article/2092988/how-white-russian-refugee-crisis-unfolded-china.

things the state either could not or would not do.

4.D.1 Pre-1911

The wealthy Chinese merchant had long had a role in addressing some social problems. In addition to charity for the poor and disaster relief, construction and maintenance of major roads and bridges and even dikes and canals were substantially undertaken by wealthy merchants throughout the Ming and Qing, with similar if less systematic efforts before then.[176]

After 1843, infrastructure provision and maintenance were among the many problems in which it soon became clear that China had work to do. The besieged and ever-more financially desperate Qing state was progressively less able to provide most public services. Driven surely to some degree by patriotism, merchants familiar with foreign languages and cultures played diplomatic roles in both Opium Wars and the 1883–1885 war with France.[177] Some were also involved in the abortive 1898 reforms. Even as they were shut out until the late 1920s from governance of the Shanghai international concession some of them were living in, they were busy modernizing the city outside the concession. The Qing also had a program to reward businessmen who built factories or ran mines, or such infrastructure as bridges and power-generation facilities.[178] And local chambers of commerce provided schools to teach commercially useful knowledge, complementing the efforts of the foreigners and wealthy Chinese noted above.

4.D.2 From the revolution to the Nanjing Decade—bourgeois order amid political chaos

Despite the already extant reputation of Sun Yat-Sen's *Tóngménghuì* as an organization sympathetic to economic control in the name of social justice (further described in the next chapter), in the years leading up to the overthrow of the Qing it was far from devoid of support from the new bourgeoisie. In the last half of the first decade of the 1900s, as chambers of commerce and trade asso-

---

176. Nanny Kim, "Privatizing the Network: Private Contributions and Road Infrastructure in Late Imperial China (1500–1900)," in Susan E. Alcock, John Bodel, and Richard J. A. Talbert (eds.), *Highways, Byways, and Road Systems in the Pre-Modern World* (New York: John Wiley & Sons, 212), 66–89.

177. Hao, "A 'New Class' in China's Treaty Ports," 453–454.

178. Tang, *Merchants and Society*, 60.

ciations grew dramatically, business elites themselves were split on the need for political change. Some were involved in actively trying to overthrow the Qing, while others preferred to involve themselves in the activities mentioned above such as the provision of public infrastructure that improved the business environment (e.g., policing, public health, or firefighting services). This followed similar efforts by business leaders to provide such services after 1843 to a rapidly growing Hong Kong, efforts that were ultimately brought under colonial management in 1856. In China proper, some commercial figures also participated in the ultimately failed efforts by the Qing to form a constitutional monarchy.[179] Some business elites belonged to the *Tóngménghuì*, and Sun Yat-sen himself raised substantial amounts of money from overseas Chinese. But to them as to the others, the revolution itself came like a bolt from the blue.

The uprising that ended the Qing dynasty also ended a Chinese tradition of governance thousands of years old. The rebellion is now agreed to have begun in October 1911, in Wuchang (武昌); October 10, the day it began, is still the national day of the ROC in Taiwan. During those first chaotic days the bourgeoisie took it upon itself to preserve order, a preferred state of course for most governments but critical for the economically liberal business environment. The head of the Chamber of Commerce in Wuhan even briefly became the police chief.[180] It was agreed among the various revolutionary agents that Sun Yat-Sen would serve for a few months as the first president of the ROC. During this time Shanghai businessmen, in particular, brought to Sun's attention the obstacles still posed to their success by the still-extant imperial monopolies. (Sun also saw the costs of these monopolies as a major problem, though from a more socialist perspective.) These monopolies had persisted through the self-strengthening period and the war with Japan. Businessmen also complained about legal restrictions on imports outside the concessions, and obstacles to purely in-country commerce such as the *líjīn* tax. It had been imposed in 1853 to fund military action but persisted until 1931.[181]

By previous arrangement the presidency passed on March 10, 1912, to

---

179. Zhongping Chen, *Modern China's Network Revolution: Chambers of Commerce and Sociopolitical Change in the Early 20th Century* (Palo Alto: Stanford University Press, 2011), Ch. 6.

180. Bergère, *The Golden Age of the Chinese Bourgeoisie*, 197.

181. *Ibid.*, 199.

Yuan Shikai (袁世凱, 1859–1916), who had successfully navigated Qing politics and even suppressed the initial uprising in Wuchang before switching sides. He demanded that he become president as soon as the last emperor abdicated.

To the extent Yuan Shikai had any economic philosophy it could best be described as favoring heavy industry and import substitution, a recipe that would become popular throughout the decolonized world after World War II. He believed in the role of business in helping modernize China, and he believed that China needed to develop modern industry as quickly as possible, both to build up national strength and to provide his central government with steady revenue. In general, Yuan proclaimed his belief in free commerce, but he also believed that foreign investment in strategic industries was good while individual Chinese buying foreign products was bad. This was music to the ears of Chinese entrepreneurs who faced foreign competition, a number of whom were advising Yuan from the beginning. He appointed the businessmen Zhou Xuexi (週學熙, 1866–1947) and Zhang Jian (張謇, 1853–1926) as ministers. But conversely, as a split developed between northern China, where Yuan's government was based in Beijing, and southern China, especially Canton, the home base of Sun Yat-Sen, wealthy businessmen in the south began funding the KMT and allied groups.[182] And yet, once the so-called second revolution was launched in July of 1913 by KMT loyalists and resentful members of 1911 revolutionary armies that Yuan had dissolved, it received little business support. This was partly because of what Zhongping Chen called "insatiable demands for merchant contributions to cover military and administrative expenses," a criticism that would return under KMT rule.[183] The revolutionaries were dispatched quickly, and Sun fled to Japan, not to return until 1917. In the meantime, regional governments were established throughout the country, beginning the so-called warlord period.

Business owners now faced an environment where it was not meaningful to speak of "the Chinese government." Rather than waiting for a stable government to emerge, and facing a breakdown of public order, they began their

182. Stephanie Po-yin Chung. *Chinese Business Groups in Hong Kong and Political Change in South China, 1900–1925* (New York: St. Martin's Press, 1998).

183. *Modern China's Network Revolution*, 200.

most active period of self-governance. The fragmentation of political power, both regionally and in terms of the ability to make and enforce decrees, was for the business community a double-edged sword. On the one hand local authorities eager for revenue had to give them more freedom, but on the other there were numerous cases in which they were shaken down by these political leaders or their roving armies for money, especially in the interior. Particularly now, when political chaos was all around them, Chinese businessman both domestically and overseas were driven at least as much by patriotism as by opportunity for profit, an attitude building on widespread resentment of what was increasingly seen as foreign exploitation. In addition to the efforts to strengthen commercial capacity in China, these businessmen participated in boycotts against goods produced in the United States and Japan. In 1905 they protested the U.S. further tightening its already almost total ban on immigration from China, and in 1915 and 1919 they protested Japanese diplomatic pressure against exploitation of a weak China.

Different businessmen chose different strategies and tactics in the face of this complex environment. Bergère has written, referring to this period between Yuan Shikai's death and 1927, that "[n]ow that the bourgeoisie could no longer operate through their defunct institutions, their actions took on a more radical slant. For awhile, the bourgeoisie became the most influential group in an alliance between all the urban classes, based upon a common desire for national independence, openness toward the West, individual liberty and economic and social progress."[184] Their social entrepreneurship included founding model towns to escape the chaos and participation in the May 4 movement (discussed in the next chapter). In addition, business activists moved the Shanghai General Chamber of Commerce (上海總商會) in a new, practical, more open, and future-focused direction. (The existing one had been established under the authority of the Qing in 1902.)[185]

Finance circles in Shanghai were particularly aggressive not just in acting independently in the ways outlined above but in actively defying the state on

---

184. Bryna Goodman, "Democratic Calisthenics: The Culture of Urban Associations in the New Republic," in *Changing Meanings of Citizenship in Modern China*, eds. Merle Goldman and Elizabeth J. Perry (-Cambridge, MA: Harvard University Press, 2002), 70–109, 76–77.

185. Bergère, *Golden Age*, 207 (model towns), 208 (national chamber), 212 (new cooperative firms), 212-3 (Shanghai chamber).

occasion. Yuan Shikai had soon after taking power pressured two state-owned banks, the Bank of China (中國銀行) and the Bank of Communications (交通銀行) to issue bank notes to allow the government to acquire silver from the banks. This was of course inflationary, and in Yuan Shikai's brief period as self-proclaimed emperor (Jan. 1–March 22, 1916) he first increased pressure on the banks to cough up more silver. Then, following a major bank run (after he abandoned his imperial title but not the effect of his rule itself), he suspended redemption of the banks' notes. Before the suspension decree could take effect, the Bank of China privatized itself, setting up a shareholders' association, transferring the bank's property to shareholders, and renewing freedom to exchange its notes for silver. The bank run was over in a week. Given the government's need to borrow from other banks while using its own shares in the Bank of China as collateral, this bank was able to take the initiative to increase private ownership when it came into possession of these shares.

In the early 1920s, as governance continued to fall apart, there were more voices among the business community in Beijing and Shanghai urging businesses to take a more active role in politics. In 1923, the reformed Shanghai General Chamber of Commerce actually declared itself an alternate government, now free of the so-called Beiyang (北洋) central government, although the political effect was negligible. While the Chamber, the broadest representative of the Shanghai business community, never called for the return of the foreign settlements, it did demand and eventually get for the Chinese international-settlement residents (who by now were the vast majority of the population there) 25 percent of the seats on its Municipal Council. (In the French settlement, governed as it was by diplomats rather than businessmen, this did not happen.) R. Keith Schoppa has provided numerous examples during this time of business associations arranging in many places beyond Shanghai to provide education and sanitation, and even negotiating peace among different militias already engaged in or threatening to engage in violence, extending the range of public services they had started providing in Shanghai before the Qing fell.[186]

The rise of business activism was a part of a larger increase in private-sector

---

186. R. Keith Schoppa, *Chinese Elites and Political Change: Zhejiang Province in the Early Twentieth Century* (Cambridge, MA: Harvard University Press, 1982), 65-66.

group agency, itself deriving from a belief in individual agency. The increase in volunteerism was described in the previous section, and labor activism also grew in the treaty ports in the late Qing and early Republic. And while business activism was often driven by self-interest, it was also future-oriented, and thus often took the form of personally funding and building institutions and infrastructure, from which many of the benefits were reaped by others, now (roads, sanitation, etc.) and later (students in the schools). And it was funded not by some faraway national government, but through local entrepreneurs, in response to their local assessments of what was needed. While it was mostly confined to the vicinity of the coastal treaty ports, it was, at a time of seeming national disintegration, no less productive.

4.E A case study of three famines between 1843 and 1949

China struggled for centuries with sometimes staggering famines. They were usually spawned by drought and usually afflicted the northern half of the country. Three are of interest here. From 1876–1879 Henan, Shandong, Shanxi, Shaanxi and Zhili (a province that no longer exists, but which roughly corresponds to today's Hebei) and the northern part of Jiangsu suffered from a famine that killed perhaps ten million people. In 1920 and 1921, famine in roughly the same area killed half a million. Finally, from 1928 to 1930, perhaps as many as 10 million died in Chahar and Suiyuan (both now part of Inner Mongolia), Gansu, Hebei, Henan, Rehe (now part of Hebei and Shaanxi), and Shandong.[187] Of the three, the 1920–1921 famine has been characterized by Pierre Fuller, who has long studied major disasters in China, as the least damaging, measured by death rates among the endangered population.[188] Part of the reason is surely the greater flexibility of response, deriving from the fruits of a half-century of economic liberalism. These include, for example, the greater production of and access to information relevant to famine relief, improved transportation technology, and the growing wealth, including agricultural productivity, of Chinese society over this time.

---

187. The famines' spans and estimated tolls are reported in Pierre Fuller, "Changing Disaster Relief Regimes in China: An Analysis Using Four Famines Between 1876 and 1962," *Disasters* 39 (S2), Supplemental Issue 2015, S146-S165, S154.

188. Pierre Fuller, "North China Famine, 1920-21," http://www.disasterhistory.org/north-china-famine-1920-21.

For centuries during Chinese famines, government and nearby merchants had been expected to exert great effort to decrease deaths. And the 1876 famine was no exception. There was a new element now, namely foreign missionaries and their organizations and the small but growing new Chinese business elite in the lower Yangzi cities. Traditional Chinese merchants were spurred to do more because they saw Westerners as shaming China by claiming Chinese inability to respond to such disasters. Compared to local traditional relief channels, the contribution of the new groups was relatively modest, however. The response relied heavily on traditional methods, although the new channel of relief funds from overseas Chinese was tapped heavily.

In the past, the state had generally released or sold grain cheaply from its granaries (partly maintained for this very purpose), both to directly provide food to the starving and to force down local grain prices. The government was aware of grain taxes collected, and therefore had a good sense, with some delay, of harvest conditions. Once a famine was detected, authorities would go door to door in the stricken jurisdictions to assess its seriousness. Merchants were then charged with finding grain to buy in other places, and their ability to do this was noted over 2000 years ago in the Guanzi. But in 1876 the canals were dry, so that traditional shipping was severely handicapped in delivering relief. In addition, traditional carts for shipping grain had a hard time getting through mountain passes.[189]

Overall, with a widespread drought, large numbers of people died in this famine, but the traditional system, supplemented by the new resources from abroad and domestically, and despite the recent national trauma of the Taiping Rebellion, did well, all things considered. Perhaps unavoidably "corruption, exploitation, or inaction" among merchants and officials hampered performance, but genuine, effective efforts were made. Other elements of the traditional response still in play included provision of clothing and cash and an extensive amount of funding by the local wealthy.[190]

By the famine of 1920, southern coastal China was considerably wealthier. In addition, numerous rail lines had been built since 1878 (the first rail network, recall, was finished in 1871), and added to rather than replaced the

---

189. Ibid.

190. Fuller, "Changing Disaster Relief Regimes" S148 ("corruption"), S149–S150.

traditional transport technologies of carts and canal ships. Under the decentralized, liberal economic environment of the time, other elements of the old relief system proceeded without any impediment from these new relief methods. Rural families in Zhili and Henan were also able to earn income by producing handicrafts and mining salt; the marketing of such goods outside the famine area, through middlemen, was much easier in 1920 China than before. There was migration of the suffering to Beijing or southern Hubei, Hangzhou, Shanxi and Manchuria. Such migration, while not unprecedented, was now greater in scale. In all places relief efforts increased, as refugees did. Fuller has credited the railroads, the shorter length of the drought (one year and not three), and the contributions of Chinese businesses, foreign diplomats, and a far more thorough network of foreign missionaries for saving many. Overall, he described the 1920-1921 famine, relative to what might have been expected, as having "modest mortality overall."[191]

So the very openness and spontaneous building of networks common in Chinese society in 1920 was a key factor. Not just the trains but new communications technology and networks, including the vastly richer media environment, allowed more information to be generated, transmitted, and used more quickly. Fuller cites 34 private (Chinese) relief organizations providing relief to southern Zhili alone by December 1920.[192] (Famine had been acknowledged by resident foreigners and Beijing authorities alike by July of that year.) Critically, people who wanted to enable or provide relief could do so through a much more diverse social structure in an environment where the single best solution did not need to be chosen from on high. As in 1876, new technology and foreigners did not have to substitute for local effort but could complement it. This new capacity had grown a great deal between 1876 and 1920. Each relief group was now more able to identify and learn from the strengths and weaknesses of other groups, be they geographic or technological, strategic or tactical.

While the 1920–1921 famine occurred during civil war among many military leaders, by 1928 the form of internal warfare had changed. By the end of 1927, most of the local armies that had sprouted after Yuan Shikai's death had

191. Pierre Fuller, "North China Famine Revisited: Unsung Native Relief in the Warlord Era," *Modern Asian Studies* 47, no. 3 (May 2013): 820–850, 837 ("modest mortality").

192. Ibid., 831.

been defeated by the KMT in the Northern Expeditions, the military campaign launched by Chiang Kai-Shek to defeat the warlord armies, including that of the CCP. However, war with the CCP had resumed, and the KMT military had also lost consequential battles to the Japanese and Soviet militaries in Shandong and Manchuria respectively. It was difficult for trains to enter the conflict zones, which overlapped to some degree with the famine area.

Organizationally, eight large relief groups had been combined into the China International Famine Relief Commission in 1921, at the end of the prior famine. Its leadership was mixed foreign and domestic, with some Shanghai Chinese elite represented. Between 1921 and 1928, the commission had tended to approve loans for infrastructure projects from the groups' headquarters in Beijing. By 1930 the commission's project funding and famine-relief activities began to wind down, as "the government itself began to assume primary responsibility for famine relief and economic reconstruction" at the national and provincial levels.[193] The KMT organized ad hoc relief and local business groups formed relief groups. But overall the government now planned and dominated the relief effort, centrally gathering information on the extent of the famine, drawing up plans to fight it, and imposing national regulations on the delivery of relief. These rules governed distribution of national assistance, limiting relief to areas thought (from the distant KMT capital of Nanjing) to be most in need of it. The government also prioritized paid work rather than food delivery by the KMT (and the paid work itself was to build long-lasting infrastructure). When food relief was distributed, grains were prioritized at the expense of other foodstuffs. While the existing major private relief organizations both foreign and domestic continuously strove to work with the government, they were limited because they had to work through KMT relief organizations and to conform to their rules.[194] Such responses were surely better in some places but worse in others, and the desire to centralize relief efforts meant that much local information was wasted.

It would be rash to ascribe all or even most of the larger death toll of the 1928-1929 famine to centralization and authoritarian control by the KMT

193. Andrew James Nathan, *A History of the China International Famine Relief Commission* (Cambridge, MA: East Asian Research Center, Harvard University, 1965), 56.

194. Andrea Janku, "The Internationalisation of Disaster Relief in Early Twentieth-Century China," *Berliner China-Hefte / Chinese History and Society* 43 (2013): 6–28, 8.

government. The number of people subject to famine conditions compared to 1920–1921 was estimated to be five times as large, although the estimated death toll was twenty times as large.[195] Civil war with the CCP and threatened and actual military conflict with the Soviets and Japanese were also obstacles to modern famine relief—although there had been warlord violence in 1920 as well. But centralization of relief efforts came to some degree at the expense of traditional forms of famine relief involving local merchants and traditional transportation methods. Those had been unhampered and even used productively in 1920–1921 when relief was carried out in conjunction with local governments, at least in Shandong.[196] But in 1928–9, since foreign and domestic relief organizations had to work with the central administration relief efforts were undoubtedly hampered.

4.F Conclusion

In concluding this chapter, it is important to have some perspective. While the introduction and subsequent production of new technology, and institutions and ideas both economic and otherwise, was found throughout the country, the *economic* transformation radiated outward from the foreign possessions. Overall, China by 1927 was still a poor and substantially peasant economy, although introduction of new products and socioeconomic innovations were having an impact even in the countryside. It was noted in previous sections that new education styles were rapidly being developed, but the percentage of adult Chinese who were illiterate in 1937 was still quite large. (In 1982, about half of surveyed men and 90 percent of surveyed women who were born before 1932 were still illiterate, and this even after major adult-literacy campaigns after 1949.[197])

And Shanghai itself was still full of factories where wages and working conditions struck some observers, foreign and especially domestic, as so

195. Nathan, *A History of the China International Famine Relief Commission*, 48.

196.劉剛,《齊魯奇荒的一九二七年》,《農學學報》, 2015年11月, 118頁至125頁 (Liu Gang, "The Grievous Famine in Shandong Province in 1927," *Journal of Agriculture*, 2015 (5), November 2015), 118-125.

197. William Lovely, Xiao Zhenyu, Li Bohua and Ronald Freedman, "The Rise in Female Education in China: National and Regional Patterns," *China Quarterly* 121 (March 1990): 61–93, 65 (Table 1).

appalling as to be worth having a revolution over. Nor should we be naive about big business, which sometimes supplied, and sometimes was demanded to pay, bribes in exchange for special privileges, a problem as old as the mutual existence of commerce and governments itself. Shanghai and other cities were also plagued by vice and crime (suggested by the English verb "to shanghai"), and contemporary observers could be forgiven for seeing this as a result of foreign control and its implied "anything goes" attitude. The colonial police in the Shanghai concessions (initially all foreign in the early years after 1842, but with a growing presence of Chinese as time passed) were often cavalier about rights of detainees. The police would sometimes mistreat them physically and hand them over to the Shanghai police outside the concessions, where legal constraints hardly existed.[198]

In addition, of course, this transfer of ideas from the West to China was born in original sin, in the sense that the Treaty of Nanjing, and indeed the First Opium War it ended, were motivated by a desire to sell opium, whose use afflicted people at all levels of Chinese society. The treaty also resulted in the transfer of small but important pieces of imperial territory to militarily much more powerful foreigners. And these initial transfers set the stage for a competition among traditional and new powers to take advantage of a civilizationally rich but materially impoverished China.

In 1927 Shanghai, Suzhou, Tianjin, and the other parts of China centered around foreign concessions were reminiscent of 1880 Tokyo or 1970 Seoul. Wages were often low and working conditions far from modern, but, as noted above, Chinese wages had improved significantly even as the population in these cities began to surge after 1843. (It was of course greater opportunity that had drawn people there to begin with.) Greater prosperity and more liberal culture had particularly flowered in these parts of China since the country's forced opening. and it is likely that these would have sustained themselves and further spread throughout the country had history not intervened in the form of the corrupt KMT dictatorship, the Japanese invasion, and the communist triumph.

Economic research in has found that wages in Shanghai between 1843 and 1949 were determined far more by human capital among workers than by

---

198. Physical mistreatment, handing over of captives: Frederick Wakeman, Jr., *Policing Shanghai 1927–1937* (Berkeley: University of California Press, 1995), 175.

any capacity for businesses to exploit them.[199] This suggests that competition operated to pay workers close to the value of what they produced at the margin, a sign of competitive markets. Among the evidence suggesting that Shanghai became a systematically better place to live after 1843 was its exploding population, most of which was absorbed well enough. Economically and socially liberal Shanghai, and to a lesser extent other cities in China, were places where, to the extent it existed at all, the central government was substantially unable to provide the fundamental public goods of physical infrastructure and public safety. Many of these functions, as we have seen, were taken over by Chinese people and groups, acting as citizens can in an open and dynamic society. So despite all the deficiencies in the new Chinese cities, especially Shanghai, the Chinese teeming multitudes came, with many of them staying so that their grandchildren could become, and be proud of being, native Shanghainese.

The question at least deserves to be raised whether the treaty-port economic model (as opposed to the colonial political order) might have been able to peacefully, gradually and comprehensively spread throughout the country (for a variety of reasons, of course, it did not). If so, would China would have progressed as its neighbors did in the postwar era? Indeed, a certain nostalgia for the freewheeling culture of Republican China, despite its political chaos, prevails in today's China, whether expressed as wings of Shanghai shopping malls devoted to the movie culture of the 1930s or as Internet publications by people who admire writers of the bourgeois golden age.[200]

But as time went by between 1927 and 1937, there was progressively less advocacy and precious little political opportunity for this model to spread. For a time, domestic political chaos did not prevent and even to a degree promoted economic experimentation and improvement because it weakened political power. By the early 1930s, however, military threats from Japan and Stalin's U.S.S.R., combined with a radically different social model proposed by an increasingly interventionist KMT, meant that whatever innate skepticism about economic liberalism already existed could not help but grow. Now it was

199. 曾凡, (人力資本與上海近代化), 上海, 上海人民出版社, 2012年 (Ceng Fan, *Human Capital and the Modernization of Shanghai*. [Shanghai: Shanghai People's Publishing Company, 2012]).

200. Naoki Mitsuda, "Shanghainese Grow Nostalgic for 'Lost Taste' of the City," *Nikkei Asian Review*, October 2, 2018, https://asia.nikkei.com/Life-Arts/Life/Shanghainese-grow-nostalgic-for-lost-taste-of-the-city.

perfectly reasonable to believe that China *had* to industrialize, fast and by government dictate, or that industrialization and modernization were themselves exploitive and cultural poisonous. Easygoing, low-tariff, Adam Smithian liberalism and the prosperity it would surely have brought eventually would no longer suffice.

CHAPTER 5

Utopias: Embracing Post-liberal Paradises

For several decades in the late nineteenth and early twentieth centuries, many Chinese of various income and education levels, places of birth, and belief systems were trying the best they could to cooperate in pursuit of mutual gain through market exchange. But in the face of the country's still-immense poverty, its weakness in the face of foreign aggression, and its internal violence, other ideas began to percolate among Chinese thinkers, and then the broader public. People who found these ideas persuasive began to organize movements to achieve something better for the Chinese people than what they thought economic liberalism had to offer. This chapter tells that story, one which in many respects is of a slow-motion strangulation of the ideas behind the vibrancy described in the last chapter.

5.A One illness, many prescriptions

The arrival of the ideas and technology of another civilization in the face of a Chinese polity powerless to prevent it was a shocking process for many Chinese. And if self-strengthening amounted to "adopt the trappings, reject the essence" with respect to the West, after 1895 there was growing agreement that the problem *was* the essence of Chinese civilization—its traditions, its politics, its hidebound social structure.

As shown in Chapter 4, as the extraterritorial era unfolded the colonialists who directed it brought with them a package of ideas, and Chinese themselves more and more sought these ideas out. Meanwhile, as the number of treaty ports expanded over the second half of the 19th century, politically the process increasingly resembled the scramble for Africa occurring simultaneously,

134 MARKETS WITH CHINESE CHARACTERISTICS

although on a smaller scale. But Westerners gave as well as took. In addition to the arrival of so many Westerners in the form of businessmen, missionaries, adventurers, and others, after the Boxer Rebellion of 1899 to 1901 many more Chinese students went to Western countries, including Japan, to study. There and through contact with foreigners in China they were exposed to a host of newer Western ideas as well, including liberalism, socialism, communism, feminism, and others.

But menacingly looming over most of these isms was the new idea of nationalism, itself significantly a project of 19th-century Europe. It is commonly argued that the idea of China as one nation among many, not as a celestial empire that constituted the civilized world, with civilization radiating out in all directions from the imperial Palace, took root in the years after 1895.[201] In other words, Chinese nationalism itself was a product of this age of Western contact. After first entry, Chinese intellectuals learned that in the West China was seen by its partial conquerors as just one of many nations, merely equal under international law, therefore obligated to treat one another with equal respect. Soon Chinese understandably saw their "nation" as, like others, one of many, yet unique, and despite its military weakness worth struggling for. This nationalism merged in the Chinese intellectual mind with social Darwinism, the belief (which, recall, Yan Fu also held) that nations themselves competed in a survival of the fittest. Such beliefs were widespread in the first third of the 20th century in China. The *nation* of China had to change or die. And as we will see, there emerged for the contemplation of Chinese (and people around the world) a new, thoroughly illiberal scheme of social organization that would allow nations adopting it to triumph in this Darwinian struggle.

The story of this journey mixes intellectual movements, political changes, and new facts on the ground. In it we will see how the intellectual and political trends after the 1911 Xinhai Revolution made economic liberalism untenable for decades in China. Influenced by Western thought, which had incorporated ideas for restricting property rights and individual autonomy in the name of the broader "social interest," Chinese revolutionaries during this time would become convinced of the need for state-directed restructuring of a backward China.

---

201. See for example the description of Liang Qichao's writing on nationalism in Jonathan Spence, *Gate of Heavenly Peace*, 74.

5.B Reform before the 1911 Revolution—sources and impact

After the 1895 defeat by Japan, Chinese intellectuals more and more accepted the existence of a fundamental Chinese crisis, far beyond the grudging need to accept the Western machines advocated by the self-strengtheners. Soon two broad camps could be identified, each the fruit of the failure of self-strengthening. There were still those both within and outside the Qing government who sought to end the imperial system entirely. They wanted to overturn not just the rule of a particular family, something that had happened numerous times in China's long history, but to overturn the idea of a single divinely ordained and dictatorial paternalistic ruling house. These included those like Yan Fu, who favored retaining Chinese tradition to some degree, and a growing number of radicals, usually informed by specific knowledge of how other countries were governed,

At least while he was younger, the influential writer Kang Youwei proposed highly focused reforms. According to Jerome Greider, Kang's visit as a young man to Hong Kong and Shanghai "convinced him that these foreigners, unlike the barbarians of China's earlier acquaintance, possessed more than 'useful skills;' that these were societies founded on law; and that behind the visible aspects of Western life must lie animating ideas and principles."[202] In this sense he resembled to some degree Yan Fu, Hu Shi, and others. To make reform more palatable to conservative intellectuals, Kang in the late 1880s labored on an essay eventually published in 1897 under the title "On Confucius as a Reformer" (《孔子改制考》). It argued that China's Confucian heritage had been misunderstood for centuries, and that Confucius actually welcomed social reform and change.

Kang Youwei's arguments persuaded the Guangxu emperor to issue an edict on July 3, 1898, announcing major reforms, many of them along the lines Kang had suggested. Over the next several weeks, Kang made the economic liberal's argument that since modern economies depend on continuous creativity and growth, China needed to modernize. This required the emperor to intervene at the expense of his aunt, the Dowager Empress Cixi, to form a truly national government, including a parliament (國會). Kang wrote in one communication to the emperor that "the modernizing process must be

---

202. Greider, *Intellectuals and the State in Modern China*, 86.

left basically to the genius of private enterprise."[203] To facilitate this, intellectual property rights and rewards for creativity were recommended. Kang also argued for modernizing education. A separate document from imperial censor Chu Chengbo (褚成博, 1854–1911) drew on one of Kang's own recommendations. He proposed that the various arsenals previously established under self-strengthening (mentioned in Chapter 3) be privatized to overseas Chinese living in Southeast Asia and North America, who were ethnically the same but presumably more familiar with Western technology. In response, the emperor in 1895 wrote: "Everything is to be done in the manner of foreign countries, mercantile and trading classes are permitted to do as they please."[204] For the first time, economic liberalism was, all too momentarily, inside the citadel of power.

By 1898, Kang Youwei was taking Meiji Japan as a model for China. It had modernized spectacularly (enough to have defeated China in 1895 in war) and had reformed while preserving and in some ways even strengthening the monarchical system there. In that year, after trying unsuccessfully for several years, Kang was able to present a statement to the Guangxu emperor (a statement known in English as a memorial) that advocated more widespread reform than had been contemplated previously. Education was to be made much more widely available, and the powers of the emperor were to be circumscribed constitutionally. In the judgment of many in the imperial court, Kang and the others went too far; his proposed simultaneous changes to Chinese education, its economy, and perhaps above all its politics were too much. Owing to machinations among court officials, notably the Dowager Empress, and aided by diplomats from Great Britain and Japan, whose nations were trying to preserve their influence in the Qing court, the emperor himself was *de facto* although not *de jure* removed from power on September 22, 1898. Kang and other reformers barely escaped with their lives, and Kang's son and other

203. Kang was quoted in Young-Tsu Wong, "Revisionism Reconsidered: Kang Youwei and the Reform Movement of 1898," *Journal of Asian Studies 51*, no. 3 (August 1992): 513–544, 531. Wong cited Kung-Chuan Hsiao, *A Modern China and a New World: K'ang Yu-Wei, Reformer and Utopian*, 1858–1927 (Seattle: University of Washington Press, 1978), 208.

204. For Chu and the quotation of the Guangxi emperor, see Spence, *The Gate of Heavenly Peace*, 43.

plotters were quickly executed.[205]

This suggests that both political and economic liberalism were a significant part of Chinese reform thinking before and during this Hundred Days movement of 1898. (Recall that free trade, a common recommendation of liberal reformers then and now, had for the most part already been imposed on China in the treaty ports through the unequal treaties.) After the Dowager Empress ended the reforms and relegated the emperor to a ceremonial role, Kang Youwei spent several years promoting reforms that would preserve the imperial system, whose continuation was already in question. First in Canada, then in India, he composed his masterwork, *The Book of Great Unity* (《大同書》, *Dàtóng Shū*). This saw humanity progressing steadily toward the use of modern technology and toward world government, and contained a section, striking for its time and place, on the centuries of oppression that women had endured all over the world, and the need for and inevitability of their attaining equality. Kang's vision was that private industry or "capitalism" was right for its time, but soon to be rendered obsolete. The book was quite specific about the design of future social and political institutions and predicted a well-defined terminal stage of social evolution, so it was not fully dynamically liberal. But when Chinese reform (as opposed to revolution) was in the air, economic liberalism was part of his contribution to it. Kang returned in 1913 and continued to advocate constitutional monarchy. While in exile he spent many years raising funds from overseas Chinese for his Society for the Protection of the Emperor (保皇會).

Also liberal in his younger years was Liang Qichao, who, recall, was the first to call China "the sick man of Asia" (東方病夫 in his rendition), and who for a time walked a path very similar to Kang Youwei. He helped Kang draft the reform proposals that resulted in the abortive Hundred Days movement. Like Kang, Liang had to escape after the reforms were ended, spending 11 years in Japan. He traveled widely during this period and from Tokyo for a time published the magazine *New Citizen* (《新民叢報》). He also wrote a series of essays collectively known as "Let Us Speak of a New People" (《新民說》). In these essays he discussed a range of issues relevant to the new China he wanted to see emerge, for example *On the Nation-State* (《論國家》) and *On Self-Re-*

---

205. For a dissenting view of Cixi's attitude toward reform, see Jung Chang, *Empress Dowager Cixi: The Concubine Who Launched Modern China* (New York: Alfred A. Knopf, 2013).

spect (《論自尊敬》). Both were powerful polemics for aspects of liberalism—as was one devoted to the value of risk-taking as a critical ingredient in progress (《論進取冒險》, *On Enterprise and Risk-Taking*). In the essay *On Freedom* (《論自由)》, Liang incorporated a Smithian argument against special privileges (特權) and discussed commercial freedom as a human right.

But as economic liberalism was at its peak both in thought and action, the dramatic growth in the treaty ports and surrounding territories did not prevent even more radical attempts to cure what ailed China. Zou Rong (鄒容, 1885–1905), after taking advantage of his protection from Qing attempts to arrest him by living in the International Settlement in Shanghai for a time, chose the route of explicitly racist nationalism. He advocated violence against those he asserted were the primitive Manchus.[206] He died in his attempted suicide bombing of Qing officials, (which only wounded several of them). Qiu Jin, mentioned in Chapter 4, was part of this radical change of direction. She made the oppression of women, both globally and in China, continual themes of her work, and she was finally executed after a failed uprising in Zhejiang in 1907. Qiu too mixed her revolutionary ideas with ethnic animus, as she blamed Manchu oppression for what she saw as the pitiful state the Chinese found themselves in. (The Qing, who came from then-separate Manchuria, had been one of several peoples who vanquished a Chinese dynasty. The Mongol Yuan dynasty, established by Kublai Khan, had been another.)

Feminism too arrived in the early 20th century, its reception first dominated by self-denigrating contrast with the West. Many Chinese, both male and female, accepted that the role China gave its women was appallingly limited. Domestic activists and Western missionaries worked not just to establish women's education but to end practices such as concubinage and foot-binding. Like anarchism, which Chinese begin to encounter, especially in its Russian form, through people such as Peter Kropotkin (1832–1921) and Nikolai Bakunin (1814–1876) in the early 20th century, the growth of feminist thinking was influenced by writers who had spent time in Japan. Liang Qichao wrote in 1897 that the exclusion of women from Chinese social reconstruction would waste

---

206. Zou Rong, *The Revolutionary Army: A Chinese Nationalist Tract of 1903*, trans. John Lust (Paris: Mouton, 1968).

the talents of half the population.[207] And socialism came as well, significantly from Japan. "Socialism" is a more slippery term than feminism, since even now there is disagreement about what it means. In the decades sandwiched around the 1911 Xinhai Revolution, "socialism" in Europe had already ramified into a variety of recipes for social improvement, from establishing voluntary communities to provide models of a better way of living to proposing sweeping government measures to re-orient society in a direction other than selfish profit-seeking. It fell to the most influential self-described socialist in early 20th-century China, Jiang Kanghu (江亢虎, 1883–1954), to try to reconcile the various socialisms with which he was familiar. He finally advocated a socialism that was long on ideas and rather short on policy, although, like Chinese anarchism, it called for revolution.[208]

Politically, 1898 saw the aforementioned Hundred Days of Reform. While it may have been quite promising as a major political effort to make China fit for the modern world, we will never know what it might have accomplished because of its evanescence.

Here some words should be said about Sun Yat-sen, one of the most important figures in the ending of the imperial system. Often depicted as a rival to Kang Youwei among eager Chinese saviors, Sun was fluent in English, as he had lived in Hawaii after moving there in childhood. Returning to China after finishing high school, he became a credentialed physician in Hong Kong in 1892. There he became involved in revolutionary politics. At the same time he was becoming more familiar with socialist ideas, especially the theories of the American Henry George (1839–1897), who emphasized the tendency of markets to benefit only those who were able to capture the monopoly profits he thought those markets generated. While in Japan between 1895 and 1905 Sun learned of the growing efforts in the West, especially Europe, to provide social services through the state rather than rely on liberal forces. Sun too

---

207. An English translation of this work is Liang Qichao, "On Women's Education," in Lydia H. Liu, Rebecca H. Karl and Dorothy Ko (eds.), *The Birth of Chinese Feminism: Essential Texts in Transnational Theory* (New York: Weatherhead East Asian Institute, Columbia University, 2013), 186–203.

208. Arif Dirlik and Edward S. Krebs, "Socialism and Anarchism in Early Republican China," Modern China 7, no. 2 (April 1981): 117–151. Jiang explicitly proposed heavy inheritance taxes, free education for all and an end to most traditional or legal occupational restrictions. Only the first would have any possibility of being called specifically "socialist" in most countries today, but nonetheless this program was radical for its time and place, and was referred to by him explicitly as "socialism" (社會主義, shèhuì zhǔyì).

took a significantly racial view of China's difficulties. He commonly blamed not the dynasty per se but Manchus generally for China's desperate state and referred to the subscribers to Kang Youwei's constitutional-monarchist views as "racial traitors."[209]

Sun's most important intellectual legacy to the Chinese people was his "Three Principles of the People" (三民主義, *Sānmín zhǔyì*)—the right of the Chinese ethnicity to be free of domination by others (民族主義, *mínzú zhǔyì*, the others clearly being the Manchus and Westerners), the right of the people to have political sovereignty (政權, *zhèngquán*), and the right of the people to govern the country (治權, *zhìquán*). (Note that the rights were defined around those of a collective, that of the Chinese people or nation, not those of individuals.) But the provisional constitution of the ROC (later modified and made permanent) after the overthrow of the Qing did protect property rights. Chapter II of the constitution, in addition to acknowledging the rights of criminal procedure and prohibiting arbitrary arrest or search, guaranteed "the right of the security of their property and the freedom of trade."[210]

From 1895 (when he was associated with an abortive uprising in Canton) to just after the deposing of absolute imperial power in 1911, Sun Yat-Sen traveled worldwide, living in Japan for an extended period of time, as noted, and throughout his travels he raised money and used the funds raised to cultivated failed Chinese uprisings. Despite these difficulties, his followers grew both in number and financial power, especially after the death of the Dowager Empress Cixi and the Guangxu emperor in rapid succession in 1908. This was all the more impressive in that Kang Youwei was tapping the same networks for his program of gradual reform in lieu of radical revolution.

During this time Sun Yat-Sen's followers coalesced around the core reformist and revolutionary causes, advocating for women's rights and against the powers of financial capitalists and industrialists, always advocating at least eventual democratic governance.[211] The proximate cause of the overthrow of

209. The remark is that of Spence, in *Gate of Heavenly Peace*, 104.

210. English translation, "The Provisional Constitution of the Republic of China," *American Journal of International Law*, 6 (3), Supplement, Official Documents, July 1912, 149-154, 149.

211. Eve M.B. Armentrout-Ma, *Chinese Politics in the Western Hemisphere, 1893-1911: Rivalry Between Reformers and Revolutionaries in the Americas*. Ph.D. dissertation, University of California at Davis, 1977, cited in Spence, *Gate of Heavenly Peace*, note 3.49, 471.

the last emperor was a Qing order to allocate to foreigners the privileges to operate railroads, even though they had been financed by local governments since 1905 in exchange for a large loan from a foreign consortium. (After the Qing's hostility to railroads in the 1860s and 1870s, for some years before 1905 the Qing had given dispensation to Chinese private firms to construct and operate them.) Public outrage against this dispensation led to violence, and the Wuhan uprising in October 1911 was the final spark that burned an ancient system to the ground. Sun, having heard about the seizure of power on the way to Denver while he was raising funds and stirring up revolutionary enthusiasm, went back to China after going through Europe to raise more money and support in the new environment. The brand-new modern state was conceived in violent fragmentation, as several military forces seized local control in the chaos of the moment; the violence of the fall disappointed the more liberal, more cautious Kang Youwei.

Shortly after the Xinhai revolution (the Chinese name for the uprising that toppled the imperial government) Sun Yat-Sen's *Tóngménghuì* became the KMT, which would emerge after more than two decades of political chaos to monopolize political power in most of the country. What were Sun's economic views when he became president? Surely not liberal in the sense of Yan Fu or Hu Shi. Since Sun had raised money from overseas Chinese businessmen in the Western Hemisphere and Europe, he could not be said to be a doctrinaire anti-capitalist. But like many in Western countries he was thoroughly suspicious of the power of big business and saw a major task of the state as controlling monopoly capitalism. He (along with most, though not all, KMT members) also felt a need to do something about what he saw as the dreadful inequality of wealth in the Western countries he had visited. By 1905, Sun saw the revolution he was planning as a *social* revolution, not just independence from the hated Manchus but also addressing the harmful results for the poor of untrammeled markets, an improvement he felt had been achieved by some of the previous revolutions in Europe. By the time of the Xinhai revolution his views on such matters, despite the clause protecting property rights in the preliminary constitution, were firm. In a March 31, 1912, speech at the Nanjing headquarters of the *Tóngménghuì*, he declared that trusts, capitalists, and "international monopolies" were obstacles in modern-era countries to "social revolution," but that a China still largely preindustrial had a greater opportunity to escape this scourge.[212]

So Sun Yat-Sen's belief that economic liberalism led to monopolistic concentration seems to have been well in place by 1912. But his socialism, a word he used frequently in his writings, did not lead him to advocate that only the government make major production decisions. Rather, Sun took the position that China faced rapacious foreign monopolies with their advanced technology, creating a division of the spoils of economic growth that was dramatically unequal and unfair to the new nation. It was the job of the government to direct major industries and use its power to negotiate an arrangement with foreign firms that was fairer to the nation of China.[213] Given the available *Tóngménghuì* literature and Sun's own remarks, believers in economic liberalism, assuming they were involved in contemporaneous politics at all, could have avoided this organization but some did not. There was an alternative, the Protect the Emperor Society (保皇會), founded by Kang Youwei in Canada in 1899 and known after 1912 as the Democratic Party (民主黨).

By 1911, we may describe three lines of economic thinking about economic liberalism. The Kang Youwei view held that free markets and industrialism were important, although they would at some point be replaced by ethically superior forms of social organization. Liang Qichao understood that progress could be spectacular and unpredictable and required tolerance for risk-taking but also an implied intolerance of market-generated economic mistakes. In this view he resembled Yan Fu. And the Sun Yat-Sen/KMT camp was deeply suspicious of capitalist industrialization as it existed and fought for a remedy—substantial government planning in place of the chaos and exploitation of the market, a workable definition of socialism. So at the outset of the chaos following 1911, camps both supporting and deeply suspicious of economically liberal policies were represented among China's leading intellectuals and activists. (Hu Shi had yet to appear on the scene.) Sun Yat-Sen was himself

212. 《共和言論報》，1912 年 一拳，75頁至83頁，再出版於《在南京中國同盟會會員餞別會的演說》，以《中國革命的社會主義》為題，《孫中山文集》二券，孟庆鹏編，617頁至620頁 (Speech reported in Speeches of the Republic, 1912(1), 75–83. Reprinted as "Socialism in the Chinese Revolution," in *Collected Works of Sun-Yat Sen*, ed. Meng Qingpeng, Vol. 2, 617–620. The "international monopolies" characterization is that of Earnest P. Young, *The Presidency of Yuan Shih-Kai: Liberalism and Dictatorship in Early Republican China* (Ann Arbor: University of Michigan Press, 1977), 89.

213. A. James Gregor and Maria Hsia Chang, "Marxism, Sun Yat-sen, and the Concept of 'Imperialism,'" *Pacific Affairs*, 55 (1), Spring 1982, 54-79.

president of the ROC very temporarily, having been elected by a revolutionary assembly in Nanjing in November 1911, before stepping aside for Yuan Shikai by prior agreement and then spending the rest of his life trying to consolidate the republic as China slipped into internal warfare. He also was an advocate of a planned future that he thought could be better achieved than by liberal spontaneous order. The provisional constitution planned under Sun Yat-sen was never formally repealed under Yuan, who ruled dictatorially until his death. Yuan, like many generals throughout world history, became very wealthy and relied significantly on China's already expansive class of wealthy businessman to promote economic development.

But economic liberalism was losing favor among intellectuals from the ascent of Yuan Shikai through the consolidation of power by the KMT in the 1920s and beyond. As shown in Chapter 4, economic liberalism in action was a real, transformative phenomenon, but political discussion of it as something to be saved along with Chinese democracy was minimal, even among opponents of the authoritarian turn China had taken. Hu Shi, for all his indefatigable brilliance, was an increasingly lonely voice among the intellectual classes. (The business classes, in their desperation for order, were another matter, as Chapter 4 indicated.) At a time of growing danger from the chaos, political transformation—to be followed by economic transformation led by politicians—was seen as most urgent.

As raw material for liberal economic progress, the provisional constitution of the ROC (in effect until 1923) resembled in spirit the Declaration of the Rights of Man and of the Citizen issued by revolutionaries in the early stages of the French Revolution in August 1789. It guaranteed rights, but also indicated that those rights could be overturned when public welfare demanded it.[214] The ROC constitution was promising in its simplicity, a fact that might limit the state's ability to frustrate the spontaneous order. Its total length when translated into modern English was less than 1900 words, while the relatively simple U.S. Constitution when drafted (excluding the Bill of Rights) had well over 4000. The text in the ROC's provisional constitution was mostly concerned with rights to be free "from" government limitation of individual autonomy—unlike Europe's postwar constitutions, which tended to state what citizens had

---

214. Chapter II, Article 6.15, "Provisional Constitution," 150.

a right "to." Section II of the constitution included a variety of other "from" rights, including the right to be free from government limitation on speech and religion; the right of privacy of communication; freedom of movement; the right to vote and to petition the state. Had the constitution been meaningfully adhered to by all in China struggling for power after 1911, entrepreneurs could have contributed to an even faster transformation of China.

But while political order can be important for economic liberalism, it can also help state direction of economic activity. The first parliamentary elections in China after the Xinhai Revolution were held in August 1912 and won by the already thoroughly economically illiberal KMT. Meanwhile, after Sun Yat-sen had resigned as president in favor of Yuan Shikai, a military man and not a profound thinker, Yuan (it is widely assumed) arranged the assassination of leading KMT parliamentarian Song Jiaoren. Song was a strong defender of the constitutionally well-defined powers of the new assembly and a looming rival to Yuan. Yuan then dismissed KMT legislators in 1913 and Parliament itself in 1914. Meanwhile, Chinese intellectuals were soon to ratify existing ideological trends by turning strongly and publicly in a different direction.

5.3 The New Culture movement

Yuan Shikai first as president and then self-proclaimed emperor had to deal with a society that even before 1911 faced growing military fractionalization, with the Xinhai Revolution itself depending in part on defections of regional Qing units. After Yuan's death, feuding regional armies both struggled over central power and carved out regional domains. This chaos would go on for more than a decade. Amid this violent political fragmentation, even as Chinese intellectuals began to see new ways of organizing society from above, businesses themselves were saved from excessive harassment by military organizations (many of which thought of themselves as governments). Commercial society was already prominent enough for governments to depend on economic growth to generate taxes.[215]

Seeing mostly poverty, foreign domination, and the collapse of the dreamed-of magic bullet of democratic governance into chaos and violence all

---

215. Tang, *Merchants and Society in Modern China*, 96.

around, thinkers themselves turned to questioning the foundations of political and economic liberalism. This interval in Chinese history sometimes goes by the name of the New Culture movement (新文化運動). The term New Culture is apt in that, even after half a century of proposed and actual reform and less dramatic arguments for social reform by people like Kang Youwei and Liang Qichao, China's failures were now increasingly seen as a result of the comprehensive failure of a Chinese culture not suited to the modern world.

But these advocates of a new culture faced a challenge. In addition to the instability plaguing China, the reforms seen as desperately needed by this intellectual tribe were being resisted in the countryside. Jonathan Spence has raised, for example, the difficulty the new generation of advocates for women's equality had in getting local authorities to permit women to inherit property and to marry by choice.[216] This happened even though these authorities no longer had national law on their side. In and around the treaty ports there was a substantial presence of modern finance and industry, of social entrepreneurship, of people dressing in the Western fashion, and of rebellion against traditional family obligations. However, political trends convinced more people that Confucian ethics, still widely followed, especially inside the family and especially in the countryside, were still a major obstacle to China's modernizing and democratizing.

And what turned out to be an usually influential group of cultural critics coalesced in 1915 around a new magazine, *New Youth* (《新青年》, *Xīn Qīngnián*).[217] From the beginning, the clarion call of this movement and journal was that the culture that nurtured the Chinese people was fundamentally useless, maybe worse than useless in the new modern world they had encountered over the last several decades. The diagnosis by previous generations of earlier reformers such as Yan Fu, in other words, was deficient. The old culture was fatal to the progress and freedom of China and had to be rooted out.

The founder of *New Youth*, Chen Duxiu, like so many reformers and revolutionaries in that era, had spent some time in Japan, in his case on a Qing scholarship. Extending the anti-Qing revolutionary politics he had already

---

216. Spence, *Gate of Heavenly Peace*, 166.

217. Initially it was published as *Youth Magazine* (《青年雜誌》, *Qíngnián Zázhì*), but soon changed its name. Throughout its publication, its cover had as its alternative title La Jeunesse.

imbibed in China, he continued while in Japan to learn more about proposed ultimate solutions for China, and associated with others doing the same. Characteristically iconoclastic, he at one point during his brief time in Japan, along with two other students, seized the local Qing official responsible for minding the students from Chen's native Hubei and cut the man's mandatory hair queue, which the Manchu Qing had always imposed on Han Chinese men. Upon Chen's return to China, he helped form the Anhui Patriotic Society (安徽愛國會, Ānhuì Àiguó Huì). The term for patriotism (愛國, aìguó) was already increasing in popularity, a sign of the growing nationalism in China. In the society's statement of purpose Chen wrote that while individual freedom was valuable, it could be curtailed if it "interfered with the national welfare," although at the same time he rejected "blindly hating all foreigners."[218]

Chen Duxiu briefly served in the revolutionary government in 1912, and then again went for a short time to Japan after a failed armed uprising in the south—the power base of the KMT—left Yuan Shikai still in power. By 1915 Chen was in freewheeling Shanghai, in the even more open French concession in particular, and in September of that year published the first edition of the monthly *New Youth*. In addition to writing by leading intellectuals, including members of its own editorial board, it published a lively series of communications from its readership, both letters and essays. Its very first article in the very first edition was Chen's own "A Warning to the Young" (《敬告青年》), which had as its backdrop his conviction that China faced unprecedented danger from foreign exploitation.[219] He warned readers they must be autonomous and not slaves, progressive and not conservative, enterprising and daring and not retiring and withdrawn, practical and not abstract in philosophy, scientific and not supernatural, and have a global worldview and not a cloistered one. It was a clarion call specifically to the young, who had long been expected to bide their time, especially in government service, at the feet of the older and wiser. Now, Chen said, they should lead the remaking of China.

The journal itself was first published as Yuan Shikai's government was introducing instruction in Confucian ethics to the rapidly developing nation-

218. The words are those of Lee Feigen, in *Chen Duxiu, Founder of the Chinese Communist Party* (Princeton: Princeton University Press, 2014), 40 ("blindly"), 41 ("interfered").

219. 陳獨秀, 《警告青年》, 《新青年》, 一拳一號, 1915年9月 (Chen Duxiu, "A Warning to the Young," New Youth Magazine 1, no. 1 (September 1915)).

al school system and thus it had a subversive air to it. It was started under Yuan's extensive censorship laws. Chen initially edited *New Youth* in his home in the French concession where he lived, and its initial print runs of roughly a thousand were distributed illicitly outside the concessions. In "A Warning to the Young," Chen specifically criticized the Chinese literati's tradition of mastering classical works at the expense of learning and thinking about how to improve the country, since this would only ensure that the Chinese would remain slaves. While he did not mention Darwin by name, survival of only the fittest societies was clearly the argument he was making.

Several themes were laid out in this very first piece in the journal, themes that would evolve while retaining their essence over just a few years. Among these was that China was backward. It was obsessed with the past at the expense of embracing the future. The Chinese were citizens of the world and could not afford to be isolated. The most valuable knowledge was not to be found in abstract ethical or metaphysical musings, but in practical ideas that advanced the nation.

Chen was already a man of the left, specifically the scientific, socialist, design-a-better-future left. Despite this, to his great credit he wanted to thoroughly modernize China and he recruited other voices with different views. Hu Shi was a member of the editorial board early on, as was the political liberal and strong supporter of intellectual freedom Cai Yuanpei (蔡元培, 1868–1940). Edmund Burke's 1775 remarks to Parliament on "Conciliation with America," in which he advocated that the United Kingdom recognize the traditional British liberties of the American colonists, were translated as "Americans' Spirit of Liberty" (《美國人之自由精神》) and published in 1916.[220] Other contributors included the writer Lu Xun and the early Marxist adherent Li Dazhao (李大釗, 1888–1927) and even Mao Zedong.[221] As long as an article discussed how to break the toxic legacy of China's past or better understand its present and future, the early *New Youth* was interested in it.

"Science," the quintessential tool of first socialists and then later communists in their redesign of society, was key to Chen Duxiu's analysis of how

220. 埃德蒙·伯克,《美國人之自由精神》, 譯者劉文典,《新青年》, 二券一號, 1916 年 二月 (Edmund Burke, "Americans' Spirit of Liberty," trans. Liu Wendian, *New Youth* 2 (1), February 1916).

221. Mao's article was published pseudonymously as 二十八畫生,《體育之研究》,《新青年》, 第3卷第2号, 1917年四月 (*Èrshí Bā Huàshēng*, "A Study of Physical Education," *New Youth* 3, no. 2 April 1917).

China could progress. In an essay in the journal in January 1919, he spoke of "Mr. Democracy" and "Mr. Science." He answered the critics of the new ethics embodied in *New Youth* by arguing that it was no crime if the reason the magazine was arguing against traditional society, and in particular its Confucian manifestations, was to promote these new and indispensable concepts.[222]

Chen's 1919 essay is interesting in that while it used the word "science" (merely a phonetic transliteration) numerous times, it never referred to natural phenomena. Instead, traditional Chinese culture was seen as the enemy of "science" (i.e., modern ways of analyzing society and its problems) and when writers criticized the magazine they were criticizing "science" itself. Science was not just a tool for understanding the natural world or even just for improving technology but, critically, a tool to re-design *society* for the better. To be against "science" was to be against progress. While in Shanghai Chen had become disgusted at what he saw as the industrial cruelty there, he was already sympathetic to the idea that under socialism society's resources could be pooled to generate better outcomes than spontaneously ordered, or as he saw it, exploitive market ones.[223]

And so with this comprehensive, "scientific" improvement in mind, Chen oversaw a series of essays attacking Confucian values, because of Yuan Shikai's effort to have Confucius play a major role in the national educational curriculum. (This was not the last such effort by the central government.) Later Chen also turned the journal's attention to women's rights. But in the end his *New Youth*, a sanctuary for ideas to be debated as long as they contributed to a new China, "evolved" into its own kind of rigidity.

5.D Two shocks from Europe

In 1917, due to China's comprehensive crisis, nationwide debate on the proper function of the state was vigorous. (While Yuan Shikai and regional governments had imposed substantial censorship, the presence of the treaty ports and overall state weakness meant that these restrictions were not very effective,

---

222. 陳獨秀，《新青年罪案之答辯書》，《新青年》，6卷1號），1919年 10頁至11頁 (Chen Duxiu, "A Reply to the Charges Against this Journal," *New Youth* 6 (1), 1919, 10-11).

223. Feigen, *Chen Duxiu*, 146.

as the influence of *New Youth* indicates.) On the ground, economic liberalism held sway when it was not held back by predation by local armies of one allegiance or another. But two bolts from the West were soon to decisively change the balance, to the detriment of economic liberalism.

Since 1842, Chinese leaders public and private had always considered themselves in the light of, first, Europe and America, and then the Japanese. These modern nations did things that the Chinese could not, and so the relevant question for most was how to acquire the ability to do them. Even those who took pride in traditional Chinese society and ethics conceded that there was something marvelous although not necessarily ethically superior about the science and technology deployed by Western militaries and companies. But now this sense of sometimes-reluctant admiration evaporated in some circles.

5.D.1 *The Bolshevik Revolution*

In Russia in 1917, an event of world-historical importance (to use a Marxist phrase) occurred. In March, in the midst of World War I, the czar who had plunged Russia into the war was overthrown. In November of that year, the weak liberal successor government was overthrown by Vladimir Ilyich Lenin (1870–1924) and a handful of his subordinates.

The effect among Chinese intellectuals was electrifying. The idea of Marxism had already been introduced into China in the late 19th century by translations of foreign works discussing it, and some Chinese students in Japan were thoroughly exposed to it.[224] But the feeling had been that Chinese conditions were not suitable for a Marxist revolution, given Marxist scripture's rather rigid predicted timeline, since China was still overwhelmingly rural. But so too was Russia, with its recent history of explicit serfdom, and yet in the second Russian Revolution Lenin and his followers had managed to seize power.

And perhaps the most important thing about the Bolshevik Revolution was what it was not— capitalism and its companion, foreign exploitation. The communist triumph in Russia allowed Chinese intellectuals to have a vision of something that was morally superior to the greed and corruption of free economic competition, something even ethically pristine. While the Bolsheviks

---

224. Martin Bernal, "The Triumph of Anarchism over Marxism, 1906-1907," in Mary Clabaugh Wright (ed.), *China in Revolution: The First Phase*, 1900-1913 (New Haven: Yale University Press, 1968), 97-142.

were chased away after briefly taking over the Russian extraterritorial concessions in Harbin (which before and after was the site of a Russian/Soviet struggle with the Japanese over control), the Soviet government soon after relinquished all Russian possessions in China, thrilling many Chinese leaders.[225] Bolshevik rhetoric appealed to a *post*-capitalist vision, a world in which cutthroat competition would be ended and cooperation and thus greater human (and not merely material) achievement would prevail. This dream was far from rare elsewhere (e.g., in Kang Youwei's *The Book of Great Unity*), and so it is no surprise that many Chinese thinkers found it appealing.

Marxism was conceived as Science, and this may have been part of its appeal to people like Chen Duxiu. But it also presented a materialist vision with an outcome much preferable, for these Chinese, to the other form of historical materialism then popular in China and elsewhere—social Darwinism. As we have seen, the latter loomed large in the Chinese intellectual consciousness from the late 1890s on, and in the *New Youth* generation was still seen as a powerful reason for immediate, radical Chinese social change.

In rendering Marxism amenable to Chinese social conditions, one of the most important early interlocutors was Li Dazhao. In 1917 he published an article introducing Marxism in one of the earliest and then most influential Chinese newspapers, *Shēnbào*. The article has been identified by Zhou Liqing as a primary precursor of the editorial direction of *New Youth*,[226] where Li was already an editor. He soon thought the Russian revolution to be the possible salvation of China. He introduced it to both colleagues and students at Beijing University; among those he communicated with was Mao Zedong. By May 1919, Li, who had written several pieces in 1918 praising the second Russian Revolution, wrote an introductory article for an issue of *New Youth* entirely dedicated to Marxism.[227] Prior to this time, *New Youth*, while focusing on the need to overturn much of the legacy of Chinese ideas, had hardly spoken of economics. Only one article, "The Unifying Principle of Economics," had

---

225. But they would be back. The cities of Port Arthur and Dalian, conceded to Stalin at Yalta, were not truly returned, i.e., Soviet troops did not leave, until after his death (*Spence, Gate of Heavenly Peace*, 371).

226. Zhou Liqing, *Exploring Modern China's Political Transformation*.

227. Lee's *New Youth* article was 李大釗,《我的馬克思主義觀》,《新青年》, 6券5號 (Li Dazhao, "My Marxism," *New Youth* 6, No. 5 (May 1919)). The title of that issue of the journal was "Investigating Marxism" (《馬克思主義研究》).

Liang advised the Chinese delegation not to sign, but the government instructed the delegation to do so. When news of this outcome was published in China on May 1, 1919, students, fueled in part by the promise of protest marches that had begun in Korea in March against Japanese colonization, quickly organized demonstrations that took place on May 4. This was close to the May 7 anniversary of China's day of national humiliation in 1915, when China had accepted most of Japan's 21 demands. The demonstrations involved only a brief interlude of violence, and no deaths. But the demonstrators at one point sacked the home of the Chinese vice foreign minister Cao Rulin (曹汝霖, 1877–1966), who was seen as supinely pro-Japanese. As head of the Chinese central bank he had negotiated the Japanese provision of a series of critical loans to sustain Chinese government finances. Cao, ironically in light of the new revolutionaries' belief that China had to free itself from foreign domination, was escorted by a Japanese friend to escape through another door, but several people remaining in the house were assaulted by the students. The students were subsequently supported by the then-president of Beijing University, the strong political liberal Cai Yuanpei, and soon demonstrations spread to many cities.

The central theme of the demonstrations and many contemporary publications was that the weak nation of China was being treated contemptuously in international diplomatic circles. The need for the nation to become strong in the legal and conceptual sense, a theme that had been prominent since 1895, and had been raised by Chen Duxiu in "A Warning to the Young," now became a dominant ideology, even among those fighting for social reform, be they communists, socialists or other cultural critics. Chen Duxiu himself published an article in another journal before the month was out arguing that the Versailles conference demonstrated that international diplomacy was not about a better world but about each nation's power, and that China needed to defend its position in that light.[230] In other words, the focus of protests and activism now went beyond reforming *society* to encompass defending the *nation*, a belief reinforced by the behavior of the Western powers leading up to and during the Washington Naval Conference of 1921–1922. The conference's propping up of the imperial powers and its unfair treatment of China and other nations were

---

230. 陳獨秀 (署名隻眼),《山東問題與國民覺悟》,《每週評論》, 第23券, 1919年5月26 (Chen Duxiu, under pen name Zhi Yan, "The Shandong Problem and the Chinese People's Awakening," *Weekly Commentary* 23 [(May 26, 1919]).

part of what prompted Bertrand Russell (1872–1990) in some of his influential lectures in China in 1920 and 1921 to urge China to avoid the Western way. (During his tour, Russell also criticized Bolshevism, having learned to see it as dangerous and oppressive after visiting the newly born Soviet Union before arriving in China. Instead, he said, China should have a government of the best and brightest to build a new nation.)[231]

So by now many intellectuals in China had completed the evolution of China's vision of itself from merely the realm of emperors to a nation, and a nation whose rights were being violated by the great powers, generally in the service of international capitalists. Thus nationalism and anti-capitalism merged.[232] This was a problem for economic liberalism because almost from the doctrine's creation, economic liberals have taken a dim view of anything redolent of nationalism, anything that judges the soundness of economic policy by how "the nation" does. Instead, it asks that we judge an economic system by the welfare of individuals and seek to maximize the choices that competition can offer them.

5.E The aftermath of the Bolshevist and Versailles shocks

After hearing of the new Soviet government's renunciation of Russia's extraterritorial claims in China, intellectuals and activists understandably contrasted the positions of the "old" and "new" foreign worlds, to the conspicuous favor of the latter. The old West sought to install and preserve colonialism, but the Soviet Union now sought to fight to replace it with something better. This led to favorable coverage of the new Soviet experiment, in *New Youth* and elsewhere.

The failure in May 1919 of talks between the putatively central Beijing government of Xu Shichang (徐世昌, 1855–1939) and a government in Guangzhou associated with Sun Yat-Sen, talks that had been agreed to shortly after the armistice in Europe, also strengthened the trend toward radicalism. Capitalism was specifically discussed as something that propelled Western domination of China, and an alternative to it, be it socialism, communism, or some fusion of East and West, was needed. Here is Qu Qiubai (1899–1935), soon to

---

231. Zhou, *Exploring Modern China's Political Transformation*, 260–261.

232. Ibid., 184–5.

be an early joiner of the CCP, writing in 1921's *A Journey to the Land of Hunger* (《餓鄉紀程》). He describes his travels in the Soviet Union shortly after the November Revolution, and in one passage describes his personal journey through one solution to China's problems after another before getting it right:

> The patriotic movement actually had actually a deeper meaning than mere patriotism. The taste of colonialism, in its full bitterness, had never come home to the Chinese until then, even though we had already had the experience of several decades of foreign exploitation behind us. The sharp pain of imperialistic oppression then reached the marrow of our bones, and it awakened us from the nightmares of impractical democratic reforms. The issue of German possessions in Shantung, which started the national uproar, could not be separated from the larger problem. The industrial powers of the modern world are beset with the problems of capitalism, which takes the form of imperialism in the colonies.[233]

By September 1920, Chen Duxiu had proclaimed his support for proletarian revolution, and an acquaintance of his later recalled that the turnabout was primarily due to what Chen saw as China's (continued) colonial dependency and the abject failure that was Chinese politics at that moment.[234] *New Youth* editors Hu Shi and Lu Xun opposed the journal's general drift toward political advocacy and away from ethical and artistic evaluation, believing that the latter was critical because social enlightenment had to precede political enlightenment, an approach that they were advocating there and elsewhere during this time. Chen was now in Shanghai, center of "foreign capital's" domination, while Hu and Lu were still in Beijing, with Hu still working at Beijing University.

---

233. Translation from Tsai-An Hsia, *The Gate of Darkness: Studies on the Leftist Literary Movement in China* (Seattle: University of Washington Press, 1968), 16.

234. The Chen article proclaiming support for proletarian revolution is 陳獨秀, 《談政治》, 《新青年》, 1920 年 9 月 (Chen Duxiu, "On Politics," *New Youth* 6, no. 9 (September 1920)). The reasoning behind Chen's swift, unambiguous embrace of the Bolshevik model is given in 張國燾, 《我的回憶》, 第一冊 (香港：明報月刊出版社, 1974), 94 頁 (Zhang Guofan, *My Memories*, Volume 1 [Hong Kong: Ming Pao Monthly Publications, 1974] 94).

In this cleavage the intellectual debate over how to build China's future can perhaps be seen in microcosm. (After *New Youth*'s run of volume 9 in 1922, Chinese authorities in Shanghai arrested some of the Shanghai editorial bureau, which put an end to *New Youth* in its original "New Culture" form.) Thus, from then on, in the eyes of Chen and those influenced by him, Bolshevism was a way to liberate the Chinese nation from foreigners and their capital alike. This emphasis on liberation from foreigners qua foreigners occurred despite whatever the *Communist Manifesto* may have said about the irrelevance of national borders to the global proletariat. It was true, Chen and his sympathizers admitted, that China was predominantly rural and therefore precapitalist, but the Bolshevik Revolution had proven that communism could be established in the poorest of countries. Indeed, while he may not have thought of the idea first, using China's vast and impoverished peasantry as a base for modern revolution became a key idea of Mao Zedong.

Chen Duxiu and others after 1919 thus saw the primary Chinese need as political revolution rather than "mere" cultural transformation. The social movements accelerated by the protests after May 4 went beyond mere nationalism. Indeed, in seeking fundamental cultural change, they surely had much in common with ideas that had been in the air in China since after self-strengthening. But the combination of two ideas—that economic competition distorted human nature in ugly ways and that it was bad for the nation of China as it currently played out—would combine ultimately to diminish the horizons for economically liberal policy to almost nothing. It was certainly an unappreciated irony that the climate of free debate—free competition in ideas—that flourished in China from 1917 to 1927 did not foster a broader appreciation for free competition more generally and was instead used to debate and advocate other economically and politically illiberal doctrines.

In a war of abstractions not focused on the fate of the individual, the results of economically liberal policies were seen not as increasing the rate of individual achievement generating social progress in the manner discussed in Chapter 4, but as putting China under the control of foreign capitalism, and hence a mortal threat. In the words of the writer Xu Xunkai (許新凱, birth and death unknown) in *New Youth*, "Given the plunder of the warlords and the capitalists, if we do not change immediately, I fear China will come soon enough to the point where foreign capital has the right to plunder under color of law."[235] And in the early 1920s *New Youth* writers debated whether Leninist dictatorship, anarchism, guild socialism, or other hypothetical Utopias promised the best way forward. It is true that elsewhere the now firmly contrarian Hu Shi could still get in a few words about the need for caution. Now sounding as much like Edmund Burke as his mentor John Dewey, he continued to advocate pragmatism, the need to consider different ways of solving social problems and avoid being entranced by universal laws of human behavior. In addition, he co-signed a short article with 16 others of various persuasions, including the Marxist Li Dazhao, advocating the need for politics to both respect individual freedom and to work for social improvement.[236]

But Marxism itself was nonetheless growing. Following its widespread introduction to Chinese intellectuals shortly after the October revolution, the first agents of the Comintern, the Communist International established earlier by the U.S.S.R. to spread communist revolution, arrived in China in 1920, meeting with Chen Duxiu and Li Dazhao. The Chinese Communist Party was founded in Shanghai in 1921 (thus again confirming—ironically in light of what would follow—its reputation as the most comprehensively liberal of Chinese cities).[237]

5.F The substantial erosion of economically liberal theory and policy—the Nanjing Decade, 1927–1937

Over the next few years, the violent struggle for power continued to grow among a large number of heavily armed factions in China, some of them driven only by a desire to get or expand power and others propelled on the wings

---

235. 「軍閥的敲剝, 外國資本的侵掠, 如不趕快改造, 恐中國就要處於外國資本的公共掠奪政權之下。」。許新凱,《再論共產主義與基爾特社會主義》,《新青年》, 9卷6號, 1922年7月 (Xu Xinkai, "Again on Communism versus Guild Socialism?", *New Youth* 9, no. 6 (July 1922). (English is author's translation.)

236. 胡適等人,《我們的政治主張》,《努力週刊》, 1922年5月, 2期14號 (Hu Shi et al., "What We Stand For," *Striving Weekly* 2, no. 14 (May 1922), http://m.aisixiang.com/data/41352.html.

237. The meeting was initially held in a building in the French concession, and it is now an official historical site. Due to continued unwanted attention by the settlement police, the meeting was concluded on a rented boat on a lake. Chen Duxiu and Li Dazhao were not present at this second meeting, but Mao Zedong was.

of ideological certainty. In a climate like that, the liberal caution of Hu Shi, who preached uncertainty, humility, and a government of trained elites willing to try things tentatively to see if they worked—of steady liberal progress, uncertain in detail but certain in the aggregate—now had no chance.[238] By the middle of the decade, the earlier warlordism had distilled into two armed political movements priming for a fight, the KMT of Sun Yat-Sen, first, and then Chiang Kai-Shek, and the CCP. It was increasingly an age of absolutes, in China as elsewhere.

5.F.1 The KMT comes to power

The Xinhai Revolution had begun when local army commanders rose up against the authority of the Qing, and even before Yuan Shikai's death a whole host of regional armies, one in the south answering to Sun Yat-Sen, had sprouted up. At various points some generals claimed to be leaders of the entire country, but the map told a different story. Army brutality directed at innocents was widespread. It is not relevant to the story being told here except that it eventually resulted in KMT rule over most of the country. A series of incidents occurred in which soldiers, including foreign ones, attacked peaceful demonstrators or strikers. (Strikes had become more frequent since the death of Yuan Shikai, as labor began to take advantage of tighter labor markets in the fastest-growing cities and KMT and CCP organizers became more active.) The most notorious of these was a massacre of protesters in Shanghai in 1925 by British police in the international settlement. It cemented an impression of chaos and foreign oppression and generated a passion to unify the country. Some of the bloodshed eventually ended after Chiang Kai-shek applied great violence in the Chinese part of the city.

Having already ended hostilities against the CCP to achieve victory over the regional generals, Chiang began a military unification campaign in 1926 from Guangdong province in the south as a protégé of the now-deceased Sun Yat-Sen. He led the Northern Expeditions and eventually captured Beijing, formally unifying the country in December 1928. Some fighting among Chinese (apart from that between the KMT and CCP, which historians consider a separate case) continued until 1930. In 1931 the Japanese occupied Man-

---

238. Zhou, *Exploring Modern China's Political Transformation*, 309–310.

churia. Once the first CCP-KMT alliance was ended by Chiang in 1927, he carried out major campaigns against the CCP, which had built an intellectual and organizational infrastructure since its founding in 1921. The most infamous example of Chiang's brutality was his purge of communists in Shanghai in March 1927 shortly after his national army marched into a city that was prepared to peacefully welcome him. At a minimum hundreds of people were arrested or killed. The interval from 1927 to 1937 is generally known in English-language scholarship as the Nanjing Decade, a period when a single political party held meaningful control over much of China.

Several things should be said also about Chiang Kai-Shek, who had been educated while young in Japan, received military training in China and Japan, and joined Sun Yat-Sen's *Tóngménghui* in 1908. After 1911 he helped found the successor KMT, and after becoming a close ally of Sun Yat-Sen was sent by him to the Soviet Union. Having returned to China after Sun's death, Chiang took control of the KMT's New Revolutionary Army, which allowed him to head the Northern Expedition.

He had little to say in person about economic philosophy, but accepted Sun Yat-Sen's principle that the Chinese people needed tutelage in modernity before there could be democracy. He implemented this principle during the Nanjing Decade. But he saw wealthy businessmen and their companies as key forces in his efforts to develop the economy. He personally knew many of them, especially those from his home province of Zhejiang, and before and after 1927 made sure these businesses continued to provide money as needed for the anticommunist fighting. But had Japan not posed such a threat, one could imagine a situation where business activity would have been allowed to continue unmolested (as long as the bribes were paid on time) in areas not under CCP control. Chiang could never be confused for a revolutionary purist. He made practical alliances as needed with legitimate businessmen and with criminals, and also accepted the kidnapping of wealthy businessmen to raise money for the army. (After 1949 he ruled Taiwan dictatorially until his death, during the first stage of that island's postwar economic miracle.) As seen already, he could engage in preemptive violence against communists, and he became an extraordinarily wealthy man by 1937.

During much of the Nanjing Decade the KMT was in military conflict with the CCP. The latter was forced by assaults in Shanghai and elsewhere in

1927 to abandon its strategy of urban organization and warfare and to concentrate instead on the peasants as the focus of the organizing effort and combat, fighting not only the KMT army but forces of private landlords as well.[239] Note that the KMT was now in a rough place ideologically. Including the *Tóngménghuì*, it now had existed for over twenty years, asserting throughout an identity as a revolutionary movement. The emergence of a much larger communist movement had been initially if grudgingly accepted by the bureaucratically ossified KMT before 1925 by placing communists in a minority position within the party. But the revolutionary energy among intellectuals was clearly with the CCP.

Military conflict diminished after the CCP's retreat from KMT forces during the Long March to Yan'an in Shaanxi province from 1934 to 1936 (leading to the so-called Yan'an period, in which Mao Zedong made many proclamations on broader social questions before its end in 1945). However, the KMT government still had to build its defenses against increasingly likely conflict with Japan after the latter seized Manchuria in 1931. During the Nanjing Decade 40 percent or more of the national budget was spent on the military, a figure that grew after Japan's invasion of the rest of China in 1937. In the end, after removing the Chinese currency from any tie to a metallic standard in November 1935, Chiang Kai-Shek's resort to desperate yet irresponsible printing of paper money caused ever-higher inflation, a problem right up until the communist takeover.

So even when what had been written down was liberal, there was a significant gap between what was written and what the government did. And even at that, what was put on paper was frequently illiberal.

5.F.2 The KMT's social and economic regimentation

During our exploration of both the Nanjing Decade and the communist era, it will be worth noting that almost any government, even one largely totalitarian, can be influenced by public opinion. Pressure on the KMT to increase economic control during the Nanjing Decade was increased by the fact that the popular press (outside the concessions) frequently saw the government

---

239. One urban redoubt for communists, at least communist intellectuals, as it had been several times for other dissidents since it was established, was the Shanghai settlements.

itself as a catspaw of capitalists whom the government should bring under control.[240] The government relied on its claim that the Chinese people were still politically immature, so all manner of regulation of private business was justified. Since the last few years of the Qing there had been open special-interest groups of all sorts, including by now the large chambers of commerce throughout the country, that were both subject to and instigators of political pressure. The preferred language these groups chose for themselves was often evocative of the public interest, with names ending with words like *gòngtuán* (共團, "public association").

These *gòngtuán* provided a ready-made chance to implement illiberal economic control. From the beginning of the Nanjing Decade, the government to a significant degree sought on paper to implement Sun Yat-Sen's three principles through "social engineering," defined as "organiz[ing] Society into functional groups supervised by the party-state."[241] This was a unifying principle different from direct government production or mere regulation of the production of goods for profit. For example, beginning in 1930 the KMT attempted to impose on high school students *xùnyù* (訓育), "training" or "instruction" in a mix of Confucian ideas and Sun's three principles. This attempt to inculcate loyalty to the one-party state met with varying degrees of success. This "training" structure begat Chiang Kai-Shek's personal campaign, known as the New Life Movement (新生活運動, *Xīn shēnghuó yùndòng*), in 1934. Confucian ideas were to be deployed to combat the squalor and moral corruption for which Shanghai was a metaphor in the West.[242] As for private society, whether as already existing or new organizations, groups either applied to or were organized by the KMT state as people's (人民團體, *rénmín tuántǐ*) or mass (民眾

240. Frederick Spencer, "Chiang Kai-Shek's Dictatorship Stumbles," *China Today* 1 (December 1934): 46; Robert W. Barnett, *Economic Shanghai: Hostage to Politics, 1937–1941* (New York: Institute of Pacific Relations, 1941), 12.

241. Xiaoqun Xu, *Chinese Professionals and the Republican State: The Rise of Professional Associations in Shanghai, 1912–1937* (Cambridge: Cambridge University Press, 2000), 80.

242. On *xùnyù*, see 黃金麟, 《戰爭、身體、現代性》, 台北：聯經出版事業公司, 2009 (Huang Jinliu, *War, Body and Modernity* (Taipei: Linkage Publishing, 2009)). On the New Life campaign and its possible motivations, see Arif Dirlik, "The Ideological Foundations of the New Life Movement: A Study in Counterrevolution," *Journal of Asian Studies* 34, no. 4 (August 1975): 945–980. The ROC of course was neither the first nor the last national government to use education to try to implement standardized political instruction.

團體, *mínzhòng tuántǐ*) organizations. They accepted government control in exchange for public legitimacy. The classification system for these groups, the number of them subject to KMT control, and the scope of such control grew over the course of the Nanjing decade.[243]

Meanwhile, Chiang Kai-Shek and other elements of the KMT leadership saw to it personally that people close to him were placed on the boards of various commercial organizations. Du Yuesheng (杜月笙, 1888-1951), the powerful leader of the Shanghai criminal organization the Green Gang and longtime ally of Chiang, at various times was on the board of the Shanghai stock exchange, the Shanghai General Chamber of Commerce, and the Bank of China.

From 1928 to 1933 the posts of minister of finance and head of the central bank were both held by T. V. Soong (宋子文, 1894-1971), Chiang Kai-Shek's brother-in-law, who had received an economics degree from Harvard and was well connected in international financial circles. Soong played the role of the good cop; at a national economic conference (全國經濟會議) held in 1928, he apologized for earlier bullying of businessmen in Shanghai and elsewhere, saying that, lamentably, desperate times called for desperate measures.[244] Reflecting the left-illiberal spirit that was widespread among Chinese writers, the primary criticism of the conference by the press was that students, peasants, and unions had insufficient input.[245]

From an economically liberal point of view, there was much to regret during this time. For example the KMT directed men to go to the Chamber of Commerce office in Shanghai on April 22, 1928, and after employees of the chamber were attacked and documents removed, the chamber suspended business. The government in October 1929 also passed a law limiting each region of the country to one stock exchange. This was of course illiberal, not just in imposing a specific number, but in dividing up the map so that the KMT could plan which regions should have which kinds of economic activity, and

---

243. Xu, *Chinese Professionals*, 97-102.

244. However, by the time Soong departed China just before 1949, he had used the power of his office to increase his personal wealth substantially.

245. Parks M. Coble, Jr., *The Shanghai Capitalists*, 58.

in what quantity.[246]

Also in 1929 Soong directed the banks to buy many of the bonds issued by the government. In November 1930 at a conference of a national business organization, the National Industrial and Commercial Association (全國共商協會), considerably more limited in its freedom than the local chambers of commerce of just a few years before, the KMT announced plans for "promoting native goods, developing greater cooperation between labor and capital, and proving industrial technology, increasing China's exports, and increasing the capitalization of Chinese industry," along with construction of infrastructure.[247] At best this was industrial policy of the postwar East Asian type, but at worst a recipe for substantial state takeover of the economy.

To be fair, Soong probably did not believe the state should plan the economy to the degree Sun Yat-Sen had. For example, stock markets were not banned outright; such an action would have done even more damage to China's economic vitality. But during the Nanjing Decade the Shanghai business community outside of the settlements became subordinate to the state, precisely because the latter had so much authority. Note the difference from earlier decades, when under weaker governments the state had little power to bring free markets to heel. Now, very well-armed, it could, and did.

As a result of the Japanese invasion of Manchuria in 1931, KMT payments on government bonds were suspended, although, remarkably, for only six months. This suspension was accompanied by bank runs, since the banks were large owners of the bonds. Important people in the business community and elsewhere in Nanjing began to clamor for the return of Chiang Kai-Shek, who had been away from power since nominally resigning immediately after the invasion. He returned on January 20, 1932, replacing Sun Fo (孫科, 1891–1973, Sun Yat-Sen's son) as premier. In a gesture suggesting that economic liberalism would be respected, T. V. Soong was sent overseas to court more foreign investment, which would give foreigners a bigger stake in helping China resist the Japanese. In 1933 the government for the sole time during the Nanjing Decade imposed import tariffs for import-substitution (as opposed to

---

246. The law was the Law on Stock Exchanges (證券交易所法), discussed in Xu, *Chinese Professionals and the Republican State*, 31–32.

247. The remarks are those of Coble in *The Shanghai Capitalists*, 84.

revenue-raising) reasons. (The government had recovered near-complete tariff autonomy in the treaty ports over several months in 1928.[248]) Because Japanese factories were disproportionally impacted, most of these tariffs against Japan were undone under Japanese pressure after Soong left office later in 1933.

With its recovered tariff autonomy, the uniform tariff of 5 percent imposed in the Treaty of Nanjing in 1842 (augmented by a 2.5 percent "surcharge" authorized by the foreign powers in 1922) was over. China's new independently set tariffs, like those of most countries, varied significantly across goods and trading partners, in the case of imports from the United States ranging from nothing on cereals to 40 percent on kerosene.[249] Between 1928 and 1935, tariff revenue as a percentage of assessed import value grew steadily from under 5 percent before stabilizing at roughly 25 percent.[250] (Owing to the almost immediate capture by the Japanese of China's most economically vital ports in 1937, even as the foreign concessions were left alone until after Pearl Harbor, gross tariff revenue fell substantially in that year.)

The Great Depression came late to China, taking hold only in late 1934.[251] But it was followed by aggressive nationalization of banks and extensive intrusion by the Chinese central bank on financial activities previously substantially private. By this point, the major Chinese-owned financial institutions of Shanghai that remained in private hands were playing the rent-seeking game and not the competition game in their dealings with the government, as access to credit became largely a cronyist activity. Indeed, between 1934 and 1936, the percentage of financial assets held by the government rose nationwide from 18.2 percent to 72.8 percent. The government's goals, according to Coble, were to "eliminate the private bankers as an obstacle to deficit spend-

---

248. This was in an era before the most-favored-nation principle, so that each country negotiated tariff rates with each other country separately. Chinese tariffs had been limited to 5 percent at all treaty ports since 1844. The United States was the first country to acknowledge China's sovereignty to set its own tariffs in July 1928, and other powers followed quickly.

249. Walter H. Mallory, "China's New Tariff Autonomy," *Foreign Affairs* (April 1929), accessed at https://www.foreignaffairs.com/articles/china/1929-04-01/chinas-new-tariff-autonomy.

250. Felix Boecking, "The Bitterness of Fiscal Realism: Guomindang Tariff Policy, China's Trade in Imported Sugar and Smuggling, 1928-1937," *Harvard Asia Quarterly* 13, no. 2 (2011): 13–20.

251. Tomoko Shiroyama, *China During the Great Depression: Market, State, and the World Economy, 1929–1937* (Cambridge, MA: Harvard University Asia Center, 2008).

ing and to control of China's monetary system."[252] Similar efforts were later undertaken, starting on April 1, 1935, when Chiang Kai-Shek announced the "National Economic Reconstruction Movement" (國民經濟建設運動). On the one hand, this was designed to increase agricultural productivity (almost all agricultural production was still in private hands) and to promote domestic industry, but, in addition, to "regulate labor and capital" and "adjust finance" and lower tariffs.[253] It was a plan, in other words, driven by a belief that the economy should be planned from the capital, Nanjing, albeit while tolerating a substantially regulated private sector. Numerous companies were established in tea, vegetables, oils, and other products, with the state controlling, but also with substantial private investment. And the government's mixed attitude toward business—seeing it as a useful source of funds for weapons and talent for industrial development—was of a piece with its behavior toward intellectuals. Some writers of the left, e.g., Ding Ling (丁玲, 1904–1986), imprisoned from 1933–1936) and Qu Qiubai (executed by the KMT in 1935), were pursued and others left to live more or less unmolested.[254] And apart from some politically threatening speech that passed across the government's field of vision, as noted in Section 4.C.1, Chinese cultural vitality continued prior to 1937. This was the case even though Chiang in September 1934, announced the aforementioned New Life Movement. He was reacting to the crime and other sins for which Shanghai had become a global metaphor, but faced strong opposition from people on the KMT left such as Wang Jingwei (汪精衛, 1883–1944). In the words of Michael Dillon, the New Life Movement campaign "conspicuously failed to have any effect."[255]

What are we to make of the economic situation in the rest of China before the Japanese invasion in 1937? On the one hand, despite the Japanese threat to China beyond Manchuria, before the intensification of economic planning

---

252. Coble Jr., *The Shanghai Capitalists and the Nationalist Government*, 203.

253. Ibid., 237.

254. Lu Xun died peacefully in 1936, never having spent time in prison. Gou Dali (郭大力, 1995–1976) and Wang Yanan (王亞南, 1901–1969) got their translation of all three volumes of Marx's *Capital* published in 1937, albeit in the International Settlement. 卡爾馬克思, 《資本論》, 議郭大力和王亞南, 上海：讀書生活出版社, 1938年。(Karl Marx, *Kapital*. Trans. by Guo Dali and Wang Yanan (Shanghai: Reading Life Publishing, 1938)). This process will be described in Chapter 6.

255. Michael Dillon, *China: A Modern History* (London: I. B. Tauris, 2010), 270.

in the mid-1930s and the delayed arrival of the Great Depression, considerable evidence exists that the economy in and around the treaty ports was performing very well, for the most part continuing the general healthy trend since 1843 documented above. Debin Ma, using data on prices and output compiled by Xu Xinwu and Huang Hanming reported average annual growth of industrial production in Shanghai from 1925–1936 of five percent, down considerably from the extraordinary 12 percent rate from 1916–1925, but still very respectable. He also reported that the Shanghai economy in the early 1930s was transitioning away from labor and toward more capital-intensive production, a pattern consistent with rising wealth. As a result, more workers were more expensive because they had more options in east Asian countries as the years after World War II proceeded.[256]

The KMT during the decade before 1937 also did a defensible job, amid the surrounding violence (to which the KMT of course contributed substantially), of providing the sorts of public goods that many economic liberals, including Adam Smith, would be perfectly comfortable with. Among government efforts in this regard were the introduction of a single currency (although it would soon be debased), progress toward a single national Chinese language, and continued improvements in primary and secondary education and in transportation. The gradual peaceful absorption of several regional military commanders after the triumph of the Northern Expeditions also allowed regional governors, a few of them former military commanders themselves, to turn their attention to some degree away from actual or planned violence and toward provision of such goods.[257]

The best summary is that Chiang Kai-Shek's KMT overall was, in the trenches, not as ideologically driven in an illiberal direction as Sun Yat-Sen's had been. The KMT recognized that regulated market activities had their place for now, although capitalism would fade away in due course. At the top

---

256. Debin Ma, "Economic Growth in the Lower Yangzi Region of China in 1911–1937: A Quantitative and Historical Analysis," *Journal of Economic History* 68, no. 2 (June 2008): 355–392. Recall that this pattern is characteristic of the "product lifecycle" model of economic development, and all the postwar East Asian miracle nations went through it.

257. On evidence for regional provision of "public goods," see Edward A. McCord, "Reevaluating the Nanjing Decade: A Provincial Perspective," unpublished manuscript, https://aacs.ccny.cuny.edu/2012conference/Papers/McCord,%20Edward.pdf

of the party, vibrant market activity, especially among big businesses, was seen as needed for other reasons, sometimes genuinely related to national security and sometimes merely venal. In the last two years of the Nanjing Decade, both because of the influence of the worldwide depression and the increasingly dangerous threat from Japan, economic policy writ large became less important.

5.G The fall and legacy of KMT China

The Nanjing decade was the temporary culmination of several decades of struggle over what post-imperial China was to be, and of efforts by the single most important political organization, the KMT, to assert control over that new China. Economically the party as a whole had a strong legacy of belief in two propositions during the period it governed before 1937. First, foreign control over Chinese territory was a crime that had to end once China was strong enough to end it. Second, a strong state could and should organize the economy for the benefit of the people as a whole; private enterprise might not be swept away, but businesses, especially larger ones, would have to either be taken over or accept substantial state involvement in their affairs.

But if a bargain could have been proposed to commercial China in which business would have been given free rein (i.e., an economically liberal policy) in exchange for making the communist threat permanently go away (and perhaps for a continuing cut of the profits of big companies), as an individual, Chiang Kai-Shek might well have taken that bargain. But that was not the bargain that the Chinese people faced after 1945; instead, it was the actual performance of the actual KMT, infected as it was by violence and corruption, versus proposed complete displacement of big business (and in reality, almost all private economic activity), by the communists.

The Nanjing Decade was not totalitarian, although neither was it remotely close to a liberal ideal. While Chiang Kai-Shek's government imprisoned, executed, and massacred those (most on the left) it saw as threats, substantial pockets of dissent remained. Beijing University, whose establishment was one of the reforms that survived the Dowager Empress's counterreaction to the 1898 100 Days Reform and the turbulence that followed, was able to rely on academic freedom to continue to criticize Chinese society and the Chinese government. This was tolerated as long as the criticism was scholarly in nature, and, as we have seen, some early CCP members, including Chen Duxiu and Li Dazhao, found shelter there. (Li was executed well after he left the university, in 1927.) The foreign concessions also proved a haven for opposing ideas; those who propounded them, such as Chen Duxiu, often used their university posts for this purpose. And businesses big and small were tolerated, although all too often abused, in KMT China, in the manner of a modern kleptocracy. But of course. this was commerce as the party's servant, not as agent of spontaneously ordered progress.

To be sure, the long struggle for power with other groups and movements meant that the KMT before 1927 could not entirely impose its vision. By 1927, when it controlled the coercive apparatus of the Chinese government in much of the country, the country seemed already exhausted. And yet by 1937 the KMT's corruption, in which some favored businesses were willing partners, and the KMT's continuous, brutal, unresolvable violent conflict with the CCP made this worse and discredited the former. Meanwhile, during the Nanjing Decade itself, while there was some room for the remnant dynamism birthed by the previously liberal economic environment, few voices in the public arena supported economic liberalism. In hindsight, this shrinking of liberal voices was inevitable due to the New Culture movement and the Bolshevik Revolution.

Unsurprisingly, ideological concerns about the injustices of, first, big business and, since the New Culture movement, the liberal economy itself, both in terms of its treatment of the poor and its role as handmaiden of imperialism, doomed economic liberalism in the KMT-dominated ROC on the mainland after 1945. In the absence of a foreign threat to the nation itself (the KMT got along well enough with the Soviet government until the CCP was close to its 1949 victory in the Chinese civil war), KMT ideologues found room in the aftermath of the Japanese surrender and China's recovery of its full sovereignty (despite immense internal problems) to continue to implement illiberal policies. The government quickly nationalized all Japanese property, public and private, and increased tariffs on imports, with an eye to import substitution.

By 1947 KMT-owned firms produced 63 percent of the country's electricity, 90 percent of its steel and iron, 100 percent of its tungsten, 70 percent of its tin, 90 percent of its sugar, 45 percent of its cement, and 33 percent of its coal.[258] Whatever large-scale liberal economic activity KMT ideology and corruption had failed to snuff out (T. V. Soong and others had sold off significant amounts of allied relief immediately after the Japanese surrender) the postwar hyperinflation finished off. Of course, economic liberals would argue that the increasing politicization of the economy and the increasing amount of corruption went hand-in-hand after 1945, since the amount of corruption in the end is a function of the number of things there are to be corrupt about, the total number resulting from decisions made by the state through its tax and regulatory powers. Whatever the truth of this claim, just as the KMT had done before them, the CCP swept into power substantially on their promise to promote a more just society, this time by replacing the miserable KMT socioeconomic experiment with communism. But from the point of view of economic liberalism, under CCP rule things, already very bad, were about to get worse.

---

258. Aron Shai, *The Fate of British and French Firms in China: Imperialism Imprisoned* (Basingstoke, UK: Macmillan, 1996), 10–11.

CHAPTER 6

Flatlining: Economic Liberalism's Near-death Experience in China

I t may seem odd to investigate the trajectory of liberalism under a distinctively communist government, which China was almost completely with respect to economic policy from shortly after the 1949 taking of power to the late 1970s. But two features of interest involving economic liberalism played out during this period. First, the process by which the modestly spontaneous, liberal order was dismantled is revealing about the differences between state direction and free self-organization of the economy, as is the periodic revival of markets during crises. Second, Marxist theory in all branches does not object intrinsically to liberal economics. Even Karl Marx (1818–1883) depicted it as appropriate for its stage, although merely a soon-to-be-obsolete description of the world that he thought would soon come when he published *Capital* in 1867. This chapter investigates economic liberalism both in theoretical and policy terms under Mao's China.

6.A The coming of communism and the end of the liberal, spontaneous order

China scholars differ on the proportions, but the triumph of the CCP was a combination of their appeal in the countryside given China's vast rural poverty, a lack of American support for the KMT after 1945, hyperinflation dating back to 1937, corruption in and intimidation by the KMT, late assistance by Joseph Stalin (1878–1953) to the CCP, and the two sides' military decisions. The war was brutal, but its end brought China sustained nationwide peace for the first time in over three decades.

6.A.1 Initial conditions

The triumph of the CCP and the charismatic leadership of Mao Zedong invested Chinese communists at all levels with tremendous confidence that the better vision they had for their society could be implemented. But China's problems were immense. This literal textbook description of Chinese cities after the takeover is surely not far off the mark:

> The task of governing this largely unfamiliar [urban] terrain was compounded by the chaotic conditions which so tragically marked urban life during the last days of [KMT] rule. In addition to chronic (and now exacerbated) problems of massive unemployment and underemployment, of corrupt and inefficient local administrations, of a population preyed upon by a vast underworld of gangster organizations and secret societies, widespread opium addiction, prostitution, and the lack of elemental standards of sanitation and municipal services, conditions of war and the misrule of a dying regime imposed even more severe problems which destroyed the economic life of the cities and inflicted cruel burdens on their inhabitants.[259]

Chapter 5 indicated that if we were to imagine a night-watchman state and a complete command economy as two poles (and later under Mao the latter would come very close to fruition), before 1937 the KMT had already advanced quite a bit since 1927 toward the command pole. It must also be emphasized that even under dictatorial communism economic outcomes were not simply handed down from on high by one person, or even several. Economic outcomes in any society emerge given people's interests and the incentives provided by state power, the latter itself a function of the interests, including the ideological goals, of individuals who make up the state. So, political conflict among senior CCP leaders is part of the story. But one man for decades was the center of such conflict whenever it arose.

---

259. Maurice Meisner, *Mao's China and After: A History of the People's Republic*, 3rd edition (New York: Simon and Schuster, 1986), 76–77.

6.A.2 Mao Zedong

What kind of person was Mao Zedong? He was born in the small town of Sha-oshan (韶山) in Hunan province in 1893, to a self-made and successful father, and a mother whom he apparently loved dearly and who, like many women in China at the time, had no given name. While young, he became a better read-er than his father, and received at first a classical Confucian education from a series of tutors. Spurning his father's advice to apprentice in the rice trade, he entered a modern school near his mother's hometown. He was introduced to newspapers, a product of the liberal China, when he moved to the provin-cial capital of Changsha in 1911, eventually studying on his own in the main library there. Later he worked at the library of Beijing University.[260] There, he met Li Dazhao and Chen Duxiu, and became familiar with the then-res-ident Hu Shi. Due to his self-education and experience at several institutions of higher education, in his own description (self-servingly to a degree, cer-tainly) as recounted to the American journalist Edgar Snow, "At this time my mind was a curious mixture of ideas of liberalism, democratic reformism, and Utopian socialism. I had somewhat vague passions about 'nineteenth-centu-ry democracy,' utopianism, and old-fashioned liberalism, and I was definitely antimilitarist and anti-imperialist."[261]

For a few years starting in 1919 he shuttled among Changsha, Beijing, and Shanghai. Having participated in the Shanghai-area meetings at which the CCP was founded in 1921, during the subsequent period of cooperation between the KMT and CCP in the 1920s he served under KMT authority. But after submitting an admiring chronicle of peasant revolts in Hunan in

---

260. Jung Chang and Jon Halliday, *Mao: The Untold Story* (New York: Anchor, 2011). Readers should know that in the first few years after this book's release, it received both academic praise and criticism. A collection of reviews, many critical, is found in *Was Mao Really a Monster? The Academic Response to Chang and Halliday's "Mao: The Unknown Story,"* George Benton and Lin Chun (eds.) (London: Routledge, 2010). Other criticism, plus a quote from Chang and Halliday responding, is found in Jonathan Fenby, "Storm Rages over Bestselling Book on Monster Mao," *The Guardian*, December 3, 2005, https://www.theguardian.com/uk/2005/dec/04/china.books. None of the criticism involves the biographical informa-tion here.

261. The remarks were cited in an interview of Mao in Edgar Snow, *Red Star Over China* (New York: Grove Press, 1961), 147–148. That work too has suffered extensive criticism over the years, in this case for its naïveté, but it has never been suggested that Snow fabricated quotes from Mao.

March,1927,[262] Mao and others blamed Chiang Kai-Shek's victories over the CCP in May 1927 on Chen Duxiu's weakness as CCP leader. In the summer and fall of 1927 Mao participated in organized violence in Hunan, notably the failed Autumn Harvest Uprising (秋收起義). After this, he was expelled for a time from the CCP.

What can we learn from these events? First, the young Mao was very representative of the wandering intellectuals of this period noted in Chapters 2 and 5—China was in disastrous shape, foreign capitalists and their imperialism were a major if not the single reason why, and there was one magical answer, if only they could find it, to solve this problem. Second, by the time he made his brief speech on a platform at Tiananmen Square announcing the establishment of the People's Republic of China on October 1, 1949, as far as Mao was concerned China's future would lie in sticking to whatever revolutionary vision his CCP decided to impose. And most of the time, that vision in the end was Mao Zedong's. Third, these visions took economic classes and not individual agency as their fulcrum.

6.B Historical and ideological backdrop to the destruction of the existing order

The communist victory in 1949 was as complete as that of any Chinese internal war. The KMT and mainland refugees fled to Taiwan, and only that island and the colonial jurisdictions of Hong Kong and Macao escaped CCP control. The Chinese were exhausted by decades of nearly continuous conflict, and its leaders were determined to undo nearly a century of Western capitalist domination. For the rest of Mao's life, from the initial blockade and threats by the defeated Nationalists on Taiwan, to his decision (with Stalin's approval, which Mao sought) to fight alongside North Korea, to the opening to Japan and the U.S. in the early 1970s, events outside China's borders brought continual challenges. But within China, his only threats were from other leaders of the CCP, and those came primarily in response to Mao's own overreaching. He specifically, and the CCP more generally, unquestionably had the power to substantially

---

262. 毛澤東,《湖南農民運動考察報告》。English version available as Mao Zedong, *Report on an Investigation of the Peasant Movement in Hunan* (March 1927), https://www.marxists.org/reference/archive/mao/selected-works/volume-1/mswv1_2.htm.

impose his vision on the China they took control of in 1949.

And that vision had two powerful influences. The first was the work of Marx and Engels, especially Engels. In thinking about the communist ideal that communist national leaders everywhere at least nominally adhered to, it is worth invoking Engels' 1847 description of the progression and outcome of the proletarian revolution:

(i) Limitation of private property through progressive taxation, heavy inheritance taxes, abolition of inheritance through collateral lines (brothers, nephews, etc.) forced loans, etc.

(ii) Gradual expropriation of landowners, industrialists, railroad magnates and shipowners, partly through competition by state industry, partly directly through compensation in the form of bonds.

(iii) Confiscation of the possessions of all emigrants and rebels against the majority of the people.

(iv) Organization of labor or employment of proletarians on publicly owned land, in factories and workshops, with competition among the workers being abolished and with the factory owners, in so far as they still exist, being obliged to pay the same high wages as those paid by the state.

(v) An equal obligation on all members of society to work until such time as private property has been completely abolished. Formation of industrial armies, especially for agriculture.

(vi) Centralization of money and credit in the hands of the state through a national bank with state capital, and the suppression of all private banks and bankers.

(vii) Increase in the number of national factories, workshops, railroads, ships; bringing new lands into cultivation and improvement of land already under cultivation—all in proportion to the growth of the capital and labor force at the disposal of the nation.

(viii) Education of all children, from the moment they can leave their mother's care, in national establishments at national cost. Education and production together.

(ix) Construction, on public lands, of great palaces as communal dwellings for associated groups of citizens engaged in both industry and agriculture and combining in their way of life the advantages of urban and rural conditions while avoiding the one-sidedness and drawbacks of each.

(x) Destruction of all unhealthy and jerry-built dwellings in urban districts.

(xi) Equal inheritance rights for children born in and out of wedlock.

(xii) Concentration of all means of transportation in the hands of the nation.

It is impossible, of course, to carry out all these measures at once. But one will always bring others in its wake. Once the first radical attack on private property has been launched, the proletariat will find itself forced to go ever further, to concentrate increasingly in the hands of the state all capital, all agriculture, all transport, all trade. All the foregoing measures are directed to this end; and they will become practicable and feasible, capable of producing their centralizing effects to precisely the degree that the proletariat, through its labor, multiplies the country's productive forces.

Finally, when all capital, all production, all exchange have been brought together in the hands of the nation, private property will disappear of its own accord, money will become superfluous, and production will so expand and man so change that society will be able to slough off whatever of its old economic habits may remain.[263]

---

263. Friedrich Engels, *The Principles of Communism*, an early draft of *The Communist Manifesto* 1847 (https://www.marxists.org/archive/marx/works/1847/11/prin-com.htm).

If Marx was the economic theorist, Engels was the social engineer. And communism was at least as much a social revolution as an economic one. Communist revolutionary leaders, Mao even more than most, sought to remake society so as to purge every trace of bourgeois life from it.

In addition, recall from the last chapter that before October 1949 the KMT, which had for decades been dominated by those who saw political regimentation as generally superior to spontaneous social order, that is, to economic and social liberalism, had done much of the heavy lifting by 1949 with regard to urban industry. This suggests that the CCP upon taking power could pay more attention to bourgeois social structure and to the countryside in their plans. Liberalism—economic, political or social—was now not competition among business, ideas, and social structures. It was instead unambiguously exploitation, to be forcibly swept away by the state. Initially, "bourgeois capitalists" (資產階級, literally "propertied class" or "asset class"), especially the petty bourgeoisie, many of whom were enthusiastic about the new China, were welcomed to participate in its building. But soon enough the adjective "bourgeois" became a comprehensive description of anything objectionable in the existing order—not just economic inequality, but economic outcomes that failed to match the CCP plan. And any resistance, real or imagined, to the imposition of the communist order either revealed stubborn bourgeois attitudes in need of adjustment or outright bourgeoisie sabotage.

And there was great skepticism of spontaneously ordered cities and urban life. If Shanghai on the one hand had represented Chinese and foreign decadence, it had also represented constant evolution, a blending of influences near and far. (In today's once-again global Shanghai, the same feeling was there to a significant extent until the outbreak of COVID-19.) In May 1949, as communist soldiers entered the city following a spree of KMT-army terror in the weeks before it fell, the soldiers were on their best behavior. But they were also, like the People's Liberation Army (PLA) as a whole, overwhelmingly from China's countryside. Shanghai's prosperity was corrupt and unfairly distributed, and the price of its lifestyle in terms of Chinese dignity was too high. Soon the city, like others throughout especially coastal China, would be remade by communist planners. This involved sweeping aside of much of what had already been constructed, whether spontaneously or through previous KMT planning. And soon enough sweeping away the capitalist, or bourgeois, spontaneous order was a key requirement throughout the country.

6.C The idea of economic liberalism under communism

In China, the theory of economic liberalism as a necessary stage before communism did not disappear during China's three decades of radical communism. The opposite in fact—economic liberalism had a role in universities and in intellectual literature (although as in most intellectual arenas, access to it by literate Chinese was extremely limited) because it had a role in Marxist theory —as a museum piece, right for its time but irrelevant now.

6.C.1 Economic liberalism in Marx's eyes

The phrase "Marxist theory" requires a little clarification. As with many a revolutionary intellectual breakthrough, over time different true believers came to believe different "truths." And like every country where indigenous Marxist revolution succeeded, China was a country that had not gone through the mass, arguably cruel industrialization of the sort that Marx himself had observed in mid-19th century Europe. This perspective led him to conclude that bourgeois capitalism was a necessary stage on the road to communism. Volume I of *Capital* (two volumes were subsequently compiled from Marx's unpublished papers and released by Engels after Marx died) never promoted the idea that socialism is an intermediate stage toward communism; indeed neither "socialism" nor "socialist" even appears in the English version of the text proper, although the words do appear in a few of the footnotes. So Marx was clearly aware of the idea of "socialism," but it played no role in the theoretical apparatus of *Capital*.

Capital did teach that history was driven forward dialectically—tensions in the existing economic system will eventually lead to a new system, whose own tensions will then develop. Marx analyzed feudalism and capitalism, arguing that tensions in the former led to its replacement at the appropriate moment by bourgeois capitalism. Eventually similar tensions between the proletariat on the one hand and the bourgeoisie and capitalist classes on the other would (and indeed were about to in mid-19th-century Europe) reach a similar critical juncture, and capitalism would fail. While Marx nowhere in *Capital* discussed the utopian replacement for capitalism, in *Manifesto of the Communist Party*, published earlier, Marx and Engels did sketch the likely contours of such a society. They devoted an entire section to criticizing "socialism" and its litera-ture as backward-looking, operating in the interests of the noble or elite class-es, or representing a compromise with capitalists that would ultimately fail.[264]

Marx's dialectic timeline of political economy was thus straightforward—feudalism, capitalism, communism. Marxist scholars have sometimes argued, based on a remark in Marx's *A Contribution to the Critique of Political Economy*, that he delineated elsewhere well-defined stages before feudalism, sometimes referred to by these scholars as primitive communism and slavery.[265] (It was also these later scholars and government officials who introduced the idea of "socialism" as an intermediate stage between the overthrow of capitalism and the arrival of communism.) Feudalism though, said Marx and Engels, had not been found everywhere; Marx did specifically discuss an "Asiatic mode of production" in which despots take any surplus above subsistence throughout centuries. Nonetheless, Marxists have specifically identified primitive com-munism, slavery, feudalism, capitalism, and communism and argued that in 1949 China was in the third, capitalist stage.[266] Marxist theory can be used to argue that before the CCP triumph foreign imperialist capital had accelerated China's progress through the stages.[267]

Given this framework, when it comes to liberal economic theory, Marx's views were somewhat mixed. On the one hand, capitalism and private prop-erty were historically inevitable early on, and therefore in a sense he was eth-ically justifying the vast, forcible (as he saw it) transformation in production and distribution. But on the other, it was an economics irredeemably corrupt-ed by the monied interests. In *Capital*, Marx, a gifted polemicist, referred in several places to economists often thought today to have made distinguished contributions to economic thought as either unperceptive or servants of capi-

---

264. See section III, "Socialist and Communist Literature," in Karl Marx and Friedrich Engels, *The Com-munist Manifesto: A Modern Edition*, ed. Eric Hobsbawm (London: Verso, 2012), Section II, 61-75.

265. The remark in question is "In broad outlines Asiatic, ancient, feudal, and modern bourgeois modes of production can be designated as progressive epochs in the economic formation of society." Karl Marx, *A Contribution to the Critique of Political Economy*, 2nd ed., trans. N. I. Stone (Chicago: Charles H. Kerr & Company, 1904), 99.

266. D. Ross Gandy, *Marx and History: From Primitive Society to the Communist Future* (Austin: Universi-ty of Texas Press, 1979), 151.

267. Karl A. Wittfogel, "The Marxist View of China (Part 1)," *China Quarterly* 11 (July-September, 1962), 1–20, 1.

talists. Henry Dunning Macleod (1821–1902), sometimes credited as a founder of old-style institutional economics, was dismissed as someone "whose function it is to trick out the confused ideas of Lombard Street in the most learned finery."[268] Frédéric Bastiat (1801–1850), now seen as a pioneer in the idea of opportunity cost, was seen by Marx as "a bag man of free trade" and "the most superficial and therefore the most successful representative of apologetic vulgar economics."[269] Jeremy Bentham, as much a moral philosopher as a political economist, was "that soberly pedantic and heavy-footed oracle of common sense of the nineteenth-century bourgeoisie."[270]

The only political economists treated with the respect one might expect from someone like Marx, who argued that economists should scientifically analyze the world, were David Ricardo (1772–1823) and Adam Smith. Smith was mentioned in the first volume of *Capital* on 18 separate occasions, more than any other political economist, and only once was he criticized in anything like the personal manner revealed in the prior paragraph. And even this criticism applied only to Smith's theorizing and not to the man himself. Marx criticized Smith's "quite preposterous analysis"[271] that funds spent by a business on what economists now call intermediate inputs eventually must end up in the pocket of some laborers making something, perhaps after circulating numerous times through the economy. This analysis is not correct under standard modern economics, either, which says that given significant competition what does not go to workers or to the owners of companies making intermediate inputs (or to consumers paying lower prices) is taken by those owners as compensation for risk-taking in the event the business is successful or as reward for deferred consumption. (The distribution of revenue under limited competition is different.) But Marx viewed Smith's error as failing to see the accumulation of some of the revenue by businesses who sell these inputs not as compensation for services rendered but merely as "capital." To Marx and most Marxists, the dynamics of the residual after survival wages have been paid, i.e.,

---

268. Karl Marx, *Capital: A Critique of Political Economy*, Volume 1, trans. Ben Fowkes (New York: Vintage Books, 1977), 153.

269. Ibid., 98 ("superficial"), 153 ("bagmen").

270. Ibid., 758.

271. Ibid., 737.

the accumulation of "capital," is the key thing driving the system's expansion and eventual collapse (and the relentless desire to accumulate more capital is what drives the capitalist system in *Capital*). For economic liberals, on the other hand, what drives growth is the incentivizing function of expected profit, including innovations that directly or indirectly enhance consumer welfare.

Still, Marx's criticism of Smith was well within the bounds of standard social-science protocol, and presumably this influenced CCP theorists after 1949. Smith was seen by Marx, and therefore by the communist nations that treated the works of Marx as holy writ, not as writing in opposition to the truth but as merely theoretically immature. Marxists sometimes used some of Smith's doctrines as support for Marx's own. Shortly after the "quite preposterous analysis" remark Marx added, "It goes without saying that political economy has gone on to exploit, in the interests of the capitalist class, Adam Smith's doctrine that the whole of that part of the net product which is transformed into capital is consumed by the working class."[272] Smith's error, thus, had negative real consequences. Yet clearly, Smith and to a lesser extent Ricardo, in contrast to other liberal economists who followed them, were seen by Marx as people who advanced the theory of political economy.

6.C.2 *Economic liberalism as seen in Maoist China*
So both before and after 1949, that is how Marxist economists in China, who had much subsequent Marxist commentary to work with, treated what were seen as the two main works of liberal political economy, Smith's *Wealth of Nations* and Ricardo's *Principles of Political Economy and Taxation*, which was first published in 1817.[273] (Hu Shi, in contrast, perhaps because of the broader reach of his liberalism into the political and social spheres, and his belief in epistemological humility, was targeted by Mao and government propaganda throughout the 1950s. He fled to Taiwan before the CCP triumph, having first served a second time as president of Beijing University from 1942 to 1948.)

By 1949, a number of liberal (and other) Western books in the social sciences and humanities had been translated into Chinese, beyond the works

---

272. Ibid., 738.

273. Lenin, in section 5 of Chapter 1 of *The Development of Capitalism in Russia* (March 1899), repeated Marx's criticism of Smith. An English version is available as Vladimir Lenin, "The Development of Capitalism in Russia," https://www.marxists.org/archive/lenin/works/1899/dcr8i/i8v.htm.

of Yan Fu. In the 1930s, two scholars with training both in English and in political economy, Guo Dali (郭大力, 1905–1976) and Wang Yanan (王亞南, 1901–1969) met in Hangzhou at a temple they were both living in to save money. Guo had studied philosophy at Daxia University (大夏大學) in Shanghai, today East China Normal University (華東師範大學). Having already been exposed to Marxism, after graduating in 1927 he started what turned out to be the long process of translating *Capital* into Chinese for the first time. After 1949, he spent the rest of his career translating and teaching, although he did not join the CCP until 1957. Already dismissed from a schoolteacher's job in Shanghai, he and Wang agreed to work together to finish the translation. But in preparation they also translated two liberal works. The first was another translation of WN, using modern Chinese to improve upon Yan Fu's classical-Chinese translation. In addition, around the same time they translated Ricardo's *Principles*, also for the first time. The goal was not so much to present the masterworks of liberal political economy, but to help them prepare to completely translate the three volumes of *Capital*. They completed the latter task in 1938, after Wang had spent several years in exile in Europe, finally publishing them in the international concession in Shanghai after several publishers refused out of fear. (Recall that Shanghai was, except for the concessions, now occupied by the Japanese.) The two of them also translated *Economic History of Europe in Modern Times*, by Melvin M. Knight, Harry Elmer Barnes, and Felix Flugel.[274] Meanwhile, Guo on his own translated works from several schools of economic thought, including John Stuart Mill's liberal *Principles of Economics* (《經濟學原理》) and Johann Karl Rodbertus' (1805–1875) *Overproduction and Crises* (《生產過剩與恐慌》). Their translation of WN was modified and rereleased in 1965, and its new introductory remarks, written by Wang, provide most of the necessary information about how the CCP saw economic liberalism between 1949 and the 1990s. Whereas the 1931 version had been titled simply *The Wealth of Nations* (《國富論》), the 1965 version, reissued in 1972 and which Wang indicated in the introduction had been released to fix some deficiencies in the 1931 translation, translated the entire title literally (《國民

---

274. Melvin M. Knight, Harry Elmer Barnes and Felix Flugel, *Economic History of Europe in Modern Times* (Boston: Houghton Mifflin, 1928).

財富的性質和原因的研究》).[275]

Wang's 1965 introduction is striking because it argued why economic liberalism was something that Chinese scholars could and even should learn, even though history had inevitably passed it by. Wang described Smith as the well-known British "economist of the capitalist class" (「資本階級經濟學者」) and asserted he was critical in moving economic policies out of the shadow of mercantilism and feudalism, effects of which were still being felt in the Britain of Smith's day.[276] The capitalist class wanted to clear the obstacles to a free economy and needed a theory to justify this. WN played this role by providing a clear, systematic explanation of the economy of that era. It was, Wang said, the most influential work of political economy of the time, and indeed helped not just to develop a theory but to promote the practice of capitalism in the U.K.

And, pace Wang, while WN was initially seen as a masterwork, history soon revealed the limitations of Smith's theory. Over the subsequent near-century, the capitalism that Smith advocated became monopolistic. Less than a half century after that, Smith's "system of natural liberty" (「自由而又自然的體制」) had failed, replaced by the better model of the U.S.S.R., the world's first "socialist country" (「社會主義國家」), thus proving false Smith's claim of capitalism's eternal life (which he had never actually made). Note that by now the prevailing doctrine in China, as in all communist countries, was that "socialism" was explicitly a transitional stage toward "communism," so implicitly China was not yet a perfect communist country. While it is unlikely that Wang and Guo fully appreciated Smith's intricate philosophical, political, and economic "system" nearly as well as Yan Fu had, at least a different, superior system was in their view now available for contrast.

Continuing, Wang said that after Smith, while some "vulgar" (「庸俗」, yōngsú) economists in the 19th century tried to talk of capitalism's repair or rebirth, it was not to be. Smith's writing, so vital at the time, was now useful only in the study of the history of economic thought. Note that this reflects the materialist view of history, that historiography was the inevitable product of the state of class relations at the time, which was of course then the only

---

275. All citations used here are from the 2013 reprint of the 1965 version, 亞當·斯密, 《國民財富的性質和原因的研究》, 郭大力和王亞南譯, 北京, 商務印書館, 2013年 (Adam Smith, *An Inquiry into the Nature and Causes of the Wealth of Nations*, trans. by Guo Dali and Wang Yanan, 2013).

276. Throughout, translations of Wang's introductory remarks are the author's own.

acceptable view among historians in communist countries.

And Wang argued that WN was a reaction against mercantilism (「重商主義」), literally "emphasize commerce-ism," which is a significant part of how Western scholars view it even today. But what was mercantilism? His answer was that it was the first school of thought to ask what wealth is, where it comes from, and how it can grow. Here Wang mentioned Pierre Le Pesant (1646–1714) and the physiocrats François Quesnay (1694–1774) and Turgot. Wang also said that John Locke (1632–1704) and William Petty (1623–1687) had argued that wealth is produced through labor combined with other resources. These ideas combined to provide the foundation for Smith's breakthrough. Again, this was fairly consistent with the views of Western scholars of the history of economic thought in 1965.

Wang noted too that in the very first sentence Smith defined wealth not as the product of gold and silver mines, nor as something that increased because of trade surpluses. Instead, Wang reported, Smith said that most people's ability to consume came from their work, and then later argued that, contra the physiocrats (「重農派」), literally "those who emphasize agriculture," there was nothing special about agricultural labor per se. And society's wealth did not just depend on the amount of labor, but on its productivity. Labor combined with other resources produced wages, profits, and, for landowners, rent. The latter too came from the surplus of the product of labor. So Wang gave Smith credit for arguing something that Marx made the core of his own analysis, that the input of labor was the measure of the value of a thing, and production under capitalism created surplus value. Wang then added that Smith claimed it was the circulation and distribution of goods emanating from the structure of the relation among classes that provided the theory of economic activity during the accumulation of capital, a claim also central to Marxist analysis.

But, Wang's analysis continued, because the conditions for completely unfettered capitalism did not yet exist, Smith mistakenly thought that capitalism was the most suitable mode of production for humanity. Wang rendered Smith's view as saying that if laborers and capitalists could escape the constraints of mercantilist policy, anyone who owned capital or labor could enter the market and compete. Their interests were then satisfied to the extent possible, and so society was then as wealthy as it could be. Society would grow and flourish. Starting from the base of the feudal production and trading system,

Smith argued that it should be replaced by the capitalist system.

Again, none of this departs markedly from the mainstream of Western scholarship to this point. But Wang added several Marxist objections. In particular, Smith ignored fixed capital (「不變資本」), and this was one of his most substantial mistakes. In addition, Smith's theory of value was a mess. Sometimes, Wang said, Smith believed the value of a good depended on the amount of labor put into it, and at other times said it was a combination of the wages paid to workers, profits to the owner of capital, and rent paid to landlords. But this was an understandable mistake, Wang said, because at that primitive stage of capitalism, the conflict between capitalists and the proletariat was at an early stage. Overall, he continued, in diagnosing the fundamental character of production WN was mistaken in claiming an indispensable role for capitalists in growth, although the book still had many "scientific elements" (「科學成分」). It was Smith's mistakes and omissions that fed the arguments of the later "vulgar" economists, which ignored far more apparent class conflict and were specifically trotted out to oppose the economics of Marx and Lenin. In Wang's view Smith certainly made contributions, even if they were incomplete and later abused. (Most of the positive things Wang says about Smith he also said about Ricardo.)

Given the blinders of Marxist historiography, Wang's sketch of Smith's thinking reveals a strong grasp of the essentials. And this new translation reflected everything important about the fate of the ideas of economic liberalism in Maoist China. Books such as this of course did not circulate widely. Certain leaders and academics could access them as "internal reading material" (內部讀物), although these works often bore the stigma of being labeled as "reactionary information" (方面材料, *fǎnmiàn cáiliào* or 反動材料, *fǎndòng cái liào*). But they were published and available to academics and senior cadres who had what the authorities saw as a legitimate interest in the topic. Note also that the first printing of Wang's retranslation of WN was in 1965, on the eve of the CR, and the second in 1972, before the reform process began. Another work published during this time was Friedrich Hayek's (1899–1992) 1944 classic, *The Road to Serfdom*, despite its more damning (from the point of view of contemporaneous communist planners) indictment of state economic planning as a danger to individual rights, as well as the source of inferior economic performance. In their introductory remarks to the 1962 edition of *Road*, Teng Weizhao and Zhu Zhongfeng characterized Hayek as nothing more than a capitalist servant.[277] Hayek may have been among the "vulgar economists" that Wang alluded to in 1965. In addition, during this time two works by Eugen Böhm-Bawerk (1851–1914), *Capital and Interest* and *The Positive Theory of Capital*, were also translated, in 1963 and 1964 respectively. So too was Jean-Baptiste Say's (1767–1832) *A Treatise on Political Economy*, in 1963. Say's work emphasized, perhaps for the first time, the entrepreneur as an agent of economic change and the idea that economic progress comes in many activities beyond countable ones such as manufacturing and harvesting.

In short, economic liberalism was either to be treated as more primitive than Marxism, which was the end point of political economy, or dismissed as corrupt. But it was not to be airbrushed out of the historical record. And yet despite the fact that the CCP labored extensively to control and eventually eliminate it, economic liberalism as fact would occasionally flourish at the margins on the ground in the years between 1949 and 1979.[278] Often, it emerged during crises undoubtedly exacerbated by its absence. The next section describes the destruction after 1949 of what still remained of the spontaneous order.

6.D The near-destruction of economic liberalism outside the library

When discussing the replacement of the existing economy after 1949, it will be useful to distinguish among three sectors—the rural-agricultural sector, domestic private urban business, and foreign-owned private urban business. For both ideological and, in the latter case, emotional reasons, the treatment

---

277. 弗里德里希·哈耶克,《通向奴役的道路》, 滕維藻和朱宗風譯, 北京, 商務印書館, 1962年 (Friedrich A. Hayek, *The Road to Serfdom*, trans. Teng Weizao and Zhu Zhongfeng (Beijing: Commercial Press, 1962), 1).

278. The most vivid example is the few years after Mao's sun was temporarily eclipsed following the disaster of the GLF. In many places, there was greater tolerance of informal economic liberalism. Perhaps because of this, foodstuffs became notably more available during this time (Jung Chang, *Wild Swans: Three Daughters of China*, 2nd ed. (New York: Touchstone, 2003)), 333. Mao's anger at the ideological surrender, at least, and perhaps also the political threat to him it represented, would help motivate his campaign for a Great Proletarian CR in 1966. Frank Dikötter, *The Cultural Revolution: A People's History* (New York: Bloomsbury, 2017), Chs. 1 & 2.

of the three was meaningfully different. In addition, throughout the highest
levels of CCP leadership there was widespread agreement initially that the
transition to communism would have to play out gradually. China's provisional
constitution adopted in 1950 had a very inclusive tone. Article 3 in section 1,
"General Principles," indicated the revolutionary government would "protect
the public property of the state and of the cooperatives and must protect the
economic interests and private property of workers, peasants, the petty bourgeoisie and the national bourgeoisie." Section 4, on economic policy, generally
described a cooperative model of working toward socialism and not imposing
it immediately, in particular (Article 26) stipulating that "[t]he government
shall coordinate and regulate state-owned economy, co-operative economy, the
individual economy of peasants and handicraftsmen, private capitalist economy and state capitalist economy, in their spheres of operations, supply of raw
materials, marketing, labor conditions, technical equipment, policies of public and general finance, etc."[279] Indeed, the CCP briefly singled out for better
treatment some capitalists who were not tainted by working for or with foreign
companies or for the KMT regime; these people could play a significant role in
the transition to communism. This brief interval was known in hindsight as the
New Democracy (新民主主義, *xīn mínzhǔ zhǔyì*) period, and Mao Zedong
himself had used the term to describe this gradual-transition approach in an
essay written in 1940.[280] After taking power, he soon repudiated this period of
"new democracy" as a dilatory obstacle to the building of socialism in a lecture
at the June 15, 1953, meeting of the CCP Central Committee titled "Refute
the Right Deviationist Departure from the General Line" (《批判離開總路

---

279. From the authorized English translation ,"The Common Program of the Chinese People's Political
Consultative Conference," The Common Program and Other Documents of the First Plenary Session of
the Chinese People's Political Consultative Conference" (Peking: Foreign Language Press, 1950), 1–20, 3
("protect"), 10 ("The government").

280. The essay in English translation is contained with commentary in "On New Democracy January 15,
1940" in Timothy Cheek, *Mao Zedong and China's Revolutions: A Brief History with Documents* (London:
Palgrave Macmillan, 2002), 76–112. In the essay Mao depicted Chinese history since the May 4 demonstrations as one in which the proletariat had begun to participate in governance, and therefore the subsequent process would be one in which the final proletarian revolution unfolded. Colonized countries such
as China did not follow the orthodox Marxist route of feudalism, capitalism, and bourgeois democracy,
then communism, but instead had a period of mixed bourgeois and proletarian governance. The fact that
the bourgeoisie were themselves partly dominated by foreign imperialists made them a partly revolutionary class as well. They would deserve some, but only some, role in an early post-revolutionary government.

線的右傾觀點》).

And before the next decade was out, Mao Zedong became more enthusiastic about the possibility of completing the task quickly, and before the disaster of the GLF he even commenced bringing this about. This acceleration to communism, described below, may have long been Mao's plan, so that New Democracy was always a sham. Or, it may have been mostly due to Mao's mercurial personality and his having been overtaken by a sudden desire to complete the construction of communism. Hua-Yu Li, investigating government archives made available after Mao's death, argued that Mao was extraordinarily influenced by Stalin's own written history of the building of the new Soviet economy, and by an egotistical desire to lead the world's most progressive communist state.[281] Whatever the reasons, Mao proclaimed in late 1953, after several months of discussion with other leaders, the new "General Line" (總路線), which indicated that within an appropriate period of time the transformation of all private enterprise to socialism should be completed. This new policy was greeted with surprise if not shock by China's remaining business owners, and it justified one catastrophic policy after another. Most dramatically, the motivation for the GLF, as expressed at the 8th Party Congress in 1958, has been described as enabling the "dragging" of China into communist modernity.[282] The liquidation of China's private economy looked different for each of three sectors discussed below.

6.D.1 Regimenting the rural/agricultural sector
While Marx had made the urban factory the center of his analysis, China in 1949 was overwhelmingly agricultural. The biggest task for the CCP was thus to bring Marx's and Mao's vision about in the countryside.

6.D.1.a Stage one: land redistribution
Mao himself had seen in the 1920s that the orthodox Marx recipe for communist victory—centered around the urban proletariat—was unlikely to succeed in China. Instead, he and other senior party leaders worked to build commu-

---

281. Hua-Yu Li, *Mao and the Economic Stalinization of China, 1948–1953* (Lanham, MD: Rowman & Littlefield, 2006), 304.

282. Dillon, *China's Modern History*, 304.

nist sympathies in the countryside, significantly based on what was depicted as the oppressive domination of the landlord class. So CCP policy required the breakup of landlords' dominion over tenant farmers. In the event, after 1949 the definition of landlord went far beyond the sort of feudalistic castle resident so familiar from European history. In the end, it did not require all that much property to be classified as a member of the countryside ruling class, and the line was drawn arbitrarily, and sometimes corruptly or vindictively, from one village to the next.

And the resulting land redistribution turned out to be just the first stage. Understandably this stage was popular, and indeed across the Taiwan Straits Chiang Kai-Shek's KMT took the same steps (with much less violence) in the 1950s, generally to great acclaim.[283]

During the civil war, the CCP had previewed its likely policies in areas it controlled, and as we saw, Mao Zedong had already noted approvingly the campaigns of violent vengeance against landowners (among others) in uprisings in Hunan in 1927. The CCP founded its Jiangxi Soviet along U.S.S.R. lines in that part of China in 1930 when the party was in retreat after its losses to the KMT army in the late 1920s. The Soviet lasted until 1934 and there were violent struggles for power among factions influenced by Comintern agents in Shanghai and Mao's forces. While the initial forcible redistribution of land from designated landlords to peasants in Jiangxi was accomplished without much violence, from roughly 1933 on violence in the manner of Hunan several years earlier, which Mao had admired, became widespread.

The nationwide land-reform campaign, officially ratified in 1950 with the June passage of the "Agrarian Reform Law" (土地改革法), divided the rural population into five classes (based on previous CCP practice). It took land from those identified as being in the top classes and awarded it to those at the bottom, especially peasants. Of all the collectivization efforts in the 1950s, agricultural collectivization, even in the early stages, was the most violent. Dikötter separately reported "close to 2 million" deaths, and R. J. Rummel, merely calculating numbers based on contemporaneous reports of Chinese officials,

---

283. On land reform in Taiwan, see Jong-Sung You, *Democracy, Inequality and Corruption: Korea, Taiwan and the Philippines Compared* (Cambridge, UK: Cambridge University Press, 2014). For a critical view, see John-Ren Chen, "The Effects of Land Reform on the Rice Sector and Economic Development in Taiwan," *World Development* 22, no. 11 (November 1994), 1759–1770.

reported 7.5 million.284 Whatever the number, the killing was preceded by CCP officials reacting to or cultivating class hatred. CCP leaders, including Mao, went so far as to offer concrete estimates of how many would have to be killed to set the proper example, often after being forced to undergo public self-criticism sessions; this became a template for how the CCP dealt with its enemies through the end of the CR, a massive upheaval in Chinese society brought about by Mao and generally held to have lasted from 1966–1976.[285] When the time came, sometimes seizures of land and people were carried out by villagers themselves under the supervision of CCP cadres.

And yet in other cases, previous tenants continued to make traditional rent payments to those landlords who survived, and land often ended up explicitly in the hands of the latter.[286] To the economic liberal who believes that social institutions evolve when it makes sense, this is not surprising. The new government had inherited much in the Chinese agricultural system that was of centuries-old vintage. The general structure of very wealthy men presiding over large plots of land in which much poorer individual farming households worked the land under a sharecropping or other rental arrangement is common throughout world history. In China, historically most farmland was alienable, although there were social obligations to sell first to kinsmen.[287] Thus land reform actually involved a forcible breaking of these ancient networks. Initially it was common for tenant and landlord alike to be willing to go back to the pre-1949 arrangements where possible. In these longstanding systems farmers with local knowledge contracted with landlords with relatively less knowledge about growing crops, but relatively more on how to market them and arrange financing. Much of the product was then sold in markets elsewhere. The economic liberal's interpretation would be that this specialization worked to the benefit of both parties. Indeed, the diary of one longtime com-

---

284. Frank Dikötter, *The Tragedy of Liberation: A History of the Chinese Revolution 1945–1957* (New York: Bloomsbury, 2013), 246. Rummel's estimate, including how he calculated it, is found in Robert Rummel, *China's Bloody Century: Genocide and Mass Murder Since 1900* (London: Transaction Publishers, 2007), Chapter 7.

285. Dillon, *China: A Modern History, 290*; Dikötter, *The Tragedy of Liberation*, preface; Rummel, *China's Bloody Century*, 223.

286. Dikötter, *Tragedy of Liberation*, 210; Dillon, *China: A Modern History*, 190.

287. Pomeranz, *The Great Divergence*, 72–73.

munist cadre assigned to oversee land reform, Li Rui (李鋭, 1917–2019), indicated that it was common where he worked for tenants and workers to object to land reform. Instead, while they preferred to share revenue and not land, land was in the end divided, sometimes according to party loyalty rather than agriculture-relevant knowledge or skill.[288]

In the end, the redistribution of land, despite whatever historical rationale the existing arrangements may have had, was itself not genuinely communist. And so starting in roughly 1953 the second stage of agricultural illiberalism began to unfold throughout China.

6.D.1.b Stage two: collectivization

As noted above, upon taking power the CCP had clearly promised a gradual approach to communism. But in the countryside, the reallocation of land had only been in place a few years when the party, substantially at the instigation of Mao Zedong, moved to collectivize agricultural workers, many of whom who had just received their own land rights a few years prior.

Economically, agricultural collectivization has the same meaning as collectivization of steel production or any other productive activity. It contrasts with the liberal framework in which outputs, including crops, are produced after the firm owner secures resources often including the time and skill of other people to produce goods. This is an action that can continue as long as the resource owners are willing to cooperate, and supporters of economic liberalism generally assume this is so as long as the firm or farm makes money. The owner chooses or assigns to someone specific the choice of the number of workers and the other resources to be applied to the task (tools, more complex machines, seeds, chemicals and the like) so as, in the unromantic language of economics, to maximize his/their expected profits.

Under communist-style collective production it is a different story. Those who have the authority to decide who will work on the collective farm conscript them accordingly, and either contentedly or because the consequences of refusing are sufficiently bad, those workers show up. They do not necessarily work with the same energy as if they were working for their own account, but

288. 斯影，《毛澤東前秘書李鋭告別儀式惹爭議, 歷史資料待公開》 (Si Ying, "Farewell Ceremony for Li Hui, Former Secretary of Mao Zedong, Is Controversial; Historical Information to Be Published," *BBC Chinese News*, February 20, 2019, https://www.bbc.com/zhongwen/trad/chinese-news-47293517.

at any rate they are where the authorities want them to be. The model is the standard revealed communist one: an economic plan is drawn up by the state, and instructions are given to various groups of people, who usually have been directed by the state to be in these groups and in these places to collectively produce certain things (not just agricultural goods) according to the government plan. Critics of economic liberalism believe that political organization of worker and other resource allocation, in addition to being more just, yields more efficient resource use.

And so land reform, which proved sufficient in numerous non-communist societies, was only a first step toward the ultimate goal in China, which was collectivization. Dillon reports that the first efforts in this regard were made in 1952, even while land reform was still underway.[289] In 1953, the government tried, often successfully, to persuade peasants to sell their crops to government marketing boards. So far, they were on track with what many other developing countries would be doing in the next 20 years.

But when the Chinese campaign accelerated in 1953, farmers in a small local area would have their agricultural implements managed by production coordinators, even though these peasants retained nominal ownership of these tools. In July 1955, Mao Zedong called for an acceleration of the pace of collectivization. Over the next four years, these small associations (Mutual Aid Teams, 互助組) were combined into Agricultural Production Cooperatives (農業生產合作社) consisting of several dozen families. Families were still not yet forced to join, although many willingly did, for reasons ranging from a genuine desire to work under such an idealistic structure to the ability to benefit from whatever knowledge the teams' leadership had to dispense. By the time of the 1956 publication of a glowing compilation of party reports about collectivization, a majority of peasant households had signed up for these still often modestly sized units.[290] From 1956 to 1958 the penultimate stage of collectivization unfolded, the creation of High-Level Agricultural Production Cooperatives (高級農業生產合作社). And with the launch of the GLF in 1958, the highest level was reached, the people's communes (人民公社).

---

289. Dillon, *China: A Modern History*, 291.

290. General Office of the Central Committee of the Communist Party of China, *Socialist Upsurge in China's Countryside* (Beijing: Foreign Languages Press, 1957).

These giant institutions, with up to 20,000 people, also were found in the urban environment; that these state-owned enterprises (SOEs) provided not just pay but food, housing, retirement services, and education would prove to be a complicating factor in China's large-scale privatization efforts beginning in the 1990s. The enterprises also minutely controlled many details of workers' families' private lives.[291]

Over the course of this process, the change in rules and therefore incentives was dramatic. Previously, peasant members had still been compensated according to the grain they contributed, but by the end they were compensated (through crop distribution and not money) primarily by work points, awarded for how hard one worked. (Each member of a household got a fixed sum of points to start with and earned more by showing up to work.) In addition, land was no longer owned in any meaningful sense by individual families, a situation that as we will see in Chapter 7 didn't begin to disappear until the late 1970s.

Finally, many agriculturally relevant decisions were now made not by individual farmers or even necessarily by local administrators, who still could benefit in theory both from local farmer input and from being on the scene, but by more distant, sometimes central-government, CCP planners. The political incentives being what they were, residents of the rural communes often initially ate lavishly, and therefore were enthusiastic. But by late 1958 famine had appeared. Food was extracted at greater rates to provide food for cities, where the large SOEs were being created to facilitate industrialization à la Stalin (still the only communist model available).[292] This was feasible because the obstacles of private property had been removed and the restriction of population mobility through the residence-permit system (discussed in Chapter 7) was in place.

All of this occurred against the backdrop of Mao's first five-year plan, published in 1953, which indicated that the planners' goal was to industrialize by extracting surplus production from farmers. That such an extraction proceeded despite the lack of such a surplus was a major contributing factor, along with the inherent deficiencies of such planning in any production environment, for

291. Dillon, *China: A Modern History*, 291–293.

292. Details of commune operations can be found in Frank Dikötter, *Mao's Great Famine: The History of China's Most Devastating Catastrophe, 1958–1962* (New York: Walker & Co., 2010), Chapter 7.

the catastrophic famine.[293]

Whether the two-step collectivization process (first land reform, then eventually communes) was strategic deception or the result of a change of vision by CCP leadership to proceed to communism as quickly as possible, the result meant that liberal forces were essentially banished from agriculture by roughly 1958. What Aron Shai referred to as firms' "extensive network of domestic and foreign trade" still had extensive value even after 1949.[294] Many of these networks of farmers, middlemen, agricultural-implement makers, and rural and urban vendors, along with the contracting methods and non-contractual social customs that tied them together, had taken centuries to develop, but were swept away in just a few years, a pattern that would occur in the more urban/industrial sector as well.

6.D.2 Nationalization of domestic businesses

So too it was in the cities. In addition to the non-negligible amount of enthusiasm for communism among Western intellectuals generally, there was substantial excitement from intellectual leaders like Edgar Snow, the noted economist Joan Robinson, the French writer Simone de Beauvoir and France's later socialist president François Mitterrand.[295] A big part of the excitement that greeted the communist takeover in 1949, especially in China but also in the coming years among such foreign admirers, derived from the very visible improvements in the conditions of the country's poor. This was particularly the case for the urban poor. In addition, the homeless, the opium users, and the prostitutes

---

293. On the GLF famine, see 楊繼繩,《墓碑——一九五八-一九六二年中國大饑荒紀實》, 香港, 天地 讀書, 2008年. A somewhat shorter version of this work has been published in English as Yang Jisheng, *Tombstone: The Untold Story of Mao's Great Famine*, trans. Stacy Mosher and Guo Jian, ed. Edward Friedman, Stacy Mosher and Guo Jian (New York; Farrah, Strauss and Giroux, reprint edition, 2012).

294. Shai, Aron, *The Fate of British and French Firms in China, 1949–54: Imperialism Imprisoned* (New York: Macmillan, 1996), 14.

295. Panjak Mishra, "Staying Power: Mao and the Maoists," *New Yorker*, December 27, 2010, https://www.newyorker.com/magazine/2010/12/20/staying-power-3. Joan Robinson had evolved from a believer in mere macroeconomic planning to comprehensive social planning during her career. She traveled to China seven times, including during the CR, and wrote sympathetically of economic policy there. Her remarkably sympathetic (based on what we know now) yet scholarly account of the CR is found in Joan Robinson, *The Cultural Revolution in China* (London: Penguin, 1970). More general praise for the Chinese experiment, including the GLF, is found in Joan Robinson, "Notes from China," *Economic Weekly*, February 1964, 195–207.

were swept from China's streets, and many of these people were sent to reform facilities, to jettison the old ways and become new and better. The streets also became much cleaner, although significant homelessness would return during times of famine. Waterborne diseases fell a great amount, although that did not prevent Mao in 1956 from ordering Chinese peasants to engage in sweeping efforts to destroy the country's snails, since they were part of the process through which humans caught schistosomiasis. (Similar efforts at the same time were launched by the CCP against rats. Both efforts were equally quixotic; in the case of the campaigns against rats, people began breeding them to allow them to bring in more rat tails for the promised rewards.[296] Even in the new China, material incentives mattered.) While many owners of the largest businesses fled the country just before or soon after October 1949, others stayed and placed their faith in the revolution. Those who remained, while they became subject to minimum-wage legislation and increasing taxation, received promises that for the foreseeable future they would be part of the new governing coalition of China—the bourgeoisie too had their role to play now, so it was said. That faith was misplaced. Even before New Democracy meaningfully ended in 1953, many business owners were subject to CCP-instigated challenges from CCP unions.

In addition to Mao's enthusiasm for quick collectivization, he was also influenced by a trip he made to the Soviet Union immediately after the Chinese revolution. Mao admired Stalin greatly and correspondingly admired the industrial transformation of Soviet society he had overseen. Mao spent nine weeks in Moscow in 1949, although he spent several of those weeks waiting for Stalin, who had had many years of friendly relations with and influence over the KMT, to grant him an audience. Negotiations between the two countries forced China to let Soviet troops temporarily remain in Port Arthur (亞瑟港, *Yàsè Gǎng*, now 旅順港, *Lǚshùn Gǎng*) and Dalian (大連), which the Soviets had taken from Japanese forces in 1945, Japan having taken it from Russia in the Russo-Japanese war in 1905. Mao also had to acknowledge the independence of much of the former Qing territory of Mongolia. But the CCP leadership was convinced of the truth of the Stalinist model of economic construction.

296. Dikötter, *Tragedy of Liberation*, 271.

The Stalinist model depended on developing heavy industry as quickly as possible. By early 1950, after Mao's return from the Soviet Union, there was also a perceived imperative to establish a means to secure the food supply from the countryside so that people in the cities could do industrial factory work. In 1951, while all the universities in China that were not already public were also being taken over (almost 40 percent of institutions of higher education were private in July 1950[297]), the government begin to designate specific jobs for new university graduates based on its own estimates of where the need was greatest.

And, in the end, there would be Soviet-style nationalization throughout society. But China was different from the Soviet Union. Along the coast, especially in Shanghai, there were many more foreign firms. In addition, the Chinese, of course, had the Soviet example to learn from. That Soviet example had involved immediate, wholesale, brutal seizure of most private property of any consequence. (China's predicament was made worse by the Soviet pillaging of factory equipment during the Soviet Union's occupation of Manchuria after the end of World War II.) In contrast, China's nationalization of its domestic firms was a central-government economic edict that, perhaps for the last time over the next decades, proceeded rapidly and according to plan.

Two personal accounts of how the process played out agree on some details. In a biography of three generations of women in her family, Jung Chang (1952–) noted that her mother was a CCP activist before and after 1949 and in 1955 and 1956 participated in the campaign to turn private companies over to the state. And Robert Loh (1924–) had been sent to the United States to get a university degree. In 1950 he returned to China in the belief that he could contribute to building his country. For several years he served as a high-level manager in a grain mill, and this timespan included both the initial entry of party officials into the business and their eventual takeover in 1956.[298]

Loh reported that soon after he took the job, his mill's work became merely processing grain for the government for a fixed fee. Party officials were now onsite, a practice that has continued in larger Chinese organizations, both

297. Robert Taylor, "Education and University Enrolment Policies in China, 1949–1971," *Contemporary China Papers* (Canberra: Australian National University Press, 1973), 2.

298. Jung Chang, *Wild Swans*; Robert Loh and Humphrey Evans, *Escape from Red China* (New York: Coward-McCann, 1962).

for-profit and nonprofit, even until today. Shanghai mayor Chen Yi (陳毅, 1901–1972), proclaimed that the five types of capitalists could be segmented differently: "1) law-abiding businessmen; 2) basically law-abiding business-men; 3) semi-law-abiding, semi-guilty businessmen (which we called 'the dou-ble semi'); 4) guilty businessmen, and 5) seriously guilty businessmen."[299] Only the last two would almost certainly face criminal punishment from the CCP. The government would also start to distinguish between patriotic capitalists and other capitalists. The former were judged, especially during the war against Japan, to have previously acted in the interest of the nation.

While the New Democracy period was marked primarily by increasing regulation of businesses, that regulation is now best seen, like the initial dis-tribution of farmland to peasants, as preparation for nationalization. Private firms during this time faced a growing dependence on state firms for the pro-vision of raw materials; immediately after 1949, the CCP took over the large KMT firms, and native owners of large companies departed the country. This enabled the CCP to focus on the takeover of the remaining private firms. Fur-thermore, since the KMT had directly controlled most infrastructure such as transportation and power generation, it could be quickly absorbed by the CCP.

Nationalization of purely private domestic firms was moved along by pres-sure against business owners and, in larger firms, managers. In a tactic that would be repeated in a variety of contexts throughout the Mao era, business owners and/or people under the influence of the bourgeoisie were called to engage in struggle sessions (鬥爭大會). They faced rooms full of employees, sometimes after both sides had had preparatory sessions with CCP officials, where they were condemned in vituperative language. While these sessions had the surely useful side effect of breaking any resistance that might exist among the businessmen, it could also be squared with Marxist ideology. It was necessary to break the contradictions between workers and owners and build a communist new people; part of the communist struggle was against individuals' deficiencies inherited from the old system. While confessing to these deficiencies might take several steps, as the numbers of things to confess expanded, at some point what one confessed to might be enough, unlike the worst circumstances in Stalin's U.S.S.R. Such sessions had already occurred

299. The words of Loh and Evans, *Escape from Red China*, 101.

among CCP members themselves before 1949 to rectify ideologically stray-
ing members, and people sometimes confessed multiple times. Some business
people who faced this pressure were eventually sent to labor camps (as was
the case with many other groups who were seen as enemies of the new society). Those with needed expertise, however, were generally kept around, albeit
often at lower-status jobs with lower pay. But some, perhaps several hundred
in Shanghai alone, committed suicide. None who went through or knew about
the experience could emerge with any belief that meaningful liberty to run
one's business could remain.

By late 1952, the combined pressures meant that many of these firms were
unsustainable, and their owners, fearing things would continue to deterio-
rate, became very reluctant to take any risks, preferring instead to simply wait
for orders to be given. Facing declining production in part because of owners'
unwillingness to deploy the specialized knowledge they had, the government
thus issued "temporary regulations for private enterprise," which restored some
of the owner's control over "general management" and firm finance. Some of
the most onerous regulations were also canceled.[300]

But in June 1953, Mao gave a speech announcing his new "Mass Line" (群
眾路線). The Shanghai Chamber of Commerce, which as we saw in Chapter 4
had been a civically vital organization, was eliminated and replaced during this
time by a new organization called the All-China Federation of Industry and
Commerce (中華全國工商業聯合會). Despite the liberalization announced
the year before, the prices companies got for their output, already fixed by the
state, continued to decline even as managers were directed to pay workers the
same wages. (And these wages had been raised numerous times since 1949.)

In late 1954, the government announced that there would be selected pilot
firms to be managed and owned jointly by the state and their owners. In the
first stage, the government seized shares held by declared enemies of the people or accepted them in lieu of previously imposed fines. But for these firms,
taxes were now low and access to resources (grain, for example) was better, so
taking the state on as a partner was good business. Other firms not selected,
in addition to not getting these benefits, saw increased labor unrest.

This pre-nationalization, softening-up campaign was facilitated by two

---

300. Loh and Evans, *Escape from Red China*, 113–114.

propaganda campaigns previously launched in rapid succession in late 1952, involving print media and public announcements to large groups of people. In these campaigns, Chinese were told to assist with the implementation of the "three resists" (三反, *sānfǎn*) launched by Mao Zedong, and announced by Zhou Enlai in December 1951. The campaign was nominally against corruption, waste, and bureaucracy, and targeted both bureaucrats tempted by capitalists and those capitalists themselves. The arguably even tougher "five resists" policy (五反, *wǔfǎn*) targeted the bourgeoisie specifically, both industrialists and merchants, and was announced in January 1952. What had to be resisted now was bribery, theft of state property, tax evasion, defrauding the government, and theft of "state economic intelligence" (「盜竊國家經濟情報」). This new campaign reflected even more a general latent hostility to what was seen as unfair business treatment of workers, as well as capitalists' unwillingness to share Marx's capitalist surplus. Given the outrage and substantial economic problems caused by Western sanctions against China due to the Korean War, these campaigns gave both party and workers all the license they needed to neutralize businesspeople as a source of resistance to the new regime.

And yet even in 1952, with the exceptions of the fruit of the poisonous KMT and Japanese trees, i.e., businesses with close ties to official enemies of the people, few businesses were seized outright. (Ties to the KMT did allow the CCP to seize almost all Shanghai newspapers shortly after victory, however.[301]) This had to wait not just for the announcement of the new Mass Line in 1953, but for the arrival of whatever Mao saw as a propitious moment. When the moment came, nationalization happened with stunning speed. With business people, landlords, and intellectuals broken (the latter through struggle sessions similar to what the other two groups were already enduring), by late 1955 that moment had arrived.

After making a dramatic entry into a meeting being conducted with local political leaders and leading Shanghai businessmen, Mao Zedong proceeded to be quite charming. At the meeting, a number of factory owners, whether out of commitment or having seen the writing on the wall, pledged their businesses then and there to the government. While it was a seemingly simple matter

---

301. Sei Jeong Chin, "The Historical Origins of the Nationalization of the Newspaper Industry in Modern China: A Case Study of the Shanghai Newspaper Industry, 1937–1953," *China Review* 13, no. 2 (Fall 2013): 1–34.

to substitute CCP cadres for the previous capitalist managers, these business-es, as is true everywhere, had relied upon networks, both family-based and otherwise, to procure resources (including talent), find markets for outputs, and manage uncertainty. When the same buildings and machinery were now managed without these informal networks, which had undoubtedly decayed as pressure increased after 1949, the new managers were unable to coordi-nate the operations of these assets. The lack of the information about what to do beyond mere engineering often assured that these firms floundered under state management.[302]

After the meeting, Mao announced publicly that nationalization of will-ing firms would take place within Mao's six-day timeline. The owners would get a buyout in the form of annual payments of 5 percent of their firms' esti-mated value, with the estimate to be determined jointly by workers and man-agement. (These bonds enabled many who accepted the buyouts to live reason-ably comfortably until the CR.) To "facilitate" the persuasion process, meetings were held throughout the nation with "drums and gongs" and other totems of celebration. CCP officials attended these meetings to persuade holdouts to agree to sell. Remarkably, within six days, almost all businesses large and small were turned over to the state.[303] (The very few that were not soon failed.) Given that foreign businesses had already been captured through a different process described below, this six-day process meant that the obituary of eco-nomic liberalism in China was ready to be written, having passed away after a quarter-century's illness.

6.D.3 Foreign firms

Foreign businesses, many of which were located in Shanghai, in principle were subject to the same laws as Chinese-owned businesses were. But they had sev-eral distinctive characteristics that meant they were treated differently. First, whereas Marxist ideology saw all private businesses as accumulating capital

---

302. See, for example, Zhaojin Zeng, "Enterprise Archives and Business History in Contemporary Chi-na: The Case of the Baojin Company Archive," *Entreprises et Histoire* 90 (April 2018), 145–48.

303. Loh and Evans, *Escape from Red China*, 178–205; Chang, *Wild Swans*, 244–246 (drums and gongs). On the standard of living after the buyouts, see Hanchao Lu, "Bourgeois Comfort under Proletarian Dic-tatorship: Home Life of Chinese Capitalists before the Cultural Revolution," *Journal of Social History* 52, no. 1 (September 2018): 74–100.

merely to expand at the expense of the proletariat, this effect was seen as particularly pronounced in the very large, global firms found in China. The profits they had made over the years were substantial, and all of them represented exploitation of Chinese workers. For the CCP to seize these profits specifically would do no harm and through redistribution could do much good.

Second, the Korean war broke out in July1950, and China joined the war in late October 1950 in alliance with North Korea as allied forces were approaching the Yalu River. Meanwhile, both the U.S. and Britain were now seizing Chinese potential military assets—ships and planes in particular—in Hong Kong and other areas these nations controlled. (While naval forces fighting in the name of the United Nations were used to blockade North Korea, this blockade was not extended to China.) The United Nations did impose an embargo on Chinese goods, which lasted until the armistice in 1953. (The U.S. embargo, a prohibition of shipping goods from the United States to China, lasted until 1972.) At the same time, the U.S. deployed its Seventh Fleet during the war to prevent a Chinese attack on Taiwan. These tensions led the campaign against British and American firms in China to be conducted much more bitterly.

Third, many of the people the CCP were dealing with in these firms were foreigners. On the one hand, to put them through struggle sessions would have been very difficult, because of the reaction it would have engendered in the U.S. and the U.K. On the other hand, the Chinese government also soon required foreigners to obtain an exit visa before they could leave the country, arguably part of the much broader campaign to limit people's freedom of movement. These visas were sometimes not granted. So this changed the dynamics of the CCP negotiation process with these foreign businesses. Finally, the leaders of foreign firms had significant knowledge of advanced technology sometimes not possessed by executives of domestic firms. Given the challenges from Western military and diplomatic pressure, and from the Soviet theft of Chinese factories after World War II, this knowledge became all the more important.

So the effort to nationalize foreign firms played out differently from that for domestic firms. In particular, there was no attempt to persuade the foreign managers of these firms of the virtues of nationalization for the Chinese people, and no surprise visits by Mao Zedong to induce acceptance of collectivization.

Remarkably in hindsight, there was at first some hope among foreign managers that their firms could continue their operations in a communist China. While many firms feared a Soviet-style immediate takeover, a British government report dated the last day of 1948 indicated that the communists planned to leave foreigners ("foreign traders") alone. The memo did indicate, however, some fear that foreign property would be seized or that the state would come to dominate the markets for the main commodities. In addition, the CCP requested that foreign businessman stay, with announcements to this effect in both Shanghai and Tianjin. There was a significant belief in the foreign community, at least in Shanghai, that it would be possible to do business with a communist China. It should be noted that some of the foreign community in Shanghai had even returned after 1949, believing that there would still be opportunities to make money.[304]

But conditions soon deteriorated. Throughout the process there was no recognition of firms as individual legal entities. Capitalist businesses, especially foreign ones, were seen merely as part of an amorphous "capitalist class." Individual contracts with individual firms thus had no meaning in communist thinking. And yet by the end of 1950, several dozen citizens of Great Britain, Canada, and the United States were also under house arrest because of financial claims on the businesses for which they worked. These claims, also faced by domestic firms, included taxes and mandated minimum compensation, were ever-higher and firms' customer and supplier bases were reduced quickly to various organs of the Chinese government. Fines for violating Chinese rules were also common. By the middle of 1952, as the British chargé d'affaires Humphrey Trevelyan put it, according to Shai's summary, the exploiting foreign businesses were "completely in the hands of the Chinese government, having to obtain raw materials from it and sell their products to it."[305]

In April 1951 the Chinese tanker ship *Yung Hao* was seized in Hong Kog, at the request of the American government; also, under American pressure, the British government had refused to return several airplanes it had come into possession of after the revolution. In retaliation, the Chinese govern-

304. Thomas N. Thompson, *China's Nationalization of Foreign Firms: The Politics of Hostage Capitalism, 1949–57* (Baltimore: University of Maryland School of Law, Occasional Paper/Reprint Series in Contemporary Asian Studies, 1979), 13.

305. Quoted in Shai, *The Fate of British and French Firms*, 32.

ment nationalized all property belonging to the Asiatic Petroleum Company, a joint venture in China of the Shell and Royal Dutch corporations. This
process took over two years. In addition, the Korean war generated retaliatory
Chinese seizures of various stockyards, shipbuilding facilities, and utilities.
The aforementioned "Five Resists" campaign also led to further pressure on
foreign as well as domestic firms.

Foreign firms were subject to price controls, prohibitions on letting workers go, and other restrictions on their operations. In this too they were no different from domestic firms. From 1950 any business decision now had to be
approved by the government, and in particular firms could not close without
government permission. This was particularly problematic for foreigners, since
they already needed exit permits to leave the country.

In 1952 liquidation fees (liquidation, of course, was required by the CCP)
were introduced, and the government became less willing to issue exit visas.
During this "hostage capitalism" phase, most of the foreigners who remained
by 1954, mainly in banking, were still not being allowed to leave. The Chinese
government had decided that much of the money in these banks' accounts was
owed to the Chinese government (in the name of the Chinese people) because
of various transgressions by the banks. By December 1954, the foreign firms
had decided to stop sending money to China to support continued operations,
especially since much of the need for such funds came from CCP edicts of one
sort or another. Eventually it was agreed that what foreign firms owed could be
settled by surrendering assets. It was later estimated that the legendary financial firm Jardine Matheson left behind assets worth £30,000,000, and British
American Tobacco surrendered £50,000,000 worth.[306]

By the time of the announcement of the six-day domestic-nationalization
drive, the foreign firms had already settled their claims by selling assets to the
Chinese government at far less than the value a competitive market would have
given them. The most parsimonious interpretation of the difference between
the treatment of foreign and domestic businesses here is that because of some
combination of generic xenophobic resentment of the foreigner and a belief
that foreigners had unjustly accumulated extraordinary wealth at the expense
of the Chinese masses, the new China could spend seized resources as it saw

---

306. Ibid., 101.

fit, and it was perfectly natural to treat them this way—notably worse than the way Chinese entrepreneurs were at least nominally supposed to be treated.

It is remarkable how much all of this is by the book, if the book is Engels' *The Principles of Communism*, written in 1847.[307] While little is said on the transition to communism in *Capital*, elsewhere Marx and Engels mostly laid out a gradual, though violent if need be, transition away from private property and competition. Agriculture should be produced not by private property owners, often peasants whose control over "their" property was actually quite limited, but it should be channeled eventually into large (collective) farms, to be managed by the former peasants themselves. Private businesses would for a time pay wages equal to those paid in state factories, but the businesses would gradually be converted to state property once the urgency of the transition from capitalism was past. Food was to be produced and eaten communally.[308] Many of the transformations in China between 1949 and the GLF resembled this blueprint.

6.E The Costs of Illiberalism

From roughly 1953 to 1978, China became one of the most economically illiberal societies the modern world has seen. When an economic order has been built through people's voluntary cooperation, with their individual plans arrived at equally voluntarily, but a political authority decides that this order must be changed, force must inevitably be used. So we should not be surprised that the imposition of the new CCP order required a great amount of coercion, as it did in numerous other communist societies. All societies face the question of where and how to limit people's property rights. Despite the KMT having done significant preliminary work in building a centrally planned economy, building the new order in China required extensive threatened and actual violence. It is true that as a matter of paperwork the nationalization of private property was conducted nonviolently; this was a stark contrast to the immediate, forced nationalization in the first few years after the Russian revolution, to the brutality of Stalin's industrialization and collectivization in the 1930s,

---

307. Available at https://www.marxists.org/archive/marx/works/1847/11/prin-com.htm.

308. See Gandy, *Marx and History*, Ch. 4.

and even to the CCP's own anti-landlord campaign of the early 1950s. But two traits of China's post-revolution deliberalization make clear that what people had chosen to build themselves had to be forcibly torn down, and new designs imposed.

The first way this substitution of central plans for decentralized, spontaneous order played out was the frequent use of numerical goals in setting CCP policy. All economic planners, whether in the government or in the private sector, sometimes set numerical targets. But in Maoist China this was taken to extremes. As far back as 1951, the CCP proclaimed that one goal of the ongoing campaign against counterrevolutionaries as a class was to cultivate the appropriate atmosphere rather than merely to purge individual malefactors.[309] During the New Democracy period before nationalization, Mao himself gave directives that a certain number of capitalists and counterrevolutionaries should be killed to set the example for the others whose cooperation was still needed, with a specific quota (one percent) in the case of accused counterrevolutionaries.[310] Less violently, after the CCP monopolized the grain trade in 1953, experts estimated productivity for each unit of land, calculated how much nutrition each peasant needed and how much grain was needed by each person in the cities, and set production quotas accordingly. State grain demands, defined using calculations of urban needs, were binding and taken off the top.[311] Later, during the GLF, grain continued to be provided to Soviet-bloc countries (and to Chinese cities) even as rural famine worsened.

The second manifestation of Mao's new order was the frequent invocation in government propaganda of the One True Way, and especially the danger of deviation from it. At various times during the Mao era, the government inveighed against enemies such as bourgeois liberalism, rightism, and capitalism. This process necessitated inspecting prevailing culture to see if it conformed or not to the inevitable Chinese future. And so soon Chinese culture was completely and centrally reshaped by the CCP. During the CR—the endpoint—communism (still) was the goal, and endless experiments were to

---

309. Laszlo Ladany, *The Communist Party of China and Marxism 1921–1985: A Self-Portrait* (Hong Kong: Hong Kong University Press, 1992), 178–185, citing various contemporaneous Chinese media reports.

310. Dikötter, *Tragedy of Liberation*, 87 (counterrevolutionaries), 170 (capitalists).

311. Ibid., 250.

be tried to get there. The criterion for success was not profit, but victory over enemies of the revolution.

The problem of nearly complete economic illiberalism is easy to see, particularly if it reaches the level it did in China prior to the beginning of economic reform in 1978. But broader social illiberalism has costs too, if not necessarily so immediate. Cultural liberalism causes culture to be more diverse, thus generating more insights into the human condition, and therefore is more generative of human progress. Many examples of this process in socioeconomically liberal China from 1842 to 1927 were provided in Chapter 4. This happens for the same reason that economic liberalism promotes a higher standard of living—dynamism. If the function of culture is to help us think about ourselves, then the more competition there is in offering cultural "products," the more and better such insights will be (at least over the long term).

But in Maoist China all such alternative outlets for ideas were swept away. China, and Shanghai in particular, had preserved vibrant cinema and publishing during the Nanjing Decade and even to some degree during the Japanese occupation. Under the KMT, both before and after war with Japan, some political themes, even communism, could be raised, although only within the confines of the Shanghai foreign concessions. Yet many printed works published there quickly made their way into the rest of urban China. But in the runup to and in roughly the first year after the revolution, a number of China's greatest intellectuals left. And within the next few years, unauthorized cultural activity came to a complete stop.

Religions too had long been evolving ideas not consistent with Mao's One Great Truth (indeed, many of them proclaimed alternate truths), and they therefore came under CCP control. After 1843, foreign missionaries had been a big part of the foreign contingent in China, and some Chinese thinkers, as in Japan, saw Christianity as part of the explanation for Western economic success. Even KMT China was not particularly hostile to religion. (Chiang Kai-Shek's fiancée, along with her brother T. V. Soong, was from a Methodist family, and her parents demanded Chiang convert if they were to approve their marriage.) And as noted in Chapter 4, despite being controlled by an ally of Nazi Germany, Japanese-run Shanghai during World War II had a population of several thousand Jewish refugees who had escaped from Nazi persecution. Yet almost immediately after taking power, the CCP forced believers of all organized "foreign" religions (primarily Islam and several Christian denominations) to participate through government-controlled religious organizations.[312] Many churches were closed, and sometimes mosques were even used to house pigs. The seizure of religious organizations providing social services, from poverty relief to education, followed soon after.

And as is well known, particularly in the first few years the CR was at least nominally based on the idea that the entire Chinese past had to be eradicated; in addition, even after nationalization in the early 1950s and almost two decades of CCP rule, it was necessary to eliminate "bourgeois" and "capitalist" enemies lurking even within CCP leadership circles.[313] Most traditional Chinese and imported foreign art forms were outlawed as "capitalist." The fate of Chinese culture and intellectuals after the CR was launched is well-known—rampant destruction of China's cultural inheritance simply because it was inherited, and purges, sometimes fatal, of those who stood in Mao's way. As we have seen, skepticism about traditional Chinese culture was by 1949 not new. But culture was subject to regimentation in the name of the One True Way, and culturally what followed was ghastly. In the liberal view, spontaneous economic and cultural order are of a piece. What China (and the world) lost because of Chinese intellectual illiberalism from 1949 to Mao's death in 1976 will never be known.

6.F Markets in the shadows under Mao

Despite having only a single political party after 1949, and this party and especially its leader being committed to the dream of moving beyond private property, market activities sometimes emerged in China even after they were legally terminated in 1956 with the completion of all commercial and agricultural collectivization. Usually catastrophe brought them out. For example, several scholars of the GLF have documented the emergence of black markets in

---

312. Rensselaer, W. Lee III, "General Aspects of Chinese Communist Religious Policy, With Soviet Comparisons," *China Quarterly* 19 (1964): 161–173.

313. The CR is often dated as beginning in 1966, but the article in which Mao called for it actually appeared in a Shanghai newspaper in 1965.

food during the famine.[314] Jung Chang described her experience in Chengdu in 1959, when some peasants violated instructions to hand over all their chickens to the commune, and secretly sold chicken and eggs.[315] She also described her brother's participation in a market for, remarkably, books during the CR, with prices differing, as one would expect, by genre and where the books came from. Dikötter documented black markets during the same period in, among many other goods, timber, health care services, doors and windows, and, of all things, the Mao badges very popular among Red Guards at the time. Some of these goods were produced or offered directly, and others stolen from state factories.[316] Authorities frequently tried to eliminate all such black markets and punish who participated in them, but market traders were indefatigable. In addition, whereas during the GLF it was desperation that drove people to ignore CCP dictates, during and after the CR this behavior reflected the disintegration of state authority amidst the surrounding chaos. In China, Adam Smith's natural instinct to "truck, barter and exchange" reemerged, the first chance it got.[317]

But while disaster did lead to toleration or lack of policing, it was not sufficient to bring economic liberalism back. For example, in August 1963 the large city of Tianjin was threatened by flooding because of days of torrential rain. Black markets in food items in the city—which had sprung up during the GLF famine—had been legalized in 1962, at its tail end. But during the flooding, officials in Tianjin feared precisely what would happen, that prices in these black markets would rise, perhaps substantially. They thus ended them.[318]

By the time most of China's revolutionary generation was passing from the scene in the late 1970s, China was a painful exception to the unprecedented economic growth going on in its global neighborhood. Having first suffered roughly a century of political humiliation and oppression, and its people then

314. Zhou Xu, Zhou Xun, ed., *The Great Famine in China, 1958–1962: A Documentary History* (New Haven: Yale University Press, 2011), 129–31, 132, 134, 135–37.

315. Chang, *Wild Swans*, 229 (food), 367–369 (books).

316. Frank Dikötter, *The Cultural Revolution: A People's History*, 1962–1976 (New York: Bloomsbury, 2016), 225, 239, 270, 278, 289, 290, 298. Smith (1976), Book I, Vol. 1, 17.

317. WN, I.1.2. Smith (1976), 17.

318. Lauri Paltemaa, "The Maoist Urban State and Crisis: Comparing Disaster Management in the Great Tianjin Flood in 1963 and the GLF Famine," *China Journal* 66 (July 2011): 25-51, 38.

brought catastrophically low by almost three decades of near-total economic illiberalism, once the chance presented itself they were eager to try anything different. And so once Mao's Utopian economic illiberalism passed from the scene, they did.

CHAPTER 7

Rebirth: Economic Liberalism, Communist-style

I n 1978, Yan Hongchang (嚴宏昌, 1949–) was a farmer for the state, as were most of the people in Xiaogang (小崗村), his small village in Anhui province in northern China. Everyone there was poor, and even though farming was the dominant economic activity, many were chronically malnourished; children would sometimes go to neighboring villages to beg. So after one miserable harvest too many (in 1978), several men gathered secretly in a farmer's house to discuss a new (yet old) way of growing food. They would divide up the collectively farmed land and individual families would make their own decisions about how to cultivate particular pieces of the collective farm. Each family would have an amount of crops they would have to turn over to the state as usual, but anything above that they could keep for themselves and do with as they wished.

As recounted to U.S. journalists in 2012, one of the farmers, describing the risk involved of growing crops on one's own initiative for one's own benefit, used the analogy of a "high-voltage wire," even though, the farmer added, no one in the village had ever seen one. They made an agreement, today on display at a museum in the village, where they pledged not just to allow each other to keep the fruits of their own labor, but to take care of the children of any among them who were caught and imprisoned or executed.[319]

And lest readers think that government officials can only damage the spontaneous order of economic liberalism, the years of early Chinese economic

319. David Kestenbaum and Jacob Goldstein, "The Secret Document that Transformed China," National Public Radio, January 20, 2012, https://www.npr.org/sections/money/2012/01/20/145360447/the-secret-document-that-transformed-china.

reform had their share of bold and ultimately admirable politicians. In 2018 several Chinese media celebrated 40 years of reform and openness by publishing a list of "reform pioneers" (改革先鋒). One of them was Xie Gaohua (謝高華, 1931–2019), who in 1982 was party secretary in Yiwu county (義烏縣) in Zhejiang province. As he and Feng Aiqian (馮愛倩, 1940–) recounted the events to the government Xinhua news agency in 2018,[320] Feng had been one of a few people operating a stall *sub rosa* for several years, selling simple household items such as shoelaces and buttons that she had purchased from government stores elsewhere. She was doing this to provide income for her desperately impoverished family and was frequently harassed by local police. She plaintively asked Xie at a public meeting why, China being as poor as it was, peasants like her could not legally operate such businesses. Xie, perhaps struck by the compelling simplicity of Feng's question, which could not be answered without invoking abstract theory very distantly removed from people's daily concerns, by the end of the year had legalized such businesses, despite their inconsistency with prevailing ideology.

Since then, the Chinese state has continued to praise the boldness of reformers such as these. (Although, perhaps revealingly, it was the communist functionary Xie and not the bold questioner Feng who made the pioneers' list.) How such people ceased to be capitalist roaders and became "pioneers" is the theme of this chapter.

The entire Chinese experience pre-liberalization vindicates the notion that there is much in individual and national flourishing that is not captured in GDP. The legacy of both unreasonable devotion to ever-changing but always thoroughly illiberal economic doctrines and concentration on whatever was countable (e.g., output of steel) rather than what people wanted was profound by the time Mao Zedong died in 1976. Equally compelling was the disastrous poverty of the Chinese people. With the Chinese people having undergone the catastrophic famine of 1959–1961, it could quite reasonably be said that the standard of living in much of China in 1976 was no better than when the Communists took power, and in some places worse. (In 1978, after almost forty years of extreme economic illiberalism, China qualified as one of the poorest

---

320. Feng and Xie's story is told (in Chinese) at 新華網時整,《義烏市場是人民創造出來的——記義烏小商品市場的催生培育者謝高華》, 2018年12月20日 (*Xinhua Politics*, "The Yiwu Marketplace is the People's Creation," December 20, 2018).

countries in the world, with a per capita GDP of just over [2010] US\$300.[321])

Devotion to the core ideals of the revolution was almost universally shared among Chinese leaders. For those who had personally fought for it, who had seen and sacrificed so much for what had been their explicit goal—a classless, post-capitalist society—the fact that their attempts to build it had led to so much destruction in the intervening 30 years must have created a fair amount of cognitive dissonance. But as the value of people working for their own purposes on their own initiative became more accepted, an economically much more liberal environment developed. Because of the large reservoir of hostility to economic liberalism, it did so in a two-steps-forward, one-step-back sort of way. But the process, still ongoing in part even now amid more recent challenges, has been one of the most consequential global events of the postwar era. The journey is unfinished (and has arguably reversed somewhat in recent years), but the distance between where the Chinese people were and are is vast.

7.A Coping with the ideological legacy after Mao

Recall that from no later than 1940 the senior leadership of the CCP had been explicitly resolved to build a Marxist society, leavened though this goal was ultimately proven to be by Mao's own radical departures. After Mao's death, a tentative advocacy of and experimentation with real economic liberalism emerged. But it would have to struggle with two legacies of the revolution—a heavy dependence on Soviet-style state-owned enterprises (SOEs) and the residue of the policy gyrations during the Mao years.

With respect to subsequent economic liberalization, one of the most influential decisions was a negative one that many sought later to reverse. At the outset of the GLF, under the slogan "decentralization is revolution," the CCP created thousands of new SOEs.[322] This was a catastrophe. These companies, behaving as SOEs often behave, proceeded to "plunder land, resources and tax revenues." Uncountable numbers of rural homes were demolished, the air and water were polluted, and land was given away to the well-connected

---

321. Throughout this and the subsequent chapter, figures on the level and growth of national income come from the World Bank's World Development Indicators.

322. Cited in English in Jinglian Wu and Guochuan Ma, *Whither China? Restarting the Reform Agenda*, trans. Xiaofeng Hua and Nancy Hearst (Oxford: Oxford University Press, 2016), 54.

at the whims of local leaders.[323] Until the end, Mao and other CCP leaders under his sway continuously engaged in radical experimentation, but not the competitive profit-driven, bottom-up, freewheeling sort that is at the heart of economic liberalism.

Although it did not officially end (by historical reckoning) until 1976, the CR's worst excesses were in the first few years, nearly a decade earlier. The Maoist left had been in charge of economic policy since 1966. After having been purged during the CR, Deng Xiaoping had been named Vice Premier of the State Council in 1974 at the recommendation of Mao Zedong's long-time second-in-command Zhou Enlai and with Mao's explicit approval. Zhou wanted Deng in part for his economic understanding, and Mao because he had support in the army, which had been unsettled since the death, quite possible murder, of Mao's rival, Marshal Lin Biao (林彪, 1907–1971). Deng and Chen Yun (陳雲, 1904–1995) were prominent among CCP leaders in advocating economic change. While often associated with Deng, the phrase "four modernizations" (四個現代化) had been raised in a report submitted by Zhou in preparation for a new constitution that was put before the National People's Congress in January 1975. Zhou died on January 9, 1976, and Mao later that year on September 9. In the spring, there had been a series of demonstrations, notably in Beijing, in the wake of Zhou's death. In Mao's last months, as he became unable to meaningfully participate in day-to-day governance, his wife Jiang Qing (江青, 1914–1991) and other radicals tried to increase their power, not just in terms of official political positions but in directing the entire country, including its economic policy. Thus, for those who wished to try a new Chinese path for escaping poverty, the first order of business was a struggle over power with the orthodox left wing of the CCP. On October 4, 1976 the radical leaders known as the Gang of Four were arrested in Zhongnanhai (中南海), the CCP central leadership's residential compound in Beijing. The four were Jiang Qing; Zhang Chunqiao (張春橋, 1917–2005); Yao Wenyuan (姚文元, 1931–2005), whose 1965 newspaper article is credited with helping to launch the CR;[324] and Wang Hongwen, (王洪文, 1931–1995). Over the next several

---

323. Ibid., 57.

324.姚文元,《評新編歷史劇〈海瑞罷官〉》,《文匯報》, 1965年11月10日 (Yao Wenyuan, Review of the Historical Drama "Hai Rui Dismissed from Office," *Wenhui Bao*, Nov. 11, 1965).

days, under the direction of Mao Zedong's chosen successor, Hua Guofeng (華國鋒, 1921-2008), other arrests were made there and in Shanghai of both individual CCP leaders and members of radical workers' groups. Stories were then released to the public vaguely describing significant crimes committed by unnamed people on the left. Because of the need to wait for changes to the Chinese legal system, the major trial of the Gang of Four and six others was not held until 1980, and in the end all of the charges involved political rather than economic questions. Optimists saw the long delay in the light of the overall legal reform that followed the death of Mao and the overthrow of the top tier of the radical left. China had been living with a cult of personality for decades, and there was some desire to institute the rule of law. Economic reform was thus initially part of the construction of an overall legal framework, which included criminal and broader civil law. A comprehensive new legal code was enacted in 1979.

7.B Getting started

Arguably the initial attitude of Chinese decision-makers with respect to economic liberalization resembled that of the old self-strengtheners in their instinctive hostility to foreigners, and the view that all they needed to do was copy the West's machines. In 1972, the government authorized the construction by duplication of an American color-television factory (just as 100 years ago the Chinese built their own factories using Western plans and machinery, although often under Western supervision). Subsequently, a team of Chinese officials went to a U. S. Corning factory in the U.S., when the company was a world leader in the production of some industrial glass and ceramics products. The Corning team gave them paperweights with snails inside as mementos, which insulted the Chinese team because they took it to mean that they were regarded as moving at a snail's pace. Somewhat remarkably, a mass meeting was organized in protest after the delegation returned, and government officials vowed not to yield to "imperialist" pressure.[325]

From this unpromising start, after Mao's death there developed an initial consensus about the need to import important technology, something that

---

325. Wu and Ma, *Whither China*, 108.

had been impossible ever since the China-Soviet split in the late 1950s. In a speech in July 1978 Hu Qiaomu (胡喬木, 1912--992) raised the possibility of allowing SOEs to sign contracts to charge prices different from those assigned to them by central planners. Hu, like Chen Yun, would later emerge as an opponent of further economic reform. In 1979 Dong Fureng (董輔礽, 1927– 2004) proposed much broader SOE independence—allowing the enterprises to decide on their own how much to make, and what to charge.

Meanwhile, as has so often been the case in China since 1978, at the local level things were already in motion. It would take until 1983 for national authorities to ratify the now rapidly spreading Xiaogang farmers' disobedient experiment of managing their own plots as consistent with a communist China, but after the results of their reforms became known in 1979, nearby local authorities began to change the way CCP leaders defined peasants' obligations to the state. (Indeed, at one point Wan Li (萬里, 1916–2015), the CCP general secretary in Anhui, the province where Xiaogang is located, intervened to save the Xiaogang arrangement itself.)[326]

Whereas previously adults were responsible for providing a certain amount of work time to collective farms (and these obligations were often substantial), increasingly the arrangement was the household joint-contract system (家庭聯產承包責任制). Under this system, individual families already registered under the Chinese national-identification system were now responsible not for providing time but the results of time, i.e., foodstuffs. Anything they produced in excess of their obligation was theirs to do with as they wished. This was an official ratification of the spreading Xiaogang-type arrangements. Farmers did not own the land, title to which was still vested in the collective organization of which they were a part, but they could claim "land use rights" (土地使用權) and "land management rights" (土地經營權). In many respects this amounted to the same thing—what and how much to plant and how to plant it were now decisions that households could make as if they owned the land outright. Food production soared, even as agricultural workers soon began moving to the cities, a practice that, as described below, had been practically prohibited before. By 1992, China would end ration tickets for food, the last vestige of

326. Kent G. Deng, *China's Political Economy in Modern Times: Changes and Economic Consequences, 1800– 2000* (London: Routledge, 2011), 75–77.

communist food rationing, which had been in effect since shortly after 1949.

In October 1979 the Sichuan provincial government put Hu Qiaomu's plan into action and gave six of its manufacturing SOEs some freedom from the state plan. As was happening with farmers in what was now several provinces, these six firms were free to produce more and sell it once they had satisfied their output obligations according to the state plan. The firms would keep a percentage of the surplus and send the rest to the state. In July 1979 this freedom was enshrined in provincial regulations, as were instructions to provincial planners to find new SOEs to grant such liberty to.

This enterprise-responsibility system was implemented nationwide in 1984 and the number of such enterprises grew from 12,000 in 1978 to roughly 12,000,000 in 1986.[327] Whether because of tolerance or torpor, throughout the first twenty years of reform a key theme continued to be decentralization, expressed as provincial or local governments, often without explicitly being given the authority by the center, taking the initiative to liberalize. As happened in Anhui and neighboring Shandong, such local initiative also often involved a mentality of act first, get permission later. Note that for the Yiwu market in 1982, the sequence of events was, first, people like Feng Aiqing setting up stalls without authorization, and then the bureaucrat Xie Gaohua proclaiming the "four permissions" (四個充許). These were: for people to operate businesses; for rural residents to enter the city; for goods to be transported across jurisdictional lines for commercial purposes; and for different producers in different stages of the production process to cooperate.[328] That such simple steps required authorization was a sign of how illiberal China was in 1982.

In this simultaneously bold yet cautious post-Mao spirit, in 1979 the economist Xue Muqiao (薛暮橋, 1904–2005), was able to publish a book called *Research in Problems in Chinese Socialist Economics* (《中國社會主義經濟問題研究》). It is now credited as the first text to seriously analyze how under a "socialist" framework China could arrange incentives and structures in order

---

327. 陳寶榮,《中國個體經濟》, 上海社會科學院出版社, 1頁至2頁 (Chen Baorong, *China's Private Household Economy*, (Shanghai: Shanghai Social Science Academy Press, 1990)), 1–2.

328. The Chinese was「四個充許通告：充許一名經商, 充許農民進城, 充許長途販運, 充許多渠道競爭」(author's translation). *Xinhua Politics* (2018).

to move forward.[329] This was written by a man who had joined the CCP in 1927, had written works on orthodox command economics, and who had been purged from an academic position during the CR. Having been restored to academic circles, he formally 《proposed in this text》 different but theoretically permissible forms for SOEs. He also explicitly took to task the economic model inherited from Stalin, which was centered around Party ownership *and* operation *and* coordination of all production.

In the meantime, true to the spirit of experimentation, the new jurisdiction of Shenzhen, adjacent to then-British Hong Kong, in 1980 became the first experimental economic zone. Here entrepreneurial and managerial freedom was expanded further, and foreign firms were allowed to engage in joint enterprises with local Chinese. (The attitude toward foreign "capital" had certainly changed since the "hostage capitalism" of the early 1950s.) Even so, in 1982 the official plan of the 12th National Congress of the CCP said that the planned economy was primary. But in 1983, the term of art became "contract responsibility" (合同責任), and it was required of SOEs throughout China. Throughout and beyond manufacturing, SOEs could legally commit to provide A to another SOE in exchange for B, with consequences if they failed to perform, the basic premise of contract law.

Alas, government planners' legislated incentives were sometimes insufficient. Freedom to set wages and let workers go or hire new ones had yet to be established. And in Sichuan, the reforms were such that the enterprises got to keep a share of profits, but were not responsible for losses, which instead fell to the provincial government as a whole (a practice common in recent decades in some Western countries, especially in finance). As the 1980s proceeded, SOEs nationwide continued to be responsible for meeting state plans but acquired more managerial independence. They too were gradually allowed both to sell on the market whatever they could produce beyond the demands of the plan and sometimes to provide a fixed monetary amount to the central authorities, while using other funds as managers thought best.[330] Yet they continued to have guaranteed, cheap prices for resource inputs provided by the state (albeit in

---

329. Originally published as 薛暮橋, 《中國社會主義經濟問題研究》, 北京, 人民出版社, 1979年 (Xue Muqiao, *Research in Problems in Chinese Socialist Economics* (Beijing: People's Publishing, 1979).

330. Yongnian Zheng and Yanjie Huang, *Market in State: The Political Economy of Domination in China* (Cambridge, UK: Cambridge University Press, 2018), 268.

plan-determined quantities) while being required to guarantee a fixed amount of output at planned prices, which as it turned out were above those being charged by private firms. Thus, they often could not sell what they produced.

To solve problems like these Chinese reformers tended to favor providing additional freedom rather than increasing restraints. (Barry Naughton has referred to this principle as "growing out of the plan."[331]) What we may by this point defensibly call small private enterprises—ventures established by individuals outside the SOE framework—were allowed over time to do things that were prohibited before. To this point state economic entities, notably SOEs, had experienced gradual reform, rather than being forced to conform to market conditions or die. This gradual reform in China differed from some of what occurred in Eastern Europe and the Soviet Union starting in the late 1980s. At that time, sudden exposure to market forces was favored by foreign governments dispensing funds and reform advice, as well as international organizations—both in communist nations and developing countries. A key founder of a private firm that evolved into the Lenovo computer firm, Liu Chuanzhi (柳傳志, 1944-), cut his teeth in an SOE during this period.

7.C Early ideological opposition

Gradualism was not necessarily done because of a theoretical commitment to it, but because moving toward "capitalism" had been demonized by the CCP for decades. There was substantial, true-believer domestic political opposition to such movement, and thus all reforms proposed had to be small. Deng Xiaoping himself is sometimes credited with describing the best attitude toward (badly needed) reform as 摸着石頭過河 ("Touch the stones to cross the river"), although there is no record of his saying it in his published remarks.[332] (A joke that the increasingly prosperous Chinese told in the 2010s to mock the government was, "We've all crossed the river, the government is still back there touching the stones" 我們都過河了, 他們還在那摸石頭呢.

331. Barry Naughton, *The Chinese Economy: Transitions and Growth* (Cambridge, MA: MIT Press, 2007), 9.

332. The assertion that the multifaceted experimental attitude captured by the saying was and is key to economic reform but that the remark itself was never made by Deng is found in the CCP publication *Study Times*. 王大陽, 《"摸着石頭過河"的來歷》,《學習時報》, 04月09日 (Wang Dayang, "The Origins of 'Touch the Stones to Cross the River,'" *Study Times*, April 9, 2018).

And what was the political reaction to the reforms early on? In the first few years of so-called "reform and openness" they had been limited to modest adjustments of the existing communist structure in just a few parts of the country, amid calls to preserve the status quo. And the new system, tentative though it was, generated social problems that were used to indict economic reform itself. Had the early reforms been materially costly, or had they generated indifferent results, it would have been easy for CCP leaders to dismiss them as a betrayal of communism. But the evidence of success was irrefutable. Per capita consumption of food, measured in mass, had been unchanged from 1957 to 1978, but grew over ten percent a year between 1978 and 1984.[333] Unlike Mao Zedong's boasts about steel production as virtuous in its own right and hence a measure of the superiority of his rule, now all the food produced above state quotas was sold by specific farmers to specific customers because those customers desired it. This of course does not happen when production increases only because of bureaucratic commands and in defiance of local knowledge that would have been produced and used through profit-driven competition.

But in the early steps of reform, opposition from important CCP officials had appeared almost immediately. In a speech at the 11th CCP Congress in August 1977, the first held since the deaths of Zhou Enlai and Mao Zedong, then-Central Committee Vice Chair Ye Jianying (葉劍英, 1897–1986) got the anti-reform ball rolling before reform had even meaningfully begun, praising the CR in particular as a "vital weapon against capitalist restoration."[334] And the general nervousness about reform was undoubtedly spiked by an outbreak of free speech in 1978, when a number of "big character posters" (大字報) made politically alarming demands for "freedom" and "democracy." (Such posters had been used in the early stages of the CR.) Even though the right to display such posters had recently been enshrined in the new Chinese constitution, a crackdown both on posters and those who put them up followed, indicating that for now political liberalism was not in the offing. CCP nervousness about this "Democracy Wall" also extended to discomfort with anything that would threaten social stability.

333. Wu and Ma, *Whither China?*, 75.

334. Richard Baum, *Burying Mao: Chinese Politics in the Age of Deng Xiaoping* (Princeton, NJ: Princeton University Press, 1994), 49. (Baum quotes the remark in English translation as Ye's words.)

A frequent specific, ideological objection raised in the early years of liber-al economic reform was its putative adulation of "bourgeois liberalization" (資產階級自由化).[335] The charge was a damning one in the Marxist framework, because seducing the people with anti-socialist cultural propaganda had long been said to be a favorite tactic of the bourgeoisie. In his book *New Democracy* Mao Zedong had condemned bourgeois liberalism as at most an obsolete form of bourgeois world revolution (舊的資產階級世界革命). Such liberalism was, he said, to be replaced by a new socialist world revolution (新的社會主義的世界革命). In January 1981, amid military objections to reformers' attacks on military budgets and privileges, the Politburo member and military veteran Wei Guoqing (韋國清, 1913–1989) harshly criticized reform in an address at a military conference. The next month, the military launched another propa-ganda campaign to "emulate Lei Feng" (模仿雷鋒), a young soldier who was said to have died in a vehicle accident in 1962. His example was used, and indeed continues to be used today even in China's most modern urban districts, to encourage self-sacrifice for the greater social good. The campaign against reformers' attacks on the military broadened to target writers specifically, and Deng Xiaoping expressed some sympathy for it. Even then-CCP General Secretary Hu Yaobang (胡耀邦, 1915–1989), who had then and would con-tinue to have a reputation of being pro-reform, acknowledged the legitimacy of the anti-liberal campaign. Wei also criticized unacceptable cultural works, although he would later say in a separate meeting with cultural figures that he had been misunderstood. Thus for now, many people, both for and against reform, saw political and economic liberalism as two sides of the same coin.

And so sometimes this is the way it went in the new China—give entre-preneurs some space, then take part of it back. Other phrases at other times were used to oppose further liberalization, often for not obviously "econom-ic" reasons. At the second plenary session of the 12th Central Committee in October 1983, Deng Xiaoping endorsed an ongoing campaign against "spiri-

---

335. Note that while in English and French the term "bourgeois" was derived from burg or town, it came in French to mean urban and correspondingly wealthier members of the Third Estate. A common Chi-nese term for the bourgeoisie since the arrival of communist thinking has been "the asset class" (資產階級, *zīchǎn jiējí*). Perhaps indicating the detachment of the idea of the bourgeoisie from that of "enemies of the working class," the word 中產階級, *zhōngchǎn jiējí* (literally "middle-or intermediate-asset class") is now common.

tual pollution" (精神污染), but reformist Chinese leaders such as Hu Yaobang and Zhao Ziyang (趙紫陽, 1919–2005) worried that the campaign was so clearly targeted that it was frightening foreign investors, and in the end Deng ended the campaign before much harm was done.[336] In the meantime, Deng and other reformers were in constant conflict with the camp that favored continued economic planning. But, on balance, the drive was forward. In 1984, Deng and the reformers expanded the number of Shenzhen-like special economic zones to 14. Even so, up to the 1989 nationwide demonstrations he and Chen Yun, who had begun to oppose further economic liberalization, would continue to joust on the role of unpredictable competition versus political planning in economic decision-making.

The political turmoil of 1989 was partly a product of this tension over economic liberalism. The year 1987 had seen a revival of the campaign against "bourgeois freedom ideology" (資產階級自由主義), although by this point the targeted liberalism was mostly political. After students in that year burned copies of the Beijing Daily (北京時報) newspaper—the culmination of months of protest—a decision was taken to crack down.[337]

But unrest continued, and in 1989, in the months before students and others began to gather and protest in Tiananmen Square in Beijing and elsewhere throughout the country, rising prices and fear of more of the same generated public alarm and protest. Here the link between opposition to economic liberalism and fear of dynamic social change is clear—the higher prices reflected the rise to market-clearing price levels of goods that had previously been price-controlled.

Following several years of advocacy by reformer Zhao Ziyang, in June 1988 the Politburo committed to studying the appropriate time frame for freeing up consumer prices and soon chose to liberalize them over four years. After Deng Xiaoping had swung behind price reform, the prices of several core consumer foodstuffs (although not grains) were decontrolled in April and those of cigarettes and alcohol in June. Many urban residents engaged in aggressive preemptive buying before price increases took effect, which led to substantial-

---

336. Baum, *Burying Mao*, 161.

337. Even before 1989, Chinese college students were prone to protesting, targets of their protest ranging from their housing on campus to the threat of Japanese economic colonialism.

ly depleted monetary reserves. In response, banks (all still state-owned and operating at least nominally not for profit) raised interest rates substantially. As a result of this economic discontent, further price decontrol was postponed indefinitely. Zhao, by now a major advocate for more liberal policies, was damaged goods bureaucratically, and the protests in spring 1989 finished him off.

7.D Saving at least economic liberalism

A problem genuinely emanating from the reforms, possibly from their gradual (as opposed to sudden and complete) implementation, was spreading corruption. Substantial corruption has a long history in communist (and of course other) societies. But taking advantage of political power rankles morally, while also frustrating the better reconciling of competing wants that is a main argument for economic liberalism. And so despite efforts to write laws to control profiteering as part of the new reformed criminal law promulgated on July 1, 1979, public complaints about and official campaigns against corruption occurred in 1981. And throughout the late 1980s leaders of SOEs who interacted with the world business community were able to leverage their connections to reap substantial rewards for nothing more than being who, when, and where they were.

A major anticorruption campaign followed the 1989 political crackdown. This campaign, framed as it could easily be as resulting from the dilution of the socialist spirit through the temptation of capitalist lucre, fit well into a broader post-Tiananmen campaign against liberalization of all sorts. At a meeting of CCP leadership in summer 1990, Chen Yun explicitly argued that corruption was the result of the stench of "bourgeois liberalization" that had been allowed to ferment under two leaders (the already forced-out Hu Yaobang and Zhao Ziyang), who had specifically advanced with the protection of Deng Xiaoping. The 1989 protests, Chen said, had been the result of "public anger over official corruption."[338] The *People's Daily*, in a series of articles in 1990, editorially linked 1988's economic turbulence to 1989's political turbulence, and specifically trotted out the phrase "peaceful evolution" (和平演變). This term was originally translated from a phrase American Secretary of State John Fos-

---

338. Baum, *Burying Mao*, 319 (Baum's own words).

ter Dulles (1888–1959) used several times during the 1950s by the CCP as a conspiratorial explanation for China's turmoil. In Chen's view, political and economic liberalization together were designed to generate discord and therefore instability, which would eventually result in the end of communist rule.

And so at the seventh Plenary Session of the 13th CCP Central Committee in December 1990, Deng Xiaoping felt compelled to argue that in fact increasing the rate of economic reform increased the ability to handle all sorts of risks, political and economic. In 1991, his righthand man, Jiang Zemin (江澤民, 1926–2022), at that time the CCP General Secretary and soon to be the Chinese president, was tasked with meeting with scholars to analyze the global economic growth and rising prosperity after World War II from a Marxist perspective, then the recent changes in Eastern Europe, and how to develop "socialism with Chinese characteristics" (中國特色社會主義), a term still used by the government today. (It might be noted that the post-World War II prosperity was seemingly in contradiction to orthodox Marxist analysis.) Economic liberalism now seemed to be losing on the policy front, as more loans were made available to money-losing SOEs, while private firms were subject to greater scrutiny by the authorities on taxes and other grounds.[339]

In response, in early 1992, just before the Lunar New Year holiday, Deng Xiaoping took a trip to southeast China, the place where all the special economic zones were and where economically liberal policies could therefore most fairly be judged. He is said to have invited Chen Yun to travel with him, an invitation which a recuperating Chen tartly declined because of the pollution problems in that part of the country.[340] While on the trip Deng spoke critically of "imperialists" and "peaceful evolution"; he strongly endorsed further economic reform. In a series of speeches in Wuhan, Shenzhen, Zhuhai, and Shanghai, Deng argued among other things that planning and markets existed under both capitalism and socialism, so it was a mistake to get caught up in rigid definitions. He praised reform in Shenzhen in particular.[341] Among the people who got the message was Jiang Zemin. Within days of the remarks, he

339. Wu and Ma, *Whither China*, 135.

340. Baum, *Burying Mao*, 342.

341. English translation from "Excerpts from talks given in Wuchang, Shenzhen, Zhuhai and Shanghai," *Selected Works of Deng Xiaoping* (Beijing: People's Publishing House, 358–370), 360–361 (Shenzhen), 368 ("imperialists," "peaceful evolution").

came out for the first time in favor of further economic reform, a significant political victory for economic liberalism.

Deng Xiaoping's southern speeches, while made before a significant number of people, were not reported domestically. But unofficial transcripts of his remarks in Shenzhen in particular very quickly made their way to Hong Kong, and from there back to China itself.[342] He succeeded in persuading enough other members of the CCP leadership of three propositions: Economic activity resulting from economically liberal policies was not "capitalism"; the primary threat to China's future was the "left" and not the "right"; and China could have economic liberalism without having to accept political liberalism.

7.E Subsequent reform, and reform yet undone

The bridge player Deng Xiaoping played his cards right, and from this point on, taking the long view with the late 1970s as a starting point, the group favoring economic liberalism advanced it relentlessly (even to some extent in recent years, as will be seen). Jiang Zemin in a speech prior to the 14th Communist Party Congress that was to take place in October 1992 described a market economy the way a Western undergraduate microeconomics textbook might. He said that "[m]arkets are an effective way to allocate resources and provide incentives. They use competition and price levels to allocate scarce resources to wherever they will have the greatest benefit, and not only put pressure on but also stimulate enterprises."[343] In October 1993 the 14th Congress adopted as a goal the development of a "socialist market economy" (社會主義市場經濟), a term that is still in use today. In hindsight, this was a decisive turning point; China was now committed to an economy where market forces would play a major role in what got made (and therefore what didn't), what innovations should be tried and should succeed, and who got the fruits of individual contributions to economic growth. As we will see, this did not mean that the government would play no substantial role in these questions, but that competition among nonstate actors would do the majority of the heavy lifting. For decades beyond this point, Chinese entrepreneurs and private-sector employ-

---

342. Baum, *Burying Mao*, 344-345.

343. The Jiang quote is cited in Wu and Ma, *Whither China?*, 140.

ees would be ever freer to take the initiative, to learn things that China needed them to learn, and to move the country forward through competition. Local governments too took the initiative in officially and aggressively courting foreign direct investment. The hostility to private enterprise that had loomed so large in Chinese politics since the rise of Sun Yat-Sen and the KMT was now meaningfully in reverse. The gradual, long-term continuous but incomplete reform that followed over the next forty years can be investigated in several particulars. In each case, work remaining left undone is also noted.

7.E.1 Privatizing SOEs

As the nations in the Warsaw Pact, and nations that had been Soviet republics, were learning at about the same time, there are numerous ways to move assets from state to private control. In China, privatization was substantial, although accompanied by corruption of a sort, although not of a degree, seen in the former Soviet Union,

7.E.1.a The original local/regional SOEs

Recall that when initially given greater freedom, SOEs had been cosseted from the full effects of private competition. But even though these firms obtained guaranteed superior prices for their outputs and paid lower prices for their inputs, private entrepreneurs found a way (innumerable ways, actually) to outcompete them. Thus, many of these enterprises were losing ever-larger amounts of money in the early stages of reform in the 1980s. And so in 1993 the smaller city of Zhucheng (諸城) in Shandong started a program in which its smaller SOEs issued shares to their employees, giving them a more direct stake in firm success. More comprehensive SOE reforms were unveiled in the city of Shunde (順德) (then a distinct city, now part of a larger district in Guangdong province), where SOE ownership possibilities included similar arrangements, along with joint ventures with foreign corporations or domestically chartered ones. In 1996, a report was issued indicating that continued support of money-losing SOEs was unsustainable, and thus similar conversions of larger companies took place on a much greater scale throughout the nation. In September 1997, the 15th CCP Congress declared that many ownership structures were consistent with "the development of productive forces" (發展生產力), one way that Deng Xiaoping had framed a socialist economy in his speeches in 1992. Many former quantitative restrictions and bureaucratic obstacles to commercial activity were also swept away during this time.[344] In addition, privatization was generally carried out at the local level, where most SOEs were managed. National SOEs did not develop as an important economic force until later. Localities differed in the extent to which they gave small numbers of owners the greatest amount of ownership and control. Greater concentration in combination with confidence that these owners would bear the consequences, good and bad, of their decision-making, was the incentive to operate firms more effectively.[345]

The results of the substantial SOE privatizations that followed were what dynamic liberalism looks like, especially when the flow of new information is unusually large and sudden: New resources, including workers, were released for potentially more valuable, if yet undiscovered, activities. Seen another way, however, millions of workers, as many as 18 million between 1992 and 2012, lost their jobs.[346] Many of these workers were older and therefore had presumably started work believing they had lifetime employment. They were often terminated with minimal severance, and a loss of access to health, housing, and other services that had been given them through the SOE. As reform unfolded, even the SOEs that remained often offloaded these services to separate entities such as schools and hospitals, either public or private, which increasingly operated on a fee-for-service basis.[347]

Naturally these costs generated considerable dissent, causing provincial and local governments sometimes to decelerate the process (although not actually reverse it) and sometimes to make alternate arrangements for workers whose political strength was sufficiently hefty. This cycle confirmed that even without meaningful elections post-Mao China to some degree had to take account of public opinion in its deliberations, a phenomenon we will see again.

---

344. Zheng and Huang, *Market in State*, 272., 272.

345. Local governments also privatized more completely as their room for political maneuver, in the sense of facing less local opposition, was greater. Jie Gan and Yan Guo, "Decentralized Privatization and Change of Control Rights in China," *Review of Financial Studies* 31, no. 10 (October 2018): 3854–3894.

346. Zheng and Huang, *Market in State*, 278, citing figures from the China Statistical Yearbook.

347. Zheng and Huang, *Market in State*, 379. Private, state, and mixed provision of medical treatment are all now common in urban China. Completely private provision of education is rarer, but exists, as noted below for migrants.

If initial uncertainty about the wisdom of reform was a brake on how quickly it could occur, now concern about too much instability at any particular moment had the same effect.

7.E.1.b Today's national SOEs

So, due to greater entrepreneurial freedom from the combined effects of economic liberalization, the street view of Chinese cities over time increasingly resembled those of other cities in northeast Asia in the degree to which private enterprises coordinated the operation of daily economic activity. But even before 2019 (the time after then is the theme of the final chapter), CCP control of the operation of some larger firms was a significant and growing phenomenon, e.g., the state oil company, the Sinopec group (中國石油天然氣集團公司). Such multinational companies, in whatever countries they are based, are often termed "national champions." Whether or not they compete internationally, the CCP believes that SOEs should continue to be majority or entirely state-owned, in order to preserve its control of industries occupying the "commanding heights" of the economy (a term used by India's first prime minister, Jawaharlal Nehru [1889–1964].) In addition, in China privatization of SOEs was often only partial, as shares were floated to the general public, but public investors were not given majority or sometimes even meaningful control.

This scheme was the result of the fact that when initial mass privatization occurred in the years after 1992, it was against the backdrop of *zhuādà fàngxiǎo* (抓大放小), the framework adopted in the mid-1990s in which the state would let go of the smaller firms but retain control over key industries. These are industries that are seen as critical to the national interest while also subject to economies of scale and scope. They are thus theoretically prone to subpar performance if left to market forces to sculpt. Sometimes state control is necessary to generate significant revenue for state coffers (tobacco being the classic case in China). Throughout more than four decades of privatization Chinese authorities have generally seemed to be more friendly to economic liberalism when consumer interface is particularly important. Foreign-brand auto companies and, since June 2018, foreign gasoline brands have been permitted to sell directly to consumers; the four largest automobile makers, all state-owned, must compete vigorously with each other, with other private domestic companies, and foreign brands. Thus, given the need to compete under partial private ownership, SOEs are simultaneously private-sector and not. And many of the largely or wholly owned SOEs participate in global commerce—not just buying and selling all over the world but, until recently, raising funds without difficulty in world stock and bond markets. Today's national SOEs are thus not leadenly uncompetitive in the way that the SOEs before 1993 were, or that Soviet-bloc SOEs were throughout the Soviet era. They are a clear hybrid, they often make money, and they are unlikely in the near future to face the same privatization pressures that smaller SOEs faced previously.

Overall the CCP's attitude in the years after 1978 was somewhat reminiscent of that of other postwar Northeast Asian economies, according to James Fallows, who says that the state was using its tools to channel at least some resources to its favored destinations, while also encouraging competition at the consumer level.[348] In China, activities subject to extensive state ownership currently include, among others, finance, aerospace, shipbuilding, natural resources, power generation, and heavy industries such as chemicals and metals, a phenomenon further discussed in the final chapter. Some of these activities have obvious military implications. But others are generally provided by markets in modern, mainly economically liberal societies.

Blurring the line between SOEs and private enterprise have been nominally private companies that have received or currently receive a critical amount of assistance from, or are significantly controlled by, state authorities. Three examples that both have grown to spectacular size and that receive a great deal of attention from foreign media are Alibaba (阿里巴巴集团控股有限公司), Tencent (騰訊控股有限公司), and Huawei (華為技術有限公司), companies involved in different ways in information technology. The former two became dominant domestically in e-commerce and social networking, and the latter in telecommunications hardware. Each has a classic Horatio Alger story involving people who started out with not much money and then built giant companies. In many respects firms such as these compete against one another in the market of providing information to Chinese netizens—a market whose content is constrained.

And yet it certainly cannot be said that these companies are private in

---

348. James Fallows, *Looking at the Sun: The Rise of the New East Asian Economic and Political System* (New York: Pantheon, 1994).

230 MARKETS WITH CHINESE CHARACTERISTICS

the same way as, say, Apple or Google. Huawei received a contract to provide telephone networks to the People's Liberation Army at a critical time in its growth, and its founder and current CEO Ren Zhengfei (任正非, 1944–) has a military engineering background. Huawei must compete for most of the business it receives around the world, and it has research facilities and well-known technology centers in many countries. And yet it has faced accusations of selling equipment that enables monitoring of the buyer's communications by the company and therefore the Chinese government. These accusations have unquestionably become stronger since summer 2019. The implications of this development are discussed in the final chapter. Ren has pledged the company will never monitor the users of its equipment, a necessary promise as a global competitor. But it is far from certain that if push came to shove it could resist any demand by the CCP that it do so, and in any event it is widely feared to be willing and able to do what the CCP asks.

The Tencent platform WeChat is globally innovative in many ways, a leader in combining social networks and e-commerce in a single platform. It is extraordinary to see the extent to which Chinese use the platform to communicate through a wide and growing variety of media and to buy and sell things. The economies of scope made available to consumers by this combination of capacities was already being described by the economist Tyler Cowen in 2015 as "one of China's first major innovations in the classic sense."[349] And yet the Chinese government can monitor all messages on WeChat, a power many Western technology companies do not concede to the state. This allows the CCP to monitor trends in communication among Chinese citizens, and thus to keep track of fermenting protest movements. Both Alibaba, founded in 1999, and Tencent are expected to participate, along with other Chinese apps used for routine tasks such as ordering plane or train tickets, in the growing Chinese government social-credit system (社會信用體系). This system, its spread accelerated by the harsh crackdown against the spread of Covid-19, increasingly keeps track of such day-to-day matters as citizens' tendency to pay bills on time, violate traffic laws, default on loans, etc. The Chinese government already uses these social-credit scores to allocate access to goods and

---

349. Tyler Cowen, "Is WeChat the Future?" *Marginal Revolution*, August 11, 2015, https://marginalrevolution.com/marginalrevolution/2015/08/is-wechat-the-future.html.

services it has control over, such as transportation and bank credit. And as we will see in the final chapter, the CCP has recently used antitrust law to bring both Tencent and Alibaba to heel.

Overall, the wave of privatization in the 1990s described in this chapter was a bold step, if we assume that there was among Chinese leadership circles significant ideological attachment to the idea of state production. But the work was unfinished. The extensive list of activities influenced or dominated by state production indicates that to become more liberal, the Chinese would need to finish the privatization they started in the early 1990s to the maximum extent consistent with CCP national-security demands. As will be seen in the concluding chapter, private economic activity has continued to expand even recently, but the above analysis suggests that there is a core set of activities that the government is so far unwilling to relinquish, and many large, nominally private, companies that the government embraces rather closely. This is not without precedent. During the later self-strengthening era, when the Qing bureaucracy began to see the importance of large-scale private enterprise in producing what they saw as critical goods, it adopted in many cases the system of *guāndū* (官督). In this system, the government exercised some control over commercial ventures funded by private capital. The same thing happened to a much greater degree during the KMT's Nanjing Decade, with associated corruption also tellingly severe. Perhaps this experience gives some guidance to future trends in Chinese-government control of its largest non-SOE businesses.

7.E.1.c Liquidating economic mistakes

Prior to Covid-19 and the devastating effect it had on Chinese business activity, one could stroll around the streets of any Chinese city and see legions of businesses that are as subject to competition as any in the developed world—small restaurants, large retail chains, investment management, animal-feed manufacturers, on and on. Food, clothing, and to a significant extent housing and medicine, much of the material stuff of life, was essentially 100 percent state-provided in 1978, and by 2019 was primarily provided via market processes, especially in the cities. Achieving economic dynamism in China has two sides: the right to private entry to replace a retreating state and the ability to shut down failed businesses in an orderly way, thus releasing their resources for use by others. This has become increasingly formalized in China. In 2007 the Enterprise Bankruptcy Law (中國人民共和國企業破產法), enacted by the National People's Congress in 2006, took effect. Initially designed, and over time brought more into harmony with, international bankruptcy rules, it distinguishes between secure and unsecured creditors (the latter including workers, even in a workers' state).[350] The contrast with the nationalization of domestic and foreign private businesses discussed in Chapter 6 is obvious.

It should be noted that the number of Chinese companies that liquidate through formal bankruptcy is still minuscule next to those that merely "exit the market," which means either that owners cancel their business registrations or have them canceled by the authorities. In 2015, 2058 businesses went formally bankrupt but over 800,000 of them merely exited.[351] The latter method makes it easier to escape debt obligations, and the unpopularity of formal bankruptcy, along with the easy availability of market exit, is a significant obstacle to doing business with strangers. An analogy would be to Hernando De Soto's analysis of how the lack of reliable property and contract rights in many developing countries limits the radius of one's circle of potential trading partners to family and close acquaintances.[352] So while entry and exit are easy and common, it is likely that further formalization of them will help Chinese economic dynamism.

7.E.2 Liberalizing mobility – the hùkŏu system

With substantial privatization after 1992 came a large decline in jobs in state-owned enterprises. How was the private labor market prepared to accept discharged employees? In a liberal labor market the answer is to allow people to search freely for work until they find a job they are willing to accept, while employers search freely to fill vacancies until they find an applicant they are willing to hire. (What to do in the case of a long-term, high rate of unemployment in a liberal economy is a separate controversy.)

But the Chinese labor market even well before 1949 had been subject

---

350. Shaowei Lin, "The Empirical Studies of China's Enterprise Bankruptcy Law: Problems and Improvements," *International Insolvency Review* 27 (2018): 77–109.

351. Ibid., 85.

352. Hernando De Soto, *The Mystery of Capital: Why Capitalism Triumphs in the West and Fails Everywhere Else* (New York: Basic Books, 2000).

to one significant friction arising from government policy. China, like other long-standing literate, complex societies, has a long history of rulers controlling population movement. Imperial authorities sometimes kept records of the agricultural population either to keep people where they were and grow food, or to move them to frontier areas, including newly conquered ones. Such record-keeping was inherited by the ROC in 1912.

But recall from Chapter 4 that during the first great wave of economic liberalization in the late 19th and early 20th centuries, Chinese achieved unprecedented mobility of residence and social status. But after 1949, the effort to limit freedom of movement expanded substantially with the use of of *hùkǒu* (戶口) documents, which began to record where individuals were authorized to live under what was officially called the household registration system (戶籍制度, *hùjízhìdù*). By 1957, the core features of the new system were in place. Each household and its individual members at birth were classified as urban or rural. As we saw, the rural population was to produce the food, and the urban population was to eat its share of it while producing other goods and services. And all according to the plan, of course—urban was urban and rural was rural, and seldom the twain would meet. The relaxation of these rules after 1978 was one of the key, if under-appreciated, liberal economic reforms.

China's long heritage of keeping track, to the extent possible, of who its people were and where they lived helped make the post-1949 *hùkǒu* system seem somewhat normal, but far more stringent controls heralded the arrival of comprehensive economic planning. In contrast, in an economically liberal society, how many people and their skills combine with how many machines, chemicals, and other resources to produce food is like every other decision—self-organized through market prices and individuals' pursuit of self-interest. Such restructuring of Chinese agriculture had been dramatically facilitated during China's transformative growth before 1937, but now under communist planning there was no guarantee that at any time there would be sufficient amounts of food to prevent widespread malnutrition or even starvation. Famines were common worldwide, including in China, before modernity, especially in areas where only the primary grain and a handful of vegetables and fruits could be grown locally ("monoculture") combined with an inability to buy much in the way of crops grown elsewhere.

But after completion of the collectivization of the economy described in

Chapter 6, decisions about which resources were to be used to produce and dis-
tribute food and which for other purposes were almost entirely a matter of central calculation, frequently influenced by political considerations extraneous
to the purpose of producing satisfying food for the most people. The threat of
famine, despite improved technology, was back. (Contrast the dynamic, multifaceted responses to the 1921 famine discussed in Chapter 5 with the political
decision during the GLF famine to maintain food exports to the Soviet bloc.)
And so once it was politically decided who should produce the food, the need
to keep people in their place was stronger than it had ever been in Chinese
history. Urban collective enterprises (all of them government organizations,
recall) were forbidden from hiring anybody without an urban *hùkǒu*, and one
for that jurisdiction to boot. After vagrants and peddlers had been swept off
the streets after 1949, it was very difficult to eat, reside, and therefore survive
in an urban area without an urban *hùkǒu*, just as it was very difficult to escape
from the countryside with a rural one.

Yet after tentative economic reform began, it emerged that people were
"living outside the plan."[353] The material gains from moving to the city (which
have existed in all places for as long as there have been cities) increased substantially, even if migration was illegal. As economic liberals see the world,
these gains exist because of greater opportunity for division of labor. Technological progress (in other words, newly discovered ways of dividing labor) is
generated when more people in a given space have the opportunity to exchange
funds, time, and, most importantly, ideas. The gains, of course, proved irre-
sistible in China after 1978, and so the government's sharp division between
"yes, you have permission to work here" and "no, you don't" was not feasible.
(For the same reason, illegal immigration occurs all over the world when areas
with high standards of living are within feasible traveling distance of areas
with low ones.)

As violations grew, both market responses and legal changes began to ease
the lives of those born with the wrong *hùkǒu*. The political response was, as
usual, gradual. As large-scale migration to the cities was renewed in the early
1980s, private markets emerged to provide migrants with food, housing, med-

---

353. The phrase is that of Jason Young in *China's Hukou System: Markets, Migrants and Institutional Change*
(London: Palgrave Macmillan, 2013), 165.

icine, and education for migrants' children—although the housing has long
been more tentative and the education of lower quality, opening fewer doors
for advancement. It became possible to live (for as long as one could get away
with it) according to one's own plan rather than the state's, albeit with obstacles.

On the legal side, in 1985 the central government both introduced a
national identification card and allowed Chinese citizens to obtain a permit
for temporary residence (暫住證). Starting in the second half of the 1990s, it
became possible both for the agricultural class to apply for a permanent change
to an urban *hùkǒu*, and for people with urban *hùkǒu* to apply to transfer them to
some other urban jurisdictions. Combining the increasingly familiar patterns
of decentralization and of "act first, ask permission later," by this time some
municipalities, notably Shenzhen, were already acting independently, aggressively issuing local urban *hùkǒu* to attract residents from all over the country. They attracted many more entrepreneurs and much more physical capital.

The decisions about how many temporary permits and how many permanent urban *hùkǒu* to issue were generally left to local authorities. And to be
sure, not all localities were as generous as some of the boomtowns along the
coast in granting *hùkǒu* transfer. While Shenzhen since its establishment as a
special economic zone was always enthusiastic about using all available tools to
promote growth, officials in Beijing, Shanghai, and other very large cities were
reluctant to legitimize longtime residents without the proper *hùkǒu*. They were
driven in part by opposition from people who were already living in these cities.
(The historical irony in the case of Shanghai is notable—many of those who
today consider themselves thoroughly Shanghainese are descended from those
who arrived as recently as between 1843 and 1949.) More recently, the ability
to "legalize" such residents, or to attract them from elsewhere with the promise of an urban *hùkǒu*, led major cities to attempt to sculpt their populations
by handing out *hùkǒu* to those with high education levels and desired skills.

And initially, many new migrants were content to live in cities illegally. As
the 1980s unfolded, it became inevitable that they and the children they had
in the cities were a permanent presence. As the state substantially retreated
in producing housing and other core goods and services, people without the
proper *hùkǒu* found that their money spent as well as anyone else's, so unequal

access to such goods and services diminished substantially.[354] Legalizing access to housing and other services allowed people born with rural *hùkǒu* to build permanent lives in most cities and to be free to change employment within it. Yet even now an urban *hùkǒu* tied to one of the largest cities is a credential that makes it easier to access the elite employment track. In short, while the effects of the *hùkǒu* system on labor mobility have fallen significantly, where it is enforced it does generate urban legal inequality.

Despite the presence of the *hùkǒu* system, hundreds of millions of people moved from the countryside after 1978, and both they and some of the workers discharged from SOEs were efficiently absorbed by the private sector. The significance of this move must be understood in the light of the vastness and complexity of "the" Chinese labor market (the term an economic oversimplification if ever there was one). There was churn at lower levels of the labor market, in which lower-level workers were fired or quit and found new jobs, and it was matched by an explosion of SOE managers, government scientists and others taking the plunge into the private sector, known as "jumping into the sea" (下海). Once economic reform began, people transitioned into and out of the state and private sectors, became entrepreneurs, and did the other things that people in countries where employment is primarily market-determined do.

Unlike privatization of large SOEs, the task of freeing movement was trending in the right direction and had become nearly complete before COVID-19. What remains is potentially the most useful step, however. In April 2019, the National Development and Reform Commission of China (中國國家發展和改革委員會) announced that almost all Chinese cities would henceforth place no restrictions on migration. But as of this writing the 13 cities with populations above 5 million are still exempt. Yet in these cities too there have been periodic normalizations of *hùkǒu*, and so further liberalization is likely even there.

7.E.3 *Agricultural land and urban expansion*
The market for land was liberalized after the market for labor. Strictly speaking, it is the market for things on the land that has been gradually liberalized; the state still owns all the land. But in 1994 legal arrangements were estab-

---

354. Ibid., 151.

lished in which residences could be bought and sold through licensed but otherwise independent real estate agents. As for new land uses both residential and commercial, local governments first define use rights in a manner somewhat similar to zoning in the U.S., and then generally auction these rights off. The incentives here are problematic, as such a system opens the door to corruption by giving local government officials reason to seize agricultural land, change use rights, and then auction those rights off. The latter has been a source of considerable public frustration in recent years.

In addition, in rural areas land-use rights are still limited. While the right to farmland is transferable among households, owners of agricultural rights are not generally allowed to convert the land to other uses. (Whereas after 1978 the rural areas were briefly leaders in freedom of land use, now they trail the cities.) The CCP's still-widespread restriction of land to specific uses without clear market-failure justification (such as environmental protection or mitigation of congestion) continues to generate significant waste in land use. In the countryside how to navigate between the Scylla of lost opportunities for using land more efficiently and the Charybdis of generating more local corruption is a challenge.

7.E.4 Finance

A primary area of liberal but incomplete reform has been finance. Turbulence in financial markets is simultaneously evidence of the government's instinctive gradualism, the inability of regulators to keep up with breakneck innovation, and the intrinsic nature of the financial beast. Finance, recall, is the trading of wealth, or claims to wealth, across periods of time and potential states of nature; especially in rapidly evolving economic environments it is prone to instability, to booms and crashes. Finance in China was also a latecomer to liberalization. By the definition above, at the dawn of the reform era, finance in China essentially did not exist. SOEs accrued revenue and disbursed expenses at planned prices, and the People's Bank of China (PBC) was the means for mediating this exchange process. The bank had the task of implementing the economic plan through storing and dispensing *renminbi* (RMB), in theory a medium of exchange. In practice, however, possession of RMB sometimes could not obtain goods because in a politically planned economy they often were not there. SOEs and individuals could deposit RMB at the PBC, and planners could transfer

RMB from the account of one SOE to another. But that was most of what "finance" consisted of. And whereas central banks in modern liberalized economies are significant, substantially politically independent organizations, the PBC in contrast was merely a branch of the finance ministry.

7.E.4.a Banking

But after 1978 finance had to be liberalized, and was, albeit slowly. Nationally, between 1978 and 1984 the PBC was restructured into several large state banks, which would again engage in lending and borrowing. While the PBC continued to exist and would come to somewhat resemble the central banks in developed economies, several large banks, still under state control today, were spun off from the it. While still answerable to the CCP, state banks now transact commercially in the manner of large commercial banks worldwide. They have also become a powerful rent-seeking group.

But as in other arenas, more advanced financial liberalization was already being implemented regionally as the center was confining itself to bureaucratic reorganization. The first province to liberalize finance was Zhejiang, particularly the city of Wenzhou, which by 1986 had some arrangements of flexible interest rates and, notably, had permitted some private joint-stock companies, which provided a model for later SOE reform. Fang Peilin (方培林, 1952–) opened what may have been the first post-1949 private bank in China, Fangxing Money Lenders (方興錢莊) in Wenzhou. Many of these institutional innovations were later authorized nationwide. The national 1995 Guaranty Law (擔保法) and the 2005 Securities Law (證券法) were landmarks in this process. And, of course, these legal innovations were designed with ideological probity in mind. For example, the joint-stock companies in the early 1980s could circumvent ideological barriers to raising private funds, but only because such companies could be regarded as nominally collective.

Now, according to estimates published in 2018 by Yiping Huang and Xun Wang:

> In the banking sector, there are three policy banks, five large commercial banks, 12 national joint stock banks, 133 city commercial banks, five private banks and 859 rural commercial banks. In 2016, the 'big four' were all among the world's five largest banks and were

identified by the Financial Stability Board as globally systemically important (Table 16.1). At the same time, Chinese financial markets and assets grew exponentially. Domestic credit provided to the private sector rose from 49 per cent of gross domestic product (GDP) in 1979 to 199 per cent in 2016. Broad money supply (M2) is already greater than in the United States and its proportion to GDP—208 per cent at the end of 2016—is among the highest in the world.[355]

In other words, Chinese finance has not been entirely liberal in form or in substance (being plagued by significant national, regional, and local CCP intervention in lending decisions) and is thus potentially more unstable to the extent that politicized lending is more perilous lending. Yet Chinese borrowers large and small as time goes by have had ever-more options for access to funds through conventional channels. However, because the CCP fears major financial instability and does not wish to see alternative centers of money and power develop, the potential for fundamental changes to the financial game now draws skepticism from financial-market participants, as will be seen in the last chapter.

7.E.4.b Securities markets
The 2005 Securities Law set up a bureaucratic structure to regulate stock issuance nationwide, authorized futures and options trading, and allowed private litigation over securities transaction disputes—all common in financially sophisticated economies. Collectively, this created at least a theoretical structure to help Chinese firms keep their wealth in more liquid forms in order to more easily manage, and possibly make money on, uncertainty.

For stocks in particular, the form has moved forward, but with respect to substance there is still some way to go. While the experimental stock markets of the early 1990s that seemed to enchant Deng Xiaoping have been brought under more effective governance, Chinese firms that list in China generally perform more poorly than those that list overseas, suggesting some kind of

355. Yiping Huang and Xun Wang, "Strong on Quantity, Weak on Quality: China's Financial Reform Between 1998 and 2018," in Ross Garnaut, Ligang Song and Cai Fang, eds., *China's 40 Years of Reform and Development: 1978–2018* (Acton, Australia: ANU Press, 2018), 291–312, 293.

adverse-selection problem.[356]

Chinese market authorities are quite willing to suspend trading in shares of particular companies during times of unusual volatility. Improving company transparency and market governance is a major challenge for a variety of reasons. Since their founding in the early 1990s, Chinese stock markets have often been used to raise money for SOEs, many companies are thought to succeed or fail on the basis of the connections of their senior managers, and investment in China is quite subject to frequent herd-like behavior on the way up and the way down.

The bond market is newer and even less well-developed, currently dominated by issuances from national state-owned banks and government at all levels. In late 2017 a structure was set up to allow foreigners to participate through purchasing via Hong Kong intermediaries, taking advantage of that city's highly liquid capital markets, themselves a product of well over a century of dynamic economic liberalism.

Skepticism about foreign participation in Chinese financial markets has recently developed not so much in China as among foreign governments themselves, who increasingly fear facilitating the rise of a militarily threatening China. Yet CCP leadership recognizes that China is a relatively capital-short nation and is reacting accordingly by seeking foreign financial investment. Whether Western governments will allow their investors to continue to participate is still an open question because of recent events discussed in the next chapter. To the extent it is allowed, growing foreign participation in Chinese financial markets will increase investor demand for transparency. In the stock market in particular, as noted above, domestic investors have tended not to buy and hold. A Chinese expression for the tendency to "flip" stocks is 炒股 (chǎogǔ, "fry stocks"), a trading strategy likened to stirring food around in a pan. Individual investing in stocks with no goal other than selling them very soon after at a higher price is quite common, and when markets turn south (as

356. Franklin Allen, Jun Qian, Chenyu Shan and Julie Zhu, "Dissecting the Long-term Performance of the Chinese Stock Market (March 13, 2018)." Available at Social Science Research Network, https://ssrn.com/abstract=2880021 or http://dx.doi.org/10.2139/ssrn.2880021. Adverse selection occurs when high-quality and low-quality products are both offered, and the buyer cannot tell the difference. In the end, the high-quality product is driven out of the market because it is unable to signal that it is high-quality.

they often do), many small, perhaps unsophisticated investors find their financial position substantially damaged. If Chinese financial evolution parallels what we have seen in other more mature liberal economies, we should expect to see independent financial analysis grow in sophistication, targeting not just such "frying" gains but longer-term investment.

7.E.4.c Alternative finance

In sum, Chinese markets overall have been moving toward a financial rule of law. But limited transparency, domination of markets by well-informed insiders, and especially state domination of banking continue to be challenges. The wisdom of allowing greater flexibility and innovation—letting other (perhaps sufficiently trustworthy or well-capitalized) private institutions engage in finance—is reinforced by the fact that when finance is legally constrained as described above people who want to offer money and people who need it will find some way around those limits. That will happen even if it means neither lenders nor borrowers can appeal to the state for redress if things go badly, and the transaction costs of consummating such deals are higher than they otherwise would be. (Note that this does not per se mean that restrictions are a bad idea.)

As it is worldwide with illegal laborers or illegal gambling, so it is in China with illegal finance — activities that are desired but banned happen anyway, only shorn of legal protection. A recent example is the so-called P2P bubble, with P2P directly borrowed from the English abbreviation for "peer-to-peer." Chinese borrowers, many of them entrepreneurs and many involved in fairly large enterprises, sometimes found it nearly impossible to access more conventional funding sources, notably banks. So entrepreneurs used the Internet to create platforms through which individuals who wanted to invest were matched with individuals who wanted funds, sometimes packaged on both sides as portfolios. And the companies themselves often lent money in these lenders' names.

This new lending model arose in the second half of the 2010s. By 2015 the government, which is always concerned about financial instability, not just because it can harm individuals but because this damage can generate political protest (a theme taken up in more detail in the last chapter), began enacting regulations on these businesses. The goal was to confine their activities to more conventional lending and borrowing, providing a platform that enabled lenders to find borrowers and vice versa (for a fee, like the rough Western equivalent

GoFundMe), and requiring them to keep funds on deposit with state banks. The number of such platforms soon fell dramatically, and many platform owners absconded with funds of both lenders and borrowers.

The core lesson is that with China's growing need for financial intermediation, laws that ban things can only have so much effect; latent demand and latent supply will crop up in some other arena that entrepreneurs can conceive of and implement before the government can think of banning it. 'Twas ever thus, all over the world. Of course, substantially liberal economies differ in their levels of financial regulation, and Chinese authorities should consider the risks to the public of aggressive and fraudulent behavior versus the opportunities for wealth creation through financial entrepreneurship. But reacting after the fact, as China has, by substantially banning new, already extant financial innovations is unlikely to be the proper way of balancing these considerations. The system should progress toward placing the financial costs of mistakes on those who make them and encouraging greater access to and innovation in the financial system under such a framework.

7.E.5 Intellectual property
While in recent years much rhetoric in Western countries, especially the U.S., has depicted China as a cheater or free-rider when it comes to protecting intellectual property, this view is at best incomplete. First, China is at a stage of modernization when other countries, notably the U.S., were also quite lax about intellectual-property protection at that stage. The angry relationship between the Chinese government and Western firms about what the latter see as intellectual-property-rights violations is reminiscent of how Victorian-era authors, notably Charles Dickens, reacted to unauthorized copies of their works in the U.S., where copyright protection was not as extensive as in the United Kingdom.[357] Violations of the intellectual-property rights of an individual or business are often seen as fundamentally moral issues, but there is no absolute morality of intellectual property. Intellectual property protection is (like other property rights) defined by the state. What should be protected, and if so for how long, generates complex questions about incentives

---

357. Jessica Bulman, "Publishing Privacy: Intellectual Property, Self-Expression, and the Victorian Novel," *Hastings Communication and Entertainment Law Journal* 26, no. 1 (January 2003), 73–118.

for innovation. Should the state prevent copying after the creator has already incurred his one-time R&D costs, thus increasing the incentive for the creator to bear those costs in the first place? Will that deter future innovation and raise consumer prices by generating monopoly privileges for some length of time? Will it place obstacles in the way of people in poorer societies earning a better living and modernizing their societies? The optimal degree of protection will depend on how much complex innovative activity is likely to go on with expansive versus weak protection.

Such protection has two pieces, passing laws protecting such property and then enforcing them. On the first score, given its level of economic development there is little reason to criticize China, especially since it joined the World Trade Organization in 2002. In 2017 Lily H. Fang, Josh Lerner, and Chaopeng Wu wrote that "[t]he letter of the law governing IPR [intellectual property rights] is consistent with international standards and is the same across the entire country."[358] Enforcement is a different matter of course, but enforcing intellectual property protection is costly, as is enforcing any law. China is a vast country, and many types of rights might be protected to many degrees (patents on commercial aircraft and their components, versus T-shirts with Disney characters sold in stalls at a market in Changsha, for example). Sometimes, as has been true everywhere, the benefits accruing to the Chinese government from enforcement may not justify the costs in terms of personnel, legal expenditures, and local irritation. Chinese society as a whole has both creators of new ideas and people who benefit from selling goods based substantially on ideas created by others, including foreigners, and used domestically without authorization. But the legal apparatus is there, and China is arguably beyond where Japan was in the early 1960s or South Korea was in the early 1970s, or the United States in the late 19th century. These, again, are the proper comparisons.

Since choosing to participate in the global economy, the CCP has chosen to enact the proper rules, and as time has gone by (and as foreign governments have chosen to raise the issue more forcefully) enforcement has improved. Presumably if China wishes to stay integrated with the global economy, it will con-

---

358. Lily H. Fang, Josh Lerner and Chaopeng Wu, "Intellectual Property Rights Protection, Ownership, and Innovation: Evidence from China," *Review of Financial Studies* 30, no. 7 (July 1, 2017), 2246–2477, 2450.

244 MARKETS WITH CHINESE CHARACTERISTICS

tinue to do so as creating ideas becomes a bigger part of the Chinese economy relative to producing goods based on ideas created elsewhere. In other words, as Chinese human capital becomes more suited to domestic innovation, the value to the Chinese state of enforcing intellectual property rights will grow.

7.E.6 Internationalization

Between the split with the Soviet Union in the late 1950s and the start of reform, whatever the policy gyrations, China's economy was in near-autarky; such foreign trade as existed was limited to deals negotiated between the communist party leadership in China and in a few other countries and merely involved swapping of some goods for other goods. The establishment of Shenzhen and subsequent special economic zones led to joint ventures with foreign companies, and these expanded significantly after reform was cemented in the early 1990s. Since reform began, Hong Kong had played its role as a middleman between China and the rest of the world economy; subsequently the Chinese government acted to promote Shanghai as a substantial presence in global finance, which it has become. Hong Kong, which had grown and flourished under more than 150 years of British sovereignty, was returned to China in 1997.[359] At least economically, the "one country, two systems" (一國兩制) framework promised in the Sino-U.K. treaty negotiated in 1984 was largely kept until the political turmoil of late 2019. Although current Chinese policy thinking seems to view Hong Kong as just another Chinese city, and merely part of the entirety of the Pearl River delta along with Guangzhou and Macao, preserving Hong Kong's distinct (for China) business-law culture would better contribute to the city's and therefore China's international financial role, although that distinct culture is under growing threat. The several months of protest beginning in June 2019 and the CCP reaction to them has led to sharp limits on political freedom, although for day-to-day commercial transactions the Hong Kong legal system is still intact and highly thought of. "One country,

---

359. It must be remembered that when the British took over Hong Kong, economic activity in what had previously been a modest village expanded dramatically. By the time of the territory's return in 1997, it was a major global city. Like Shanghai, which was bigger at first entry than Hong Kong and whose flourishing under foreign political domination was documented in Chapter 4, how one evaluates these intervals depends at least partly on the importance one attaches to the prosperity generated by economic liberalism versus native sovereignty as a promoter of human happiness broadly defined.

two systems" is in decline in terms of democratic participation and in danger in terms of freedom of expression. But as long as the rule of law is preserved for contracts, property rights, and the like, the ability of Hong Kong to play a major role in Chinese planning for the larger delta region is possible. Foreign firms, however, are already weighing the value of Hong Kong as an operations base not against Shenzhen or Guangzhou but Seoul, Singapore, and Tokyo. This consideration has increased since the territory's harsh measures against COVID-19 and the crushing of dissent beginning in 2019. Whether mainland-style corruption infects Hong Kong will be a crucial factor in foreign firms' decisions.

With respect to the rest of the world, China's 2002 entry into the World Trade Organization (WTO) cemented, at least on the surface, China's commitment to a rules-based system of resolving trade disputes, at least as much as is true in any other randomly drawn member country. China's entry ended a problematic (for domestic and foreign economic actors of any size) annual exercise since 1979 in which the U.S. Congress was forced to decide whether China could retain its most-favored-nation status, which allowed its exports to enter the United States at a tariff rate similar to that of other developing nations. The importance of the CCP's acceptance of international authority over its internal policies should not be underestimated—even if (as with many countries) it is sometimes observed in the breach. How much damage the current friction between the U.S. and China, discussed in the next chapter, may do to Chinese confidence in world trading rules (in lieu of bilateral agreements with individual nations) is uncertain at this time. So far at least, elite Chinese society attaches great significance to full access to a world economic system based on reciprocity; the extent to which such public opinion can be translated into government action more generally is also discussed in the last chapter.

The Chinese government is also now a major donor, and therefore a major player, in both the International Monetary Fund and the World Bank. It has, however, also started to build alternate international structures to promote its economic leadership—at the expense of the existing ones that it sees as dominated by the West and by the U.S. in particular. One example is the Asian Infrastructure Investment Bank (AIIB) (亞洲基礎設施投資銀行), founded in 2015 by CCP initiative because the existing Asian Development Bank was seen to unfairly give China little influence. The Belt and Road Initiative (一

帶一路) was conceived by Chinese leadership in 2013 and is discussed further in the next chapter. It works to some extent with the AIIB to substantially improve infrastructure (especially transportation) in a variety of countries, for now mostly in Asia and Africa.

7.F Conclusion

At the top of a hill overlooking Lotus Mountain Park (蓮花山公園) in Shenzhen, where many people have long gone on Sunday afternoon with family or friends, stands a statue of Deng Xiaoping, like the man himself of modest stature. He appears to be walking, and moving forward, as has China, for most of the time since 1978, substantially due to his political decisions. While his lifetime moral ledger contains many troubling entries, his leadership enabled the Chinese people to use their own individual energies to change the country. The greatest achievement of what we may properly call the Deng Xiaoping era was the removal of political dogma as an obstacle to letting Chinese economic actors move forward in the ways the incentives provided by an economically liberal environment induce them to. While there is still real poverty in China, especially in the countryside, and current CCP leadership is altering in some ways economic liberalization (in a manner discussed in the next chapter), people throughout the country would find it genuinely bizarre if the pre-Deng command economy were to be restored. The Western press pays attention to current but insubstantial revanchist Marxist and Maoist voices in China, but economically the People's Republic of China has not been "communist" in the historical economic sense for some time.

By mid-2019 it was widely agreed that China had taken tremendous steps toward an economically free society since the late 1970s. And while there was some domestic disagreement, it was a very defensible position that further economic liberalization would continue, even if imperfectly so. The Chinese people and their companies were thoroughly engaged in the world economy, and while there was concern overseas over the growing political and military power of the Chinese government, economic integration was broadly accepted as a good thing. The most likely outcome would have been continued economic liberalization, combined with more friction with other nations as China rose.

And then some history happened.

CHAPTER 8

Futures: Economic Liberalism in China Moving forward, and the Consequences

T he summer of 2019 witnessed the first in a series of events that in combination appear to be rearranging China's relationship with much of the rest of the world, particularly bringing pressure on relations with the West, including Japan and South Korea. These events also threaten to largely undermine China's decades of substantial economic liberalization. The challenges began with the Donald Trump administration's protectionist measures first aimed at China's bilateral trade surplus (which many economic liberals view as a meaningless accounting artifact). This was followed by protests, some of them very large, organized in Hong Kong against a proposed law to enable the rapid extradition to the mainland of Hong Kong residents accused of crimes. Over the next several months the law was enacted anyway by Hong Kong authorities, and additional legislation was passed to substantially limit freedom of the press and the freedom to protest, both previously largely guaranteed. Then, in January 2020, the Beijing government acknowledged there was a rapidly spreading new respiratory virus in the Chinese city of Wuhan, and even though the city was sealed on January 23 of that year, the virus quickly spread around the world, killing millions. There was significant global skepticism about how the Chinese government handled matters before officially acknowledging the virus's presence, and about what was seen as its limited cooperation with later inquiries into its origins. Finally, in February 2022 Russian armed forces invaded the neighboring country of Ukraine, and the Chinese government used language that to some extent supported Russia and refused to call Russia to account in any way.

All of this occurred while a Chinese-government campaign to bring some economic forces under tighter government control was already underway. And despite facing the aforementioned rising tide of international challenges, that government under Xi Jinping has staked its legitimacy on what it asserts is the ongoing magnificent rejuvenation of the Chinese nation (中華民族偉大復興). In September 2022, on the eve of the CCP's 20th Party Congress, its periodic gathering of party representatives from around the country to nominally govern, and China's most widely watched political gathering, the party published a set of books titled "Rejuvenation Collection" (《復興文庫》). Spanning the same period of time as the story told in this book, from the First Opium War to the present, it offered an ideological interpretation, with Xi himself writing the introduction inviting the Chinese people to have confidence in the glorious new era now unfolding.

When the Congress itself unfolded in October 2022, Xi Jinping confirmed a decision he had previously engineered to abandon term limits for Chinese leaders, a policy decided roughly two decades prior. He was named to a third term as general secretary of the CCP as well as president—and thus likely to become the longest-serving Chinese national leader since Mao Zedong. But in the meantime, because of the events outlined above, much of the West has grown generally (if not unanimously) more skeptical of its long economic engagement with China. The CCP in turn now seeks to confine economic engagement with the outside world, and especially the West, to areas that promote what it sees as its own interests. The previous chapter told of a great triumph, with the vast Chinese population liberated from decades of economic madness. This one, alas, tells of progress by a still middle-income country (according to 2019 figures, Chinese per capita GDP in current U.S. dollars was $16,652, between Turkmenistan and Botswana) now under threat because the changes brought by economic liberalism endanger the CCP's monopoly on power.

8.A China's partial transformation under Xi Jinping

At the Congress's conclusion in October 2022, the global news was of Xi Jinping's retaining national leadership. But for our purposes the most important trends of the last few years can be seen as a process occurring since Xi's ascension to and consolidation of power since 2012.

As documented in Chapter 7, from the late 1970s China had first furtively and reluctantly and then with greater enthusiasm embraced economic liberalism (without calling it that). While there were twists and turns throughout, overall openness and reform had by 2019 produced a much more liberal Chinese economy than at any time since at least 1937. The effects on the Chinese standard of living constituted one of the great world postwar miracles. If one accepts the right to try to earn a living as a fundamental human right, it was a substantial triumph in this regard as well, compared to what had been before.

In 2012 Xi Jinping succeeded Hu Jintao, whose accession after the two terms of Jiang Zemin had seemingly institutionalized the routinization of Chinese leadership succession—a major goal of Deng Xiaoping following several decades of chaos after 1949. Xi's father had suffered during the CR, and Xi himself had been sent down to the countryside, like many in his generation. Upon assuming office there were no obvious signs that he meant to upend Chinese economic policy. And yet as his rule unfolded there was a sequence of proclamations, by him or in the name of the government, that indicated a desire to increase state control of some economic activities.

This desire for more control over Chinese society began in late 2013 with an unpublicized campaign to remove topics from Chinese media, a campaign known as the seven "don't says" (不講). The things to be purged from Chinese official media and online conversation were universal values (普世價值), press freedom (新聞自由), civil society (公民社會), civil rights (公民權利), past CCP mistakes (共產黨的歷史錯誤), the wealth of the rich and powerful (權貴資產階級), and the independence of the judiciary (司法獨立).

The implementation of these principles further constrained freedom of expression in CCP China; it had never been substantially protected, but subject to periodic though temporary relaxations since 1949. In pursuit of this agenda, an agency to "administer" the internet, the Cyberspace Administration of China (國家網信辦), was established in 2014, and a series of arrests against human-rights lawyers, the so-called 709 campaign, was launched in July 2015.

These events support the argument that after forty years of openness and reform the CCP under Xi Jinping's leadership had decided that threats to its political monopoly required action. Economically too, possible alternative power centers began to be eliminated. In 2015 the central government launched a plan termed "supply-side reform" (供給側改革). Unlike the American "supply-side economics" school of thought, the plan was to have the state

FIGURE 8.1 DISTRIBUTION OF EMPLOYEES AMONG THE PUBLIC
AND PRIVATE SECTORS, 1989–2017

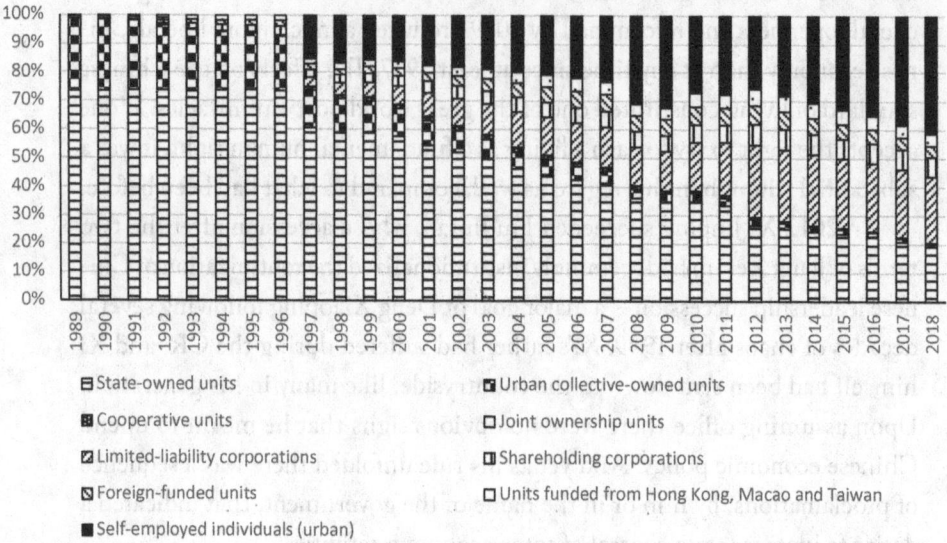

🩢 State-owned units	▨ Urban collective-owned units
▦ Cooperative units	☐ Joint ownership units
▧ Limited-liability corporations	▥ Shareholding corporations
▨ Foreign-funded units	☐ Units funded from Hong Kong, Macao and Taiwan
■ Self-employed individuals (urban)	

oversee a diminution of what was perceived as widespread Chinese industrial oversupply. Thus it would implement a state direction of overall production. In 2018, China's taxation became significantly more centralized, with provincial and local governments required to hand over more of their tax revenue to Beijing. Also, as equities in China lost a great deal of value over that year, government takeovers of majority stakes in publicly traded companies increased, leading to the growing prevalence of the idea "the state advances, the private sector retreats" (國進民退) among economic observers in China.

The Xi administration also confronted the billionaire Ma Yun (馬雲, 1964–) in October 2020, delaying and then canceling the initial public offering of his proposed Ant Group. This company planned to use the information generated through Ma's sprawling social-media and finance company Alibaba to create new ways for Chinese to raise capital through unconventional channels. Somewhat reminiscent of peer-to-peer financing, this was a technology now used widely throughout the developed world. The use of such technology, in which people can raise funds from strangers through technological intermediation rather than depending on the judgment of a lending institution's personnel, had flourished in China in the 2010s, as we saw. However, a crash in the industry in 2016 had led to government efforts to eliminate it. Ma proposed to introduce a radical new option for firms large or small to access funds. Its radical disruption lay not just in new technology enabling lenders and borrowers to link up, but in enabling them to both provide and access funds independently of the more orthodox, CCP-influenced banking system. This proposal was unacceptable to the CCP because it threatened to damage the large state-owned banks mentioned in Chapter 7, and because it would generate an independent channel that would fund broad entrepreneurial creative destruction. In addition, financial innovations that prove to be permanent are often poorly understood initially with unfortunate results, be they futures contracts introduced to facilitate tulips trading in the Netherlands in the 1630s, joint-stock companies introduced later in that century that were followed by the South Sea and Mississippi Company bubbles in the early 1700s, or the mortgage securities introduced in the 1990s in the U.S. followed by the global financial crash of 2008.[360] Learning how to use (and not use) them is painful. Technology of the Ant Group type, which undoubtedly will be tried and perfected elsewhere, would have done the same in China. That Ma, just before the IPO was about to happen, made a public speech in which he criticized the obsolete and excessively cautious nature of Chinese finance and financial regulation surely did not help. But the core problem was the threat the technology posed to government interests (including banking) and the associated economic—and soon enough perhaps—social disruption.

Since 1949 (indeed for longer than that) China has never had a sufficiently large number of key officials genuinely committed to economic liberalism, and there have been long stretches in which the only tolerated opinion was to oppose it, even remove it root and branch. This absence has certainly not changed during the Xi Jinping era. And yet there is a utilitarian commitment to limited economic liberalism because it allows the Chinese people to live a materially satisfactory life. At the same time, the government will not tolerate any developments that threaten its political monopoly. This tradeoff will significantly influence the currently diminished future of economic liberalism

---

360. On tulips, see Earl A. Thompson, "The Tulipmania: Fact or Artifact?" *Public Choice* 130, no. 1–2 (January 2007): 99–114.

for at least as long as Xi Jinping, and very probably the CCP more generally, monopolizes power.

8.B. And yet there are limits—the costs of hypothetically reimplanting socialism

And so there is much talk these days that given this lack of fundamental commitment to economic liberalism in the Chinese government, economic reform in China, as the government has actually carried it out, has failed and will not continue.[361] But the data indicate that comprehensive deliberalization would generate too much resentment to be politically feasible. As noted in Chapters 2 and 5, even before 1949 China had a significant history of state entanglement with private business. But from the late 1970s, first reluctantly and then after 1992 with the central government's blessing, the CCP has worked hard, subject to its peculiar constraints, to liberalize the economy. Even now, in the world beyond summer 2019, there are numerous government and corporate officials, along with publicly active intellectuals, who are thoroughly familiar with market mechanisms. So significant is this penetration of market ideas that even in the summer and fall of 2021, when some Chinese cities were plagued by rolling blackouts due to sharply rising coal prices, the government response was to give utilities with coal-based power plants not less but more pricing flexibility—which at least at the time brought the problem under control.[362] It is difficult to imagine going back in time to the completely planned economy of yore, although more government control over key parts of it is likely, as discussed below.

Such a return journey would have to be a very long one. The Chinese government for many years has kept track of various measures of economic activity and to what extent they occur in the public and private sectors. Figure 8.1 shows data for urban employment in a variety of ventures in each sector between 1989 (the first year for which data for both series are available) and

---

361. Daniel H. Rosen, "China's Economic Reckoning: The Price of Failed Reforms," *Foreign Affairs* 100, no. 4 (July-August 2021): 20–29.

362. Yang Jie, "China to Let Power Prices Rise in Bid to Fix Electricity Crunch," *Wall Street Journal*, October 12, 2021.

2019.[363] In the figure, "Public companies" includes employment in SOEs (國有全社會固定資), collectives (集體全社會固定資產投資), cooperative units (股份合作全社會固定資產投資), and jointly owned units (合資企業中的城市僱員). The third of these, cooperative units, took shape after Deng Xiaoping's critical trip to southern China, in which, after the massacre around Tiananmen Square in June 4, 1989, he went to that area where economic reform was already flourishing to make the case for more of it. These units vest both workers and investors with ownership rights. Legally purely private entities include limited-liability companies (有限責任公司), shareholding corporations (股份有限公司), foreign-funded units (外商投資單位), units funded from Hong Kong, Macao, and Taiwan (港澳台商投資單位), and self-employment (個體就業).

Even if we acknowledge significant state influence over some large private companies, the extraordinary degree and sustained nature of economic liberalism since 1989 is unmistakable. The private share of urban employment was only 5.4 percent in 1995, but by 2020 the share was over 90 percent. Note that this shift coincided with huge rural-to-urban migration, indicating that this migration was induced by private-employment opportunities (just as migration to Shanghai and other cities had been in the decades before 1937). The availability of these migrant workers undoubtedly made private-sector expansion easier, as existing firms increased employment, and migrants started their own businesses. Such shifts of "surplus labor" from countryside to city have occurred in modern economic development around the world. Indeed, the rising percentage of the Chinese population that lives in urban areas is itself a sign of liberal transformation; recall the earlier centrality of the hùkǒu system, whose diminution was documented in Chapter 7.[364] (According to World Bank

---

363. National Bureau of Statistics of China, http://www.stats.gov.cn/english/Statisticaldata/AnnualData/, various years.

364. The labor-surplus model of economic growth indicates that at the onset of economic development surplus labor, i.e., workers who earn a wage exceeding the value of what they can add to output, but whose employment is required by tradition, moves to the city. Wages do not rise until all such surplus labor is siphoned off, at which point the agricultural and growing industrial sectors must compete for workers in the usual way. After this turning point, wages continually rise. The idea was developed in W. Arthur Lewis, "Economic Development with Unlimited Supplies of Labour," *Manchester School* 22, no. 2 (May 1954): 139–191, and substantially extended in John C. H. Fei and Gustav Ranis, *Development of the Labor Surplus Economy: Theory and Policy* (Homewood, Illinois: Richard A. Irwin, 1964).

figures, China's population became majority urban for the first time in history in 2011.[365]) It is true that the surveillance state is much more thorough than the *hùkǒu* system. It was further enabled by COVID-era imposition of health codes limiting travel or even exit from one's home and was soon used to suppress political dissent. However, the purpose of extension is such suppression, and not facilitating Maoist central economic planning.

More broadly, in 2018 the *New York Times* surveyed figures provided by the All-China Federation of Industry and Commerce, an organization originally formed in 1953 to facilitate the transition to communism but now with a broader mission and with guaranteed representation in the National People's Congress. Its work indicated that "[t]oday, the private sector contributes nearly two-thirds of the country's growth and nine-tenths of new jobs."[366] Referring to China's "private sector," the World Economic Forum in 2019 said that these companies contribute "60% of China's GDP, and are responsible for 70% of innovation, 80% of urban employment and provide 90% of new jobs. Private wealth is also responsible for 70% of investment and 90% of exports."[367] Total market capitalization in the Shenzhen stock exchange increased at a 28.8 percent annual rate between 1995 and 2019, while the equivalent figure for the American NASDAQ index over the same time interval was just 10.83 percent.[368] The important point is not that the Chinese index grew faster than the American one over these years, despite the NASDAQ being the U.S. index where companies involved in new technologies are most highly represented. Rather, it is that (as with every other similar measure in China) growth in listed joint-stock companies indicates dramatic long-term growth in the private sector. It is true that state influence in these companies may remain; some are significantly owned by government entities or were founded by former government officials. Even from August 1, 2016, to August 1, 2019, i.e., after Xi

---

365. https://data.worldbank.org/indicator/SP.URB.TOTL.IN.ZS?locations=CN.

366. Li Yuan, "Private Businesses Built Modern China. Now the Government Is Pushing Back," *New York Times*, October 3, 2018, https://www.nytimes.com/2018/10/03/business/china-economy-private-enterprise.html.

367. Amir Guluzade, "Explained, the Role of China's State-Owned Companies," World Economic Forum, May 7, 2019, https://www.weforum.org/agenda/2019/05/why-chinas-state-owned-companies-still-have-a-key-role-to-play/.

368. Figures from both indexes calculated from data at https://www.ceicdata.com/en. The figures are based on annual growth rates calculated from August 1, 1995, to August 1, 2019.

Jinping began his second term as president, total capitalization in Shenzhen did not retreat, but grew at five percent annually, even while Chinese economic growth slowed. Despite substantial problems with corruption, the Chinese economy, particularly at the level of daily life, is vastly and probably permanently more liberal than 40 years ago.

CCP language, even under Xi Jinping, reflects the tradeoff between ideological fidelity and practicality. A recent manifestation of the path the country's leadership has set out on is the somewhat cumbersomely phrased "New-era Chinese-style socialism" (新時代中國特色社會主義). But when it comes to many of the essential things of daily life such as food, housing, clothing, energy and even—to a significant (if also significantly corrupt) extent—health care, private companies engaging in a continuous conversation with consumers will carry much of the load, particularly in Chinese cities.[369] Even the hard COVID-19 lockdowns starting in Wuhan in January 2020, and continuing throughout the country until late 2022, significantly relied on private supermarkets and food-delivery companies to provide food to mostly privately owned housing. (It must also be noted that private companies also provided the mandatory tests that Chinese were required to undergo several times a week, and some of them derived substantial profits from this captive customer base.)

Ultimately even in a dictatorial country like China public opinion matters to some extent. For example, in the last few years there have been significant efforts to bring China's urban air pollution under control, and still-limited but growing social-media echoes of the Me Too movement to try to restrain sexual-harassment problems involving Chinese business and political leaders. Most dramatically, after extensive resistance, the central government relaxed its lockdown rules in November 2022 once protests began to appear across the country, with a handful even calling for Xi Jinping and the CCP to cede power. Survey evidence indicates the Chinese people greatly value economic reform, and indeed economic and political liberalism more broadly. At least with respect to economic liberalism, to substantially roll this back by cutting

---

369. On different delivery systems in health care see Xue Han, Yuanyuan Wu and Jie Zheng, *Disruptive Innovation through Digital Transformation: Multi-Sided Platforms of E-Health in China* (Springer 2020), particularly Chapter 3.

Chinese people off from better futures would cause trouble for the CCP.[370]

8.C. Limits on the Limits — Of "Common Prosperity" and other ideas

Of course, China has different leadership than it did earlier and it faces a different domestic and international environment than it did even as recently as 2019. These changes could promote government reticence with respect to further economic liberalization. The country's working-age population is seriously declining, a trend that will slow economic growth. The decline is exacerbated to some still-unknown degree by people who are emigrating from Hong Kong and the rest of China to escape China's political and economic repression. The possibly permanent responses to COVID-19 also present challenges to continuing liberalization. The CCP's efforts to enforce zero-COVID increased substantially both its ability and the population's perhaps grudging acceptance of limits on their movement, the ability of the government to use its powers to reward businesses who did what it asked and punish those who didn't, and the nationalistic tone of its rejection of foreign advice and technology. So too did it increase dissatisfaction among China's young with the current Chinese economic model via, e.g., the recent "lying down" (躺平) movement. This movement advocates, amidst official criticism, that the young stop cooperating with the country's high-pressure "996" (9:00 to 9:00, six days a week) workplace culture. The dispiriting nature of the prolonged and stark limits on any kind of social engagement imposed during COVID-19 may increase this sentiment. And even before 2019 some economists were arguing that the miracle years were over, that China had, like other developing nations before it, fallen into the middle-income trap, where countries benefiting from years of high economic growth suddenly lack it before arriving at the development destination.[371]

---

370. On Chinese enthusiasm for liberalism in all varieties, see the survey results in Iliara Mazzocco and Scott Kennedy, "Public Opinion in China: A Liberal Silent Majority?" Center for Strategic and International Studies, February 9, 2022, https://www.csis.org/features/public-opinion-china-liberal-silent-majority.

371. See, for example, Justin Yi-fu Lin, Peter J. Morgan, and Guanghua Wan (eds), *Slowdown in the People's Republic of China: Structural Factors and the Implications for Asia* (Tokyo: Asian Development Bank Institute, 2018).

And yet the most important limitation derives from the nature of CCP governance itself. Like all absolute political monopolies, what the CCP fears most are threats to its rule and the material and other benefits its leading ranks receive from it. The party's campaigns against perceived political threats are beyond the scope of this book, but the threats the party faces from further economic liberalism are not. Economic liberalism is everywhere a disruptive force, and indeed "disruptive innovation" has become a term of art in the English-language high-technology world in recent years. Dynamic liberalism in previous centuries generated factories, the steam engine and the doors it opened to generating power for human purposes, and the telegraph and subsequent speed-of-light communication methods spurred by the discovery of electromagnetism. More recently the digitization of information is bringing tremendous changes to societies worldwide. Societies that are the most tolerant of such innovation will create most of it.

As Chapter 7 demonstrated, China was in desperate straits when reform and openness began, one of the poorest countries in the world yet with a government still committed to communist economic orthodoxy, as amended by Mao Zedong. Reform after Mao's death was thus initially slow, but as the dramatic results from even modest reforms unfolded wherever they were tried, the Chinese central government and various local governments were compelled— by both the political need to keep up and by public approval of greater economic freedom—to broaden geographically and deepen liberal reforms. Now, the Chinese people have achieved enough prosperity to remove this urgency for the CCP. As a result, its traditional desire to preserve comprehensive social stability, because instability of any social, economic, or political sort brings political risk, looms larger in its decision-making.

And so the CCP's goal is to preserve and if possible even promote a further increase in Chinese prosperity, while keeping social disruption to a minimum. Thus it will maintain ultimate government control (even if sub rosa) over not just activities with direct military uses, e.g., the production of natural resources or military matériel, but even activities where substantial change will be truly disruptive. The eminently representative example is finance. The large Chinese banks described in Chapter 7 are not just politically influential rent-seekers, although that they surely are. They are also entities that allow the government to maintain significant control over who, at the highest levels, gets investment and who does not. Anything that threatens that control is problematic, and if the risks to even short-run social stability from financial innovation are big enough, they must be prevented. This is the biggest reason why the CCP could not abide Ma Yun's Ant Group until such time as it could be sufficiently domesticated. Xi Jinping's wielding of the slogan "common prosperity" (共同富裕) actually dates back decades, and under Deng Xiaoping the phrase entered the CCP charter in 1992. But while Deng used it to advocate that the path to prosperity would benefit from some getting rich first, under Xi Jinping the emphasis has been primarily on the "common" part, with both words and deeds (e.g., a very public campaign against celebrities on charges of evading taxes) targeting China's wealthiest.[372]

In the Deng Xiaoping era the stark reality of China's poverty meant that substantially greater economic liberalism had to be accepted. But today the CCP is what it says it is, a communist party committed since its creation at least nominally to doing things on behalf of the country's working class and in reality, as needed and as seen in Chapter 6, punishing its real or imagined wealthy. In addition, China under economic reform has become a nation playing a much greater geopolitical role. Like every major power before it, its government will subordinate private economic activity to these considerations. And so the way to think about the future of economic liberalism in China is not as one of profound theoretical dedication as occurred in, say, the mid-19th-century United Kingdom. Instead, private economic activity is meant to preserve and, where feasible, promote a rise in the overall Chinese standard of living. With respect to the government's perceived political needs on the one hand and threats from dynamic liberalism on the other, there is already a mix of ongoing liberalization and deliberalization. Because China still has a relatively weak capacity to funnel funds to embryonic companies and to channel investment funds more generally, it continues even since summer 2019 to financially liberalize, although in the CCP style. In July 2019 the Shanghai stock exchange opened an auxiliary entity known in English as the SSE Star Market (科創版, the literal translation is the Science and Technology Version), designed to

---

372. 《中共二十大 習近平的「共同富裕」實質、看點與海外評論》(The 20th National Congress of the Communist Party of China: The essence, highlights and overseas remarks on Xi Jinping's "common prosperity") BBC (author not listed), November 1, 2022, https://www.bbc.com/zhongwen/trad/world-63332234.

help young domestic technology companies raise capital. In September 2021 Xi Jinping announced a similar exchange (technically an upgrade of a more modest existing exchange) in Beijing, the political capital. In July 2022, the securities-regulatory agencies in Hong Kong and the mainland authorized trading on those two stock exchanges of securities marketed to foreigners to enable them to invest in baskets of Chinese companies. And in October 2022 China's government announced rules to standardize procedures and operating rights for individual-owned and other small businesses. The goal was to encourage new ventures, although accompanied by an economically illiberal channel for local governments to fund them and a manifestly illiberal statement that in all business decisions the CCP has the last word.[373]

The events since summer 2019 have caused CCP leadership to accelerate the decoupling of China from the West, subject to the caveats of permitting needed contact, especially allowing more foreign portfolio investment on Chinese terms. Facilitating this decoupling in one way is the China-centric links being built under "One Belt, One Road," an initiative launched by the CCP in 2013 that seeks to build closer economic links primarily although not exclusively with former Soviet entities in Asia. Its goal is the construction of a network in which other countries funnel inputs, notably raw materials, into China and in exchange get both substantial infrastructure investment and access to Chinese manufacturing exports. "One Belt, One Road" is supposed to liberate China from the vagaries of international commodity markets even while providing revenue for Chinese firms, many of them outright state-owned. To critics, it reeks of a quasi-colonial arrangement, with the distant Chinese emperor ruling through local satraps, but, at any rate, it clearly serves the interests of national rulers. China is not the first regional hegemon to integrate nearby countries in this way, but carrying this out, despite encouraging more corruption inside and outside China, is increasingly the globalization road the country is currently traveling.

---

373. 新華社。《促進個體工商戶發展條例》。2022年十月二十五日。(Xinhua New Agency, Regulations on Promoting the Development of Individual Industrial and Commercial Businesses, October 22, 2022, https://baijiahao.baidu.com/s?id=1747649804510896628).

8.D. Conclusion — On China's Future Economic Model

And so the government's approach to economic liberalism in the foreseeable future will involve a belief that some of it is essential to keep the Chinese people satisfied. And some greater liberalization is even necessary to promote growth in the broader industries the CCP sees as in the national interest but for which domestic resources are inadequate. But any industries or activities that threaten a social transformation that in turn threatens the party's political power will be reined in at the first sign of trouble. In addition to the delaying and possible ending of the Ant Group's nascent major experiment in new finance, the government in 2021 substantially restricted the previously booming private-tutoring industry (教培行業). While there is probably some truth to the official account that this was done to rein in excessive competition by parents seeking to help their children get into the most highly selective Chinese universities (consistent with Xi Jinping's account of "common prosperity"), the industry also enabled unmediated parent and student contact with foreign tutors.

While once the Chinese government actively courted foreign direct investment in production facilities so that local would-be entrepreneurs could learn (as had happened in the first liberal era discussed in Chapter 3), the desire to decouple in broader economic terms, particularly with respect to strategic technology, gets stronger by the day. This desire is not unreasonable from the CCP perspective, given the accelerating suspicion in Western countries of its rule. Xi Jinping himself has spoken of the need to achieve more overall self-reliance, and the government is subsidizing specific technology companies in pursuit of this aim.[374] Especially since Russia's invasion of Ukraine, a government that recognizes the need for international economic exchange has nonetheless promoted domestic manufacturing and is attempting to promote such exchange primarily with Russia and Belt and Road countries. Economic liberalism consistent with the country's geopolitical interests and a moderate level of prosperity will be accepted, but no more. Many companies, large ones in particular, may be private on paper but nonetheless face heavy state influence. Indeed, the in-house CCP committees mentioned above in the October 2022 decree standardizing rules for new businesses were already common in

---

374. James T. Areddy, "Fearful of Getting Cut Off, China Pushes for Self-Reliance," *Wall Street Journal*, May 3, 2022.

large companies and found in all universities and other nonprofit organizations for a number of years. They are now being extended to all domestic companies of any size.[375] The word is out to the private sector: make money, but don't make trouble.

The conclusion is perhaps unsatisfying, yet seemingly unavoidable. China's miracle since the late 1970s is real, and no leader can afford to actively undo it. And yet the CCP fears the unpredictable social change that results from dynamic economic liberalism, change that is often accepted in other governments as a necessary price (the classic example is Meiji Japan in the nineteenth century). In very many spheres, the CCP is wielding an ever-broader stick. The new model has its strengths, particularly, when combined with Chinese nationalist attitudes with respect to large, prestigious projects. Thus the birthing of giant dams, space stations and likely future moon landings, staging the Olympic Games, and the rapid construction of hospitals and quarantine facilities in response to an epidemic; the CCP seems unusually good at achieving such projects. But respect for domestic entrepreneurial freedom at some point must always yield to the needs of the CCP. The cost of these limits will be borne not just by the Chinese themselves but by the rest of the world deprived of the fruit of the country's forgone innovations. Since Western first entry after the first Opium War, China has struggled to reconcile itself with economic liberalism. At first too weak to resist it, and then rejecting it for decades because it was seen as humiliating, unjust, and historically obsolete, China's hard-won acknowledgment of its virtues finally emerged after Mao Zedong's death. But its limits, at least under the country's current rulers, are now becoming clearer by the day.

---

375. Scott Livingston, "The Chinese Communist Party Targets the Private Sector," Center for Strategic and International Studies, October 8, 2020, https://www.csis.org/analysis/chinese-communist-party-targets-private-sector.

References

Alan, Robert C. *The British Industrial Revolution in Global Perspective*. Cambridge, UK: Cambridge University Press, 2009.

Allen, Franklin, Jun Qian, Chenyu Shan, and Julie Zhu, "Dissecting the Long-term Performance of the Chinese Stock Market." Social Science Research Network, https://ssrn.com/abstract=2880021 or http://dx.doi.org/10.2139/ssrn.2880021.

Allen, Robert C., Jean-Pascal Bassino, Debin Ma, Christine Moll-Murata, and Jan Luiten Van Zanden. "Wages, Prices, and Living Standards in China, 1738–1925: In Comparison with Europe, Japan, and India." *Economic History Review* 64, no. S1 (February 2011): 8–38.

Anete, A.A. "Middleman and Smallholder Farmers in Cassava Marketing in Africa." *Tropicultura* 27 (2009): 40-44.

Areddy, James T. "Fearful of Getting Cut Off, China Pushes for Self-Reliance." *Wall Street Journal*, May 3, 2022.

Armentrout-Ma, Eve M.B. "Chinese Politics in the Western Hemisphere, 1893–1911: Rivalry Between Reformers and Revolutionaries in the Americas." PhD diss., University of California at Davis, 1977.

Bailey, Paul. "Active Citizen or Efficient Housewife? The Debate over Women's Education in Early-Twentieth-Century China." In *Education, Culture, and Identity in Twentieth-Century China*, edited by Glen Peterson, Ruth Hayhoe, and Yongling Lu. Ann Arbor: University of Michigan Press, 2004, 318–347.

Barnett, Robert W. *Economic Shanghai: Hostage to Politics, 1937–1941*. New York: Institute of Pacific Relations, 1941.

Baten, Joerg, and Jan Luiten van Zanden. "Book Production and the Onset of Modern Economic Growth." *Journal of Economic Growth* 13, no. 3 (September 2008): 217–235.

Baten, Joerg, Debin Ma, Stephen Morgan, and Qing Wang. "Evolution of Living Standards and Human Capital in China in the 18–20th Centuries: Evidences from Real Wages, Age-Heaping, and Anthropometrics." *Explorations in Economic History* 47, no. 3 (July 2010): 347–359.

Baum, Richard. *Burying Mao: Chinese Politics in the Age of Deng Xiaoping*. Princeton, NJ: Princeton University Press, 1994.

Benton, George and Lin Chun, eds., *Was Mao Really a Monster? The Academic Response to Chang and Halliday's "Mao: The Unknown Story."* London: Routledge, 2010.

Bergère, Marie-Claire. *The Golden Age of the Chinese Bourgeoisie 1911–1937*. Translated by Janet Lloyd. Cambridge, UK: Cambridge University Press, 1990.

Bernal, Martin. "The Triumph of Anarchism over Marxism, 1906–1907." In *China in Revolution: The First Phase, 1900–1913*, edited by Mary Clabaugh Wright. New Haven: Yale University Press, 1968, 97-142.

Boecking, Felix, "The Bitterness of Fiscal Realism: Guomindang Tariff Policy, China's Trade in Imported Sugar and Smuggling, 1928–1937," *Harvard Asia Quarterly* 13, no. 2 (2011): 13–20.

Brandt, Loren, Debin Ma, and Thomas G. Rawski. "From Divergence to Convergence: Reevaluating the History Behind China's Economic Boom." *Journal of Economic Literature* 52, no. 1 (March 2014):

45–123.

Brewer, Anthony. "Turgot: Founder of Classical Economics." *Economica*, New Series 54, no. 216 (November 1987): 417–428.

Bulman, Jessica. "Publishing Privacy: Intellectual Property, Self-Expression, and the Victorian Novel." *Hastings Communication and Entertainment Law Journal* 26, no. 1 (January 2003): 73–118.

Chan, Florence. "The Money Making in Ancient China: A Literature Review Journey Through Ancient Texts." *Journal of Business Ethics* 91, Supplement 1 (2010): 17–35.

Chan, Wing-Tsit. *A Sourcebook in Chinese Philosophy*. Princeton, NJ: Princeton University Press,1963.

Chang, Jung, and Jon Halliday. *Mao: The Untold Story*. New York: Anchor, 2011.

Chang, Jung. *Empress Dowager Cixi: The Concubine Who Launched Modern China*. New York: Alfred A. Knopf, 2013.

Chang, Jung. *Wild Swans: Three Daughters of China*, 2nd ed. New York: Touchstone, 2003.

Cheek, Timothy. "On New Democracy January 15, 1940." In *Mao Zedong and China's Revolutions: A Brief History with Documents*, edited by Timothy Cheek, 76–112. London: Palgrave Macmillan, 2002.

Cheek, Timothy. *The Intellectual in Modern Chinese History*. Cambridge, UK: Cambridge University Press, 2015.

Chen, John-Ren. "The Effects of Land Reform on the Rice Sector and Economic Development in Taiwan." *World Development* 22, no. 11 (November 1994): 1759–1770.

Chen, Zhengping. *A Brief History of Finance in China*. Translated by Qian Suqin. Beijing: Social Sciences Academic Press, 2014.

Chen, Zhongping. *Modern China's Network Revolution: Chambers of Commerce and Sociopolitical Change in the Early 20th Century*. Palo Alto: Stanford University Press, 2011.

Chesneaux, Jean, Marianne Bastid, and Marie-Claire Bergère. *China from the Opium Wars to the 1911 Revolution*. Translated by Anne Destanay. New York: Random House, 1976.

Chin, Sei Jeong. "The Historical Origins of the Nationalization of the Newspaper Industry in Modern China: A Case Study of the Shanghai Newspaper Industry, 1937–1953." *The China Review* 13, no. 2 (Fall 2013): 1–34.

Chiu, Y. Stephen, and Ryh-Song Yeh. "Adam Smith versus Sima Qian: Comment on the Tao of Markets." *Pacific Economic Review* 4, no. 1 (February 1999): 79–84.

Choi, Alvin (Jun Young). "History of the Tomato in Italy and China: Tracing the Role of Tomatoes in Italian and Chinese Cooking." On *Noodles on the Silk Road* (blog), July 13, 2018, https://scholarblogs.emory.edu/noodles/2018/07/03/history-of-the-tomato-in-italy-and-china-tracing-the-role-of-tomatoes-in-italian-and-chinese-cooking/.

Dikötter, Frank. *The Age of Openness: China before Mao*. Berkeley: University of California Press, 2008.

Chow, Kai-Wing. *Publishing, Culture, and Power in Early Modern China*. Palo Alto: Stanford University Press, 2004.

Chung, Stephanie Po-yin. *Chinese Business Groups in Hong Kong and Political Change in South China, 1900–1925*. New York: St. Martin's Press, 1998.

Coase, Ronald. "The Lighthouse in Economics." *Journal of Law and Economics* 17, no. 2 (October 1974): 357–376.

Coble, Parks M. Jr., *The Shanghai Capitalists and the Nationalist Government 1927–1937*. Cambridge, MA: Harvard University Press, 1980.

Cochran, Sherman. *Encountering Chinese Networks: Western, Japanese, and Chinese Corporations in China, 1880–1937*. Berkeley: University of California Press, 2000.

"The Common Program of the Chinese People's Political Consultative Conference." In *The Common Program and Other Documents of the First Plenary Session of the Chinese People's Political Consultative Con-*

ference. Peking: Foreign Language Press, 1950.

Cowen, Tyler. "Is WeChat the Future?" Marginal Revolution (blog), August 11, 2015, https://marginalrevolution.com/marginalrevolution/2015/08/is-wechat-the-future.html.

Culp, Robert. "Local Entrepreneurs, Transnational Networks: Publishing Markets in the Cantonese Communities Within and Across National Borders." In *The Business of Culture: Cultural Entrepreneurs in China and Southeast Asia, 1900–1965*, edited by Christopher Rea and Nicolai Volland. Vancouver, Canada: UBC Press, 2015, 181–206.

Davis, Walter W. "China, the Confucian Ideal, and the European Age of Enlightenment." *Journal of the History of Ideas* 44, no. 4 (October-December 1983): 523–548.

De Bary, William Theodore. *The Liberal Tradition in China*. Hong Kong: City University of Hong Kong Press, 1983.

De Soto, Hernando. *The Mystery of Capital: Why Capitalism Succeeds in The West and Fails Everywhere Else*. New York: Basic Books, 2000.

Deng, Kent G., *China's Political Economy in Modern Times: Changes and Economic Consequences, 1800–2000*. London: Routledge, 2011.

Deng, Xiaoping. "Excerpts from Talks Given in Wuchang, Shenzhen, Zhuhai and Shanghai." *Selected Works of Deng Xiaoping, 1982–1992*. Beijing: People's Publishing House: 358–370.

Dikötter, Frank. *The Cultural Revolution: A People's History*. New York: Bloomsbury, 2017.

Dikötter, Frank. *The Tragedy of Liberation: A History of the Chinese Revolution 1945–1957*. New York: Bloomsbury, 2013.

Dikötter, Frank. *Mao's Great Famine: The History of China's Most Devastating Catastrophe, 1958–1962*. New York: Walker & Co., 2010.

Dillon, Michael. *China: A Modern History*.

London: I.B. Tauris, 2010.

Dirlik, Arif. "The Ideological Foundations of the New Life Movement: A Study in Counterrevolution." *Journal of Asian Studies* 34, no. 4 (August 1975): 945–980.

Dirlik, Arlif, and Edward S. Krebs. "Socialism and Anarchism in Early Republican China." *Modern China*, no. 2 (April 1981): 117–151.

Dunch, Ryan. "Mission Schools and Modernity: The Anglo-Chinese College, Fuzhou." In *Education, Culture, and Identity in Twentieth-Century China*, edited by Glen Peterson, Ruth Hayhoe, and Yongling Lu. Ann Arbor: University of Michigan Press, 2004, 109–146.

Ebrey, Patricia Buckley. "State-Forced Relocations in Imperial China, 900–1300." In *State Power in China, 900–1325*, edited by Patricia Buckley Ebrey and Paul Jakov Smith. Seattle: University of Washington Press, 2016, 307–340.

Elleman Bruce A. *Modern Chinese Warfare, 1795–1989*. London: Routledge, 2001.

Elman, Benjamin A. *A Cultural History of Modern Science in China*. Cambridge, MA: Harvard University Press, 2009.

Engels, Friedrich. *The Principles of Communism, an Early Draft of The Communist Manifesto 1847*. Study Guide for Engels's *The Principles of Communism*, Marxists International Archive, https://www.marxists.org/archive/marx/works/1847/11/prin-com.htm.

Fallows, James. *Looking at the Sun: The Rise of the New East Asian Economic and Political System*. New York: Pantheon, 1994.

Fang, Lily H., Josh Lerne and. Chaopeng Wu. "Intellectual Property Rights, Ownership, and Innovation: Evidence from China." *The Review of Financial Studies* 30, no. 7 (July 1, 2017): 2246–2477.

Fay, Peter Ward. *The Opium War: 1840–1842*, 2nd ed. Chapel Hill: University of North Carolina Press, 1997.

Fei, John C. H., and Gustav Ranis, *Development of the Labor Surplus Economy: Theory and Policy*. Homewood, Illinois: Richard A. Irwin, 1964.

Feigon, Lee. *Chen Duxiu, Founder of the Chinese Communist Party*. Princeton, NJ: Princeton University Press, 2014.

Fenby, Jonathan. "Storm Rages over Bestselling Book on Monster Mao." *The Guardian*. Dec. 3, 2005, https://www.theguardian.com/uk/2005/dec/04/china.books.

Ferdoushi, Zannatul, Xiang-Guo Zhang, and Mohammed Rajiv Husan. "Mud Crab (Scylla esp.) Marketing System in Bangladesh." *Asian Journal of Food and Agro-Industry* 3, no. 2 (2010): 248–265.

Frankel, Charles. "Does Liberalism Have a Future?» In *Relevance of Liberalism*, edited by Zbigniew Brzezinski. Boulder, CO: Westview Press, 1978, 97–134.

Fuller, Pierre. "Changing Disaster Relief Regimes in China: An Analysis Using Four Famines Between 1876 and 1962." *Disasters* 39, no. S2 (Supplemental Issue, 2015): S146–S165.

Fuller, Pierre. "North China Famine, 1920–21." Disasters.org, http://www.disaster-history.org/north-china-famine-1920-21.

Fuller, Pierre. "North China Famine Revisited: Unsung Native Relief in the Warlord Era." *Modern Asian Studies* 47, no. 3 (May 2013): 820–850.

Gan, Jie, and Yan Guo, "Decentralized Privatization and Change of Control Rights in China." *Review of Financial Studies* 31, no. 10 (October 2018): 3854–3894.

Gandy, D. Ross. *Marx and History: From Primitive Society to the Communist Future*. Austin: University of Texas Press, 1979.

Garcia, Manuel Pérez. "Challenging National Narratives: On the Origins of Sweet Potato in China as Global Commodity During the Early Modern Period." In *Global History and New Polycentric Approaches*. Palgrave Studies in Comparative Global History: Europe, Asia and America in a World Network System, edited by Manuel Perez Garcia and Lucio De Sousa, 53–80. Singapore: Palgrave Macmillan, 2017.

General Office of the Central Committee of the Communist Party of China. *Socialist Upsurge in China's Countryside*. Beijing: Foreign Languages Press, 1957.

Geng, Yunzhi. *Evolution in Ideology and Culture after the Opium Wars and Up to The Westernization Movement*. Berlin: Springer-Verlag, 2015.

Goldin, Claudia. "The U-Shaped Female Labor Force Function in Economic Development and Economic History." In *Investment in Women's Human Capital and Economic Development*, edited by T. Paul Schultz. Chicago: University of Chicago Press, 1995, 61–90.

Goldman, Merle, and Leo Ou-Fan Lee, eds. *An Intellectual History of Modern China*. Cambridge, UK: Cambridge University Press, 2002.

Goodman, Bryna. "Democratic Calisthenics: The Culture of Urban Associations in the New Republic." In *Changing Meanings of Citizenship in Modern China*, edited by Merle Goldman and Elizabeth J. Perry. Cambridge, MA: Harvard University Press, 2002, 70–109.

Gregor, A. James, and Maria Hsia Chang. "Marxism, Sun Yat-sen, and the Concept of 'Imperialism.'" *Pacific Affairs* 55, no. 1 (Spring 1982): 54–79.

Greider, Jerome. *Hu Shih and the Chinese Renaissance: Liberalism in the Chinese Revolution, 1917–1937*. Cambridge, MA: Harvard University Press, 1962.

Greider, Jerome. *Intellectuals and the State in Modern China*. New York: Free Press, 1983.

Guluzade, Amir. "Explained, the Role of China's State-Owned Companies." World Economic Forum, May 7, 2019, https://www.weforum.org/agenda/2019/05/why-chinas-state-owned-companies-still-have-a-key-role-to-play/.

Han, Xue, Yuanyuan Wu, and Jie Zheng. *Disruptive Innovation through Digital Transformation: Multi-Sided Platforms of E-Health in China*. New York: Springer, 2020.

Hao, Y'en-Ping. "Cheng Kuang-Ying: The Comprador as Reformer." *Journal of Asian Studies* 29, no. 1 (November 1969): 15–22.

Hao, Yen-p'ing. "A 'New Class' in China's Treaty Ports: The Rise of the Comprador-Merchants." *Business History Review* 44, no. 4 (Winter, 1970): 446–459.

Hardin, Garrett. "The Tragedy of the Commons." *Science* 162, no. 3859 (December 13, 1968): 1243–1248.

Harrison, Henrietta. "The Qianlong Emperor's Letter to George III and the Early-Twentieth-Century Origins of Ideas about Traditional China's Foreign Relations." *American Historical Review* 122, no. 3 (June 2017): 680–701.

Hart, Robert, and James Duncan Campbell. *The I.G. in Peking: Letters of Robert Hart, Chinese Maritime Customs, 1868–1907*, edited by John King Fairbank and Katherine F. Bruner. Cambridge, MA: Harvard University Press, 1975.

Hayek, Friedrich A. "The Uses of Knowledge in Society." *American Economic Review* 35, no. 4 (September 1945): 519–530.

Heaver, Stuart. "How the White Russian Refugee Crisis Unfolded a Century Ago, and the Lucky Ones Who Made it to Hong Kong." *South China Morning Post*, May 7, 2017, https://www.scmp.com/magazines/post-magazine/long-reads/article/2092988/how-white-russian-refugee-crisis-unfolded-china.

Hsia, C.T. *A History of Modern Chinese Fiction*, 3rd edition. New York: Columbia University Press, [1961] 2016.

Hsia, Tsai-An. *The Gate of Darkness: Studies on the Leftist Literary Movement in China*. Seattle: University of Washington Press, 1968.

Hsiao, Kung-Chuan. *A Modern China and a New World: K'ang Yu-Wei, Reformer and Utopian, 1858–927*. Seattle: University of Washington Press, 1978.

Huang, Max Ko-Wu. *The Meaning of Freedom: Yan Fu and the Origins of Chinese Liberalism*. Hong Kong: The Chinese University Press, 2008.

Huang, Yiping, and Xun Wang. "Strong on Quantity, Weak on Quality: China's Financial Reform Between 1998 and 2018." In *China's 40 Years of Reform and Development: 1978–2018*, edited by Ross Garnaut, Ligang Song, and Cai Fang. Acton, Australia: ANU Press, 2018, 291–312.

Janku, Andrea. "The Internationalisation of Disaster Relief in Early Twentieth-Century China." *Berliner China-Hefte / Chinese History and Society* 43 (2013): 6–28.

Ji, Zhaojin. *A History of Modern Shanghai Banking*. Armonk, NY: M.E. Sharpe, 2003.

Jia, Ruixue. "The Legacies of Forced Freedom: China's Treaty Ports." *Review of Economics and Statistics* 96, no. 4 (October 2014): 596–608.

Jie, Yang. "China to Let Power Prices Rise in Bid to Fix Electricity Crunch." *Wall Street Journal*, October 12, 2021.

Kestenbaum, David, and Jacob Goldstein. "Secret Document that Transformed China." National Public Radio, January 20, 2012, https://www.npr.org/sections/money/2012/01/20/145360447/the-secret-document-that-transformed-china.

Kestenbaum, David, and Jacob Goldstein. Secret Document that Transformed China." National Public Radio, January 20, 2012, https://www.npr.org/sections/money/2012/01/20/145360447/the-secret-document-that-transformed-china.

Kim, Stuart. "Privatizing the Network: Private Contributions and Road Infrastructure in Late Imperial China (1500–1900)." In *Highways, Byways, and Road Systems in the Pre-Modern World*, edited by Susan E. Alcock, John Bodel, and Richard J. A. Talbert. New York: John Wiley & Sons, 2012, 66–89.

Kim, Sungmoon. "Confucianism and Acceptable Inequalities." In *Philosophy and Social Criticism* 39, no. 10 (December 2013): 983–1004.

Kirby, William C. "China Unincorporated: Company Law and Business Enterprise in Twentieth-Century China." *Journal of*

Asian Studies 54, no. 1 (February 1995): 43–63.

Klaar, Victor C. "Ethics and Economics." In *21st Century Economics: A Reference Handbook*, edited by Rhona C. Free. London: Sage, 2010, 891–900.

Knight, Melvin M., Harry Elmer Barnes, and Felix Flugel. *Economic History of Europe in Modern Times*. Boston: Houghton Mifflin, 1928.

Kow, Simon. "Enlightenment Universalism? Bayle and Montesquieu on China." *European Legacy* 19, no. 3 (2014): 347–358.

Krueger, Anne O. «The Political Economy of the Rent-Seeking Society.» *American Economic Review* 64, no. 3 (June 1974): 291–303.

Ladany, Laszlo. *The Communist Party of China and Marxism 1921–1985: A Self-Portrait*. Hong Kong: Hong Kong University Press, 1992.

Landes, David S. "Why Europe and the West? Why not China?" *Journal of Economic Perspectives* 20, no. 2 (Spring 2006): 3–22.

Lee, Leo Ou-Fan, and Andrew J. Nathan. "The Beginning of Mass Culture: Journalism and Fiction in the late Ch'ing." In *Popular Culture in Late Imperial China*, edited by David Johnson, Andrew J. Nathan, and Evelyn S. Rawski. Berkeley: University of California Press, 1985.

Lenin, Vladimir. "The Development of Capitalism in Russia." Marxists International Archive, https://www.marxists.org/archive/lenin/works/1899/dcr8i/i8v.htm.

Leonard, Kate. *Wei Yuan and China's Rediscovery of the Maritime World*. Cambridge, MA: Harvard University Press, 1984.

Lewis, W. Arthur. "Economic Development with Unlimited Supplies of Labour." *The Manchester School* 22, no. 2 (May 1954): 139–191.

Li, Hua-Yu. *Mao and the Economic Stalinization of China, 1948–1953*. Lanham, MD: Rowman & Littlefield, 2006

Li, Yuan. "Private Businesses Built Modern China. Now the Government Is Pushing Back." *New York Times*, October 3, 2018, https://www.nytimes.com/2018/10/03/business/china-economy-private-enterprise.html.

Liang, Qichao. "On Women's Education." In *The Birth of Chinese Feminism: Essential Texts in Transnational Theory*, edited by Lydia H. Liu, Rebecca H. Karl, and Dorothy Ko. New York: Weatherhead East Asian Institute, Columbia University, 2013, 189–203.

Lin, Justin Yifu. "The Needham Puzzle: Why the Industrial Revolution Did Not Originate in China." *Economic Development and Cultural Change* 43, no. 2 (January 1995): 269–292.

Lin, Justin Yifu, Pete J. Morgan, and Guanghua Wan, eds., *Slowdown in the People's Republic of China: Structural Factors and the Implications for Asia*. Tokyo: Asian Development Bank Institute, 2018.

Lin, Shaowei. "The Empirical Studies of China's Enterprise Bankruptcy Law: Problems and Improvements." *International Insolvency Review* 27 (2018): 77–109.

Ling, Huping. "A History of Chinese Female Students in the United States, 1880s–1990s." *Journal of American Ethnic History* 16, no. 3 (Spring 1997): 81–109.

Livingston, Scott. "The Chinese Communist Party Targets the Private Sector." Center for Strategic and International Studies, October 8, 2020, https://www.csis.org/analysis/chinese-communist-party-targets-private-sector.

Loh, Rodney, and Humphrey Evans. *Escape from Red China*. New York: Coward-McCann, 1962.

Lovely, William, Xiao Zhenyu, Li Bohua, and Ronald Freedman. "The Rise in Female Education in China: National and Regional Patterns." *China Quarterly* 121 (March 1990): 61–93.

Lu, Duanfang. "Third World Modernism: Utopia, Modernity, and the People's Commune in China." *Journal of Architectural Education* 60, no. 3 (February 2007):

40–48.

Lu, Hanchao. "Bourgeois Comfort under Proletarian Dictatorship: Home Life of Chinese Capitalists before the Cultural Revolution." *Journal of Social History* 52, no. 1 (September 2018): 74–100.

Ma, Debin. "Economic Growth in the Lower Yangzi Region of China in 1911-1937: A Quantitative and Historical Analysis." *Journal of Economic History* 68, no. 2 (June 2008): 355–392.

Ma, Tao. "Confucian Thought on the Free Economy." In *The History of Ancient Chinese Economic Thought*, edited by Cheng Lin, Terry Peach, and Wang Fang, 153–165. London: Routledge, 2014.

Macartney, Robbins, Helen Henrietta, and George Macartney. *Our First Ambassador to China: An Account of the Life of George, Earl of Macartney, with Extracts from His Letters, and the Narrative of His Experience*. Cambridge, UK: Cambridge University Press, 2011.

Mallory, Walter H. "China's New Tariff Autonomy." *Foreign Affairs*, April 1929, https://www.foreignaffairs.com/articles/china/1929-04-01/chinas-new-tariff-autonomy.

Mao, Zedong. "Report on an Investigation of the Peasant Movement in Hunan (March 1927)." Marxists International Archive, https://www.marxists.org/reference/archive/mao/selected-works/volume-1/mswv1_2.htm.

Marmé, Michael. "From Suzhou to Shanghai: A Tale of Two Systems." *Journal of Chinese History* 2 (2018): 79–107.

Marx, Karl and Friedrich Engels. *The Communist Manifesto: A Modern Edition*, edited by Eric Hobsbawm. London: Verso, 2012.

Marx, Karl. *A Contribution to the Critique of Political Economy*, 2nd edition. Translated by N.I. Stone. Chicago: Charles H. Kerr & Company, 1904.

Marx, Karl. *Capital: A Critique of Political Economy, Volume 1*. Translated by Ben Fowkes. New York: Vintage Books, 1977.

Mazzocco, Iliara, and Scott Kennedy. "Public Opinion in China: A Liberal Silent Majority?" Center for Strategic and International Studies, February 9, 2022, https://www.csis.org/features/public-opinion-china-liberal-silent-majority.

McCloskey, Deirdre. *Bourgeois Dignity: Why Economics Can't Explain the Modern World*. Chicago: University of Chicago Press, 2010.

McCloskey, Deirdre. *Bourgeois Equality: How Ideas, Not Capital or Institutions, Enriched the World*. Chicago: University of Chicago Press, 2017.

McCloskey, Deirdre. *The Bourgeois Virtues: Ethics for an Age of Commerce*. Chicago: University of Chicago Press, 2006.

McCord, Edward A. "Reevaluating the Nanjing Decade: A Provincial Perspective." Unpublished manuscript, https://aacs.ccny.cuny.edu/2012conference/Papers/McCord,%20Edward.pdf.

McCormick, Ken. "Sima Qian and Adam Smith." *Pacific Economic Review* 4, no. 1 (February 1999): 85–87.

McDermott, Joseph P. *A Social History of the Chinese Book: Books and Literati Culture in Late Imperial China*. Hong Kong: Hong Kong University Press, 2006.

Meisner, Maurice. *Mao's China and After: A History of the People's Republic*, 3rd edition. New York: Simon and Schuster, 1986.

Menger, Carl. *Grundsatzë der Volkswirtschafster*. Wien: Wilhelm Braumüller, 1871. [Carl Menger, *Principles of Economics*. Vienna: Wilhelm Braumüller, 1871].

Mill, John Stuart. *On Liberty*, edited by David Bromwich and George Kate. New Haven: Yale University Press, 2003.

Mishra, Panjak. "Staying Power: Mao and the Maoists.» *New Yorker*, December 27, 2010, https://www.newyorker.com/magazine/2010/12/20/staying-power-3.

Mitsuda, Naoki. "Shanghainese Grow Nostalgic for 'Lost Taste' of the City." *Nikkei Asian Review*, October 2, 2018, https://asia.nikkei.com/Life-Arts/Life/Shanghainese-grow-nostalgic-for-lost-taste-of-the-city.

Mokyr, Joel. *A Culture of Growth: The Origins of the Modern Economy*. Princeton, NJ: Princeton University Press, 2017.

Mokyr, Joel. *The Lever of Riches: Technological Creativity and Economic Progress*. New York: Oxford University Press, 1992.

Mokyr, Joseph. *The Enlightened Economy: An Economic History of Great Britain, 1700–1859*. New Haven: Yale University Press, 2009.

Morgan, Kelly, Joel Mokyr, and Cormac Ó Gráda. "Precocious Albion: A New Interpretation of the British Industrial Revolution." *Annual Review of Economics*, no. 6 (2014): 363–391.

Morgan, Stephen L. "Economic Growth and the Biological Standard of Living in China, 1880–1930." *Economics & Human Biology* 2, no. 2 (June 2004): 197–218.

Nathan, Andrew J. *Chinese Democracy*. New York: Knopf, 1986.

Nathan, Andrew James. *A History of the China International Famine Relief Commission*. Cambridge, MA: East Asian Research Center, Harvard University, 1965.

National Bureau of Statistics of China, various years, http://www.stats.gov.cn/english/Statisticaldata/AnnualData/.

Naughton, Barry. *The Chinese Economy: Transitions and Growth*. Cambridge, MA: MIT Press, 2007.

Needham, Joseph. *Science and Civilisation in China, Vols. 1–7*. Cambridge, UK: Cambridge University Press, 1954–2007.

Needham, Joseph. *The Grand Titration: Science and Society in East and West*. Abingdon, UK: Routledge, 2013.

Osborne, Evan. *Self-Regulation and Human Progress: How Society Gains When We Govern Less*. Palo Alto, CA: Stanford University Press, 2018.

Paltemaa, Lauri. "The Maoist Urban State and Crisis: Comparing Disaster Management in the Great Tianjin Flood in 1963 and the Great Leap Forward Famine." *China Journal* 66 (July 2011): 25–51.

Pan, Lynn. *When True Love Came to China*. Hong Kong: Hong Kong University Press, 2015.

Pan, Ming-Te. "Rural Credit in Ming-Qing Jiangnan and the Concept of Peasant Petit Commodity Production." *Journal of Asian Studies* 55, no. 1 (February 1996): 94–117.

Pomeranz, Kenneth. *The Great Divergence: Europe, China, and the Making of the Modern World Economy*. Princeton, NJ: Princeton University Press, 2000.

Posner, Richard A. *Economic Analysis of Law*, 8th edition. New York: Wolters Kluwer, 2011.

"The Provisional Constitution of the Republic of China," English translation. *American Journal of International Law* 6, no. 3, Supplement, Official Documents (July 1912): 149–154.

Rensselaer, W. Lee III. "General Aspects of Chinese Communist Religious Policy, with Soviet Comparisons." *China Quarterly* 19 (1964):161–173.

Rickett, W. Allyn. *Guanzi: Political, Economic and Philosophical Essays from Early China*. Princeton: Princeton University Press, 1998.

Robinson, Joan. "Notes from China." *Economic Weekly* (February 1964): 195–207.

Robinson, Joan. *The Cultural Revolution in China*. London: Penguin, 1970.

Rong, Zou. *The Revolutionary Army: A Chinese Nationalist Tract of 1903*. Translated by John Lust. Paris: Mouton, 1968.

Rosen, Daniel H. "China's Economic Reckoning: The Price of Failed Reforms." *Foreign Affairs* 100, no. 4 (July-August 2021): 20–29.

Rummel, Robert. *China's Bloody Century: Genocide and Mass Murder Since 1900*. London: Transaction Publishers, 2007.

Samuelson, Paul A. "The Pure Theory of Public Expenditure." *Review of Economics and Statistics* 36, no. 4 (November 1954): 386–389.

Schell, Orville. "China's Hidden Democratic

Legacy." *Foreign Affairs* 83, no. 4 (August 2004): 116–124.

Schoppa, R. Keith. *Chinese Elites and Political Change: Zhejiang Province in the Early Twentieth Century*. Cambridge, MA: Harvard University Press, 1982.

Schwartz, Benjamin. *In Search of Wealth and Power: Yen Fu and the West*. Cambridge, MA: Harvard University Press, 1964.

Shai, Aron. *The Fate of British and French Firms in China: Imperialism Imprisoned*. Basingstoke, UK: Macmillan, 1996.

Shi, Hu. "Conflict of Cultures," in *Hu Shih, English Writings of Hu Shih: Chinese Philosophical and Intellectual Writing, Volume 2*, edited by Chih-Ping Chou. Berlin: Springer, [1932] 2013, 46–56.

Shi, Lei. "Moving to Shanghai: The Massive Internal Migration to the First Chinese Megacity (1927–1937)." Working paper, Spanish Association of Economic History, July 2015, https://www.aehe.es/wp-content/uploads/2015/04/dt-ae-he-1510.pdf.

Shiroyama, Tomoko. *China During the Great Depression: Market, State, and the World Economy, 1929–1937*. Cambridge, MA: Harvard University Asia Center, 2008.

Shiue, Carol H. and Wolfgang Keller. "Markets in China and Europe on the Eve of the Industrial Revolution." *American Economic Review* 97, no. 4 (September 2007): 1189–1216.

Sima, Qian. *Records of the Grand Historian, Vol. II: The Age of Emperor Wu 142 to circa 100 B.C.* Translated by Burton Watson. New York: Renditions-Columbia University Press, 1961.

Slowdown in the People's Republic of China: Structural Factors and the Implications for Asia. Tokyo: Asian Development Bank Institute, 2018.

Smith, Adam. *An Inquiry into the Nature and Causes of the Wealth of Nations*. Chicago: University of Chicago Press, [1776] 1976.

Snow, Edgar. *Red Star Over China*. New York: Grove Press, 1961.

Sowell, Thomas. *Race and Culture: A World View*. New York: Basic Books, 1994.

Spence, Jonathan. *The Gate of Heavenly Peace: The Chinese and Their Revolution*. New York: Penguin, 1982.

Spence, Jonathan. *The Search for Modern China*, 3rd edition. New York: W. W. Norton, 2012.

Spencer, Frederick. "Chiang Kai-Shek's Dictatorship Stumbles." *China Today* 1 (December 1934).

Spencer, Herbert. *The Study of Sociology*. New York: D. Appleton, 1904.

Stewart, Dugald. "Account of the Life and Writings of Adam Smith." In Dugald Stewart, *The Works of Dugald Stewart in Seven Volumes. Volume 7*. Cambridge, UK: Hilliard and Brown, 1829.

Stigler, George. "The Economics of Information." *Journal of Political Economy* 69, no. 3 (June 1961): 213–225.

Suzuki, Shinzo. *Civilization and Empire: China and Japan's Encounter with European International Society*. London: Routledge, 2009.

Taiwan Documents Project. "Treaty of Peace" (Treaty of Shimonoseki). Taiwan Documents Project, http://taiwandocuments.org/shimonoseki01.htm.

Tang, Lixing. *Merchants and Society in Modern China: From Guild to Chamber of Commerce*. London: Routledge, 2017.

Taylor, Robert. "Education and University Enrolment Policies in China, 1949-1971," *Contemporary China Papers*. Canberra: Australian National University Press, 1973.

Temple, Robert. *The Genius of China: 3000 Years of Science, Discovery and Invention*. New York: Simon and Schuster, 1986.

Thompson, Earl A. "The Tulipmania: Fact or Artifact?" *Public Choice* 130, nos. 1–2 (January 2007): 99–114.

Thompson, Thomas N. *China's Nationalization of Foreign Firms: The Politics of Hostage Capitalism, 1949-57*. Occasional Paper/Reprint Series in Contemporary Asian

Studies. Baltimore: University of Maryland School of Law, 1979.

Trescott, Paul B. *Jingji Xue: The History of the Introduction of Western Economic Ideas into China, 1850–1950*. Hong Kong: The Chinese University Press, 2007.

Tsai, Weipin. *Reading Shenbao: Nationalism, Consumerism and Individuality in China 1919–37*. London: Palgrave Macmillan, 2009.

Tsai, Jung-Fang. "The Predicament of the Comprador Ideologists: He Qi (Ho Kai, 1859–1914) and Hu Liyuan (1847–1916)." *Modern China* 7, no. 2, 191–225.

Tullock, Gordon. "The Welfare Costs of Tariffs, Monopolies, and Theft." *Western Economic Journal* 5, no. 3 (June 1967): 224–232.

Van Dyke, Paul A. *The Canton Trade: Life and Enterprise on the China Coast, 1700–1845*. Hong Kong: Hong Kong University Press, 2005.

Van Zanden, Jan Luiten. "Explaining the Global Distribution of Book Production before 1800." In *Technology, Skills in the Pre-Modern Economy in the East and West*, edited by Maarten Prak and Jan Luiten von Zanden. Leiden: Brill, 2013, 321–340.

Von Glahn, Richard. *The Economic History of China: From Antiquity to the Nineteenth Century*. Cambridge, UK: Cambridge University Press, 2016.

Wakeman, Frederic Jr. *Policing Shanghai 1927–1937*. Berkeley: University of California Press, 1995.

Wang, Hsien-Chun. "Discovering Steam Power in China, 1840s–1860s." *Technology and Culture* 51, no. 1 (January 2010): 31–54.

Wasserstrom, Jeffrey N. *Global Shanghai, 1850–2010: A History in Fragments*. London: Routledge, 2009.

Winseck, Dwayne R., and Robert M. Pike. *Communication and Empire: Media, Markets, and Globalization, 1860–1930*. Durham, NC: Duke University Press, 2007.

Wittfogel, Karl A. "The Marxist View of China (Part 1)." *China Quarterly* 11 (July-September 1962): 1–20.

Wong, Young-Tsu. "Revisionism Reconsidered: Kang Youwei and the Reform Movement of 1898." *Journal of Asian Studies* 51, no. 3 (August 1992): 513–544.

Wu, Jinglian, and Guochuan Ma. *Whither China? Restarting the Reform Agenda*. Translated by Xiaofeng Hua and Nancy Hearst. Oxford: Oxford University Press, 2016).

Xu, Xiaoqun. *Chinese Professionals and the Republican State: The Rise of Professional Associations in Shanghai, 1912–1937*. Cambridge, UK: Cambridge University Press, 2000.

Yan, Fu. "Learning from the West." In *China's Response to the West: A Documentary Survey, 1839–1923*, edited by Ssu-yü Teng and John K. Fairbank. Cambridge: Harvard University Press, 1979, 150–151.

Yang Jisheng, *Tombstone: The Untold Story of Mao's Great Famine*. Translated by. Stacy Mosher and Guo Jian, edited by Edward Friedman, Stacy Mosher, and Guo Jian. New York; Farrah, Strauss and Giroux, reprint edition, 2012.

Yang, Shu. "I Am Nora, Hear Me Roar: The Rehabilitation of the Shrew in Modern Chinese Theater." *Nan Nü* 18 (2016): 291–325.

Yeh, Wen-Hsin. "Shanghai Modernity: Commerce and Culture in a Republican City." *China Quarterly* 150 (June 1997): 375–394.

You, Jong-Sung. *Democracy, Inequality and Corruption: Korea, Taiwan and the Philippines Compared*. Cambridge, UK: Cambridge University Press, 2014.

Young, Earnest P. *The Presidency of Yuan Shih-Kai: Liberalism and Dictatorship in Early Republican China*. Ann Arbor: University of Michigan Press, 1977.

Young, Jason. *China's Hukou System: Markets, Migrants and Institutional Change*. London: Palgrave Macmillan, 2013.

Young, Leslie. "The Tao of Markets: Sima Qian

and the Invisible Hand." *Pacific Economic Review* 2, no. 1 (September 1996): 137–45.

Zeng, Zhaojin. "Enterprise Archives and Business History in Contemporary China: The Case of the Baojin Company Archive." *Entreprises et Histoire* 90 (April 2018): 145–48.

Zheng, Yongnian, and Yanjie Huang. *Market in State: The Political Economy of Domination in China*. Cambridge, UK: Cambridge University Press, 2018.

Zhou Xu. *The Great Famine in China, 1958–1962: A Documentary History*, edited by Zhou Xun. New Haven: Yale University Press, 2011.

CHINESE-LANGUAGE BIBLIOGRAPHY

《上海民族機器工業第1卷》。北京, 中華書局, 1979年 (Survey of Shanghai Machine Industry, Vol. 1. Beijing: Zhonghua Publishing, 1979)).

王大陽。《摸着石頭過河"的來歷》。《學習時報》。2018年04月09日 (Wang Dayang. "The Origins of 'Touch the Stones to Cross the River.'" *Study Times*, April 9, 2018), http://dangshi.people.com.cn/n1/2018/0409/c85037-29913289.html.

《中共二十大 習近平的「共同富裕」實質、看點與海外評論》。BBC，無名, 2022年11月1日。("The Substance of the CCP's 'Common Prosperity' Campaign." BBC (no author). November 1, 2022, https://www.bbc.com/zhongwen/trad/world-63332234.

卡爾馬克思。《資本論》, 議郭大力和王亞南, 上海：讀書生活出版社, 1938年。(Karl Marx. *Kapital*. Translated by Guo Dali and Wang Yanan. Shanghai: Reading Life Publishing, 1938).

毛澤東,《湖南農民運動考察報告》, 1927年3月。

(Mao Zedong. *Report on an Investigation of the Peasant Movement in Hunan*. March 1927, https://www.marxists.org/reference/archive/mao/selected-works/volume-1/mswv1_2.htm.)

毛澤東, 筆名二十八畫生,「體育之研究」, 新青年, 第3卷第2号, 1917年四月。(Mao Zedong, under pen name "Art Student No. 28. "A Study of Physical Education. *New Youth* 3, no. 2 (April 1917).)

老子,《道德經》, 第五十號篇 (Laozi 15, *Tao Te Ching*), https://ctext.org/dao-de-jing/zh.

弗里德里希·哈耶克。《通向奴役的道路》。滕維藻和朱宗風譯。北京, 商務印書館, 1962年 (Friedrich A. Hayek. *The Road to Serfdom*. Translated by Teng Weizao and Zhu Zhongfeng. Beijing: Commercial Press, 1962).

李大釗。《我的馬克思主義觀》。《新青年》6券5號, 1919年5月。 (Li Dazhao. "My Marxism." *New Youth* 6, no. 5 (May 1919)).

李澤厚。《中國近代思想史論。》北京, 人民出版社, 1982。 (Li Zehou, *A History of Modern Chinese Historical Debates* (Beijing: People's Publishing House, 1982)).

沈俊平。《晚清同文書局的興衰起落與經營方略》。《漢學研究》第33卷第1期, 2015年3月, 261頁至294頁 (Shen Junping. "The Development and Business Strategies of the Tongwen Press in the Late Qing Dynasty." *Chinese Studies* 33, no. 1 (March 2015: 261–294).

周麗卿。《探索現代中國的政治轉型：<新青年>與民初政治, 社會思潮》。台北：台灣學生書局, 2016 年。 (Zhou Liqing. *Exploring Modern China's Political Transformation: "New Youth," Democratic Politics, and Trends in Social Thought*. Taipei: Students Press, 2016.).

姚文元。《評新編歷史劇〈海瑞罷官〉》。《文匯報》, 1965年11月10日 (Yao Wenyuan, "Review of the Historical Drama 'Hai Rui Dismissed from Office.'" *Wenhui Bao* Nov. 11, 1965).

胡適。《美國的婦人》。 無期 (Hu Shi. "American Women." Undated.) https://zh.m.wikisource.org/zh-hant/美國的婦人。

胡適。《文學改良爭議》。《新青年》, 2 券 5 號, 1917年一月。(Hu Shi. "The Debate

Over Literary Reform." *New Youth* 2, no. 5: (January 1917)).

胡適。《我們對於西洋近代文明的態度>》。《現代評論》，第四卷第八十三期，1926年7月10日。 (Hu Shi. "Our Attitude Toward Modern Western Civilization." *Contemporary Review* 4, no. 83 (July 10, 1926). Reprinted in English in Sharon Shih-jiuan Hou and Chih-p'ing Chou. *The Hu Shi Reader*, 19–74. New Haven: Far Eastern Publications, 1990.)

胡適等人。《我們的政治主張》。《努力週刊》，1922年5月，2期14號 (Hu Shi et al. "What We Stand For." *Striving Weekly* 2, no. 14 (May 1922)), http://m.aisixiang.com/data/41352.html).

荀子。《天論》。篇第十五篇。(Xunzi 17, "On Nature" 17). https://ctext.org/xunzi/tian-lun/zh).

荀子。《王制》篇第九。(Xunzi *The Rule of a True King* 9), https://ctext.org/xunzi/wang-zhi).

荀子。《富國》篇第六。(Xunzi *Enriching the Nation* 6), https://ctext.org/xunzi/fu-guo/zh.

孫中山。《共和言論報》。1912年一拳，75頁至83頁，再出版於《在南京中國同盟會會員餞別會的演說》，以《中國革命的社會主義》為題。《孫中山文集》二券，孟庆鵬編，617頁至620頁。北京，團結出版社，1997年。 (Sun Yat-Sen. "Socialism in the Chinese Revolution." First published in Sun Yat-Sen, "Speeches of the Republic, Volume 1, 1912: 75–83. Published again in Meng Qingpeng, ed., *Collected Works of Sun-Yat Sen*, Volume 2 617–620. Beijing: Unity Publishing, 1997).

亞當·斯密。《國民財富的性質和原因的研究》。郭大力和王亞南譯。北京，商務印書館，2013年。(Adam Smith. *An Inquiry into the Nature and Causes of the Wealth of Nations*. Translated by by Guo Dali and Wang Yanan. Beijing: Commercial Press, 2013).

埃德蒙·伯克。《美國人之自由精神》，譯者劉文典。《新青年》，二券一號,, 1916年。二月 (Edmund Burke. "Americans' Spirit of Liberty." Translated by Liu Wendian. *New Youth* 2, no. 1 (February 1916)'.

徐繼畬。《瀛寰志略》，第四卷，駱驛和劉驍編輯。上海上海書店，2001年 (Xu Jishe, *Summary of the Maritime Realms*, Volume 4. Edited by Luo Yi and Liu Shao. Shanghai: Shanghai Bookstore Publishing House, 2001.)

梁廷柟。《海國四說》。北京，中華書局，1993年。(Liang Tingnan. *Four Accounts From the Maritime Countries*. Beijing: Zhonghua Publishing, 1993.)

黃金麟。《戰爭、身體、現代性》。台北：聯經出版事業公司，2009年 (Huang Jinliu. *War, Body and Modernity*. Taipei: Linkage Publishing, 2009.)

馬俊亞。《混合與發展：江南地區傳統社會經濟的現代演變》第5章。北京，社會科學文獻出版社，2003年。 (Ma Junya. *Blending and Development: The Gradual Evolution of Traditional Society and the Economy in the Jiangnan Region*. Volume 5.Beijing: Social Sciences Academic Press, 2003.)

曾凡。《人力資本與上海近代化》。上海，上海人民出版社，2012年。(Ceng Fan. *Human Capital and the Modernization of Shanghai*. Shanghai: Shanghai People's Publishing Company, 2012.)

章士釗。《經濟學之統原則：以最小之勞費，而求張大的效果》。《新青年》，3卷二號，1917年4月。(Zhang Shizhao. "The Unifying Principles of Economics: Achieving the Greatest Results at the Least Labor Cost." *New Youth* 3, no. 2 (April 1917).)

陳獨秀。《警告青年》。《新青年》，一拳一號，1915年9月。(Chen Duxiu. "A Warning to the Young." *New Youth Magazine* 1, no. 1 (September 1915).)

陳獨秀。《文學革命論》。《新青年》第二券第五期，1917年二月。 (Chen Duxiu. "On Literary Revolution." *New Youth* 2, no. 5 (February 1917).)

陳獨秀，筆名隻眼。《山東問題與國民覺悟》。《每週評論》，第23券，1919年5月26。(Chen Duxiu, under pen name Zhi Yan. "The Shandong Problem and the Chinese People's Awakening." *Weekly Commentary*

23 (May 26, 1919).)

陳獨秀。《新青年罪案之答辯書》。《新青年》, 6卷1號, 1919年, 10頁至11頁. (Chen Duxiu. "A Reply to the Charges Against this Journal." *New Youth* 6, no. 1 (Jan. 5, 1919): 10–11.)

陳獨秀。《談政治》。《新青年》, 1920 年 9月。 (Chen Duxiu. "On Politics." *New Youth* 6, no. 9 (September 1920).)

陳寶榮。《中國個體經濟》。上海社會科學院出版社, 1990年。(Chen Baorong. *China's Private Household Economy.* Shanghai: Shanghai Social Science Academy Press, 1990.)

張忠民。《近代上海工人階層的工資與生活——以20世紀30年代調查為中心的分析》。《中國經濟史研究》, 2卷2期, 1頁至16頁。(Zhang Zhongmin. "The Life and Wages of Shanghai Workers — An Analysis of 1930s Survey Data." *Researches in Chinese History* 2011, no. 2, 1–16.)

張國燾。《我的回憶》, 第一冊。香港：明報月刊出版社, 1974年。(Zhang Guofan, *My Memories,* Volume 1. Hong Kong: Ming Pao Monthly Publications, 1974.)

許新凱。《再論共產主義與基爾特社會主義》。《新青年》, 9卷6號, 1922年7月。(Xu Xinkai. "Again on Communism versus Guild Socialism?" *New Youth* 9, no. 6 (July 1922).)

馮桂芬。《校邠廬抗議》。 (Feng Guifen. *Dissenting Views from a Hut Near Bin.*) https://ctext.org/wiki.pl?if=gb&chapter=916939.

斯影。《毛澤東前秘書李銳告別儀式惹爭議, 歷史資料待公開》。BBC新聞網站。2019年二月二十日。 (Si Ying. "Farewell Ceremony for Li Hui, Former Secretary of Mao Zedong, is Controversial; Historical Information to be Published." *BBC Chinese,* February 20, 2019. Accessed January 8, 2023, https://www.bbc.com/zhongwen/trad/chinese-news-47293517.)

新華社。《促進個體工商戶發展條例》。2022年十月二十五日。(Xinhua New Agency. "Regulations on Promoting the Development of Individual Industrial and Commercial Businesses."

October 22, 2022. Accessed January 8, 2023, https://baijiahao.baidu.com/s?id=1747649804510896628).

新華網時整。《義烏市場是人民創造出來的——記義烏小商品市場的催生培育者謝高華》。2018年12月20日。(*Xinhua Politics.* "The Yiwu Marketplace is the People's Creation." December 20, 2018. Accessed January 8, 2023, http://www.xinhuanet.com/politics/2018-12/20/c_1210020618.htm.)

楊繼繩。《墓碑——一九五八-一九六二年中國大饑荒紀實》。香港, 天地讀書, 2008年。 (Shorter English version published as Yang Jisheng. *Tombstone: The Untold Story of Mao's Great Famine.* Translated by Stacy Mosher and Guo Jian, edited by. Edward Friedman, Stacy Mosher and Guo Jian. New York; Farrah, Strauss and Giroux, 2012.)

熊月之。《略論晚清上海新型文化人的產生與匯聚》。《近代史研究》。1997年04期, 257頁至271頁 (Xiong Yuezhi. "On the Emergence and Convergence of the People of Shanghai's New Culture in the late Qing Dynasty." *Research in Modern History* 1997, no. 04, 257–271.)

劉剛。《齊魯奇荒的一九二七年》。《農學學報》, 2015年11月, 118頁至125頁。 (Liu Gang. "The Grievous Famine in Shandong Province in 1927." *Journal of Agriculture* 2015, no, 5 (November 2015): 118–125.)

水羽信男。《中國自由主義者的分岐：1930年代的胡適和羅隆基》。《胡適與近代中國的理想追尋——紀念胡適先生120歲誕辰國際學術研討會論文集》, 潘光哲編輯。台北, 秀威資訊出版社, 2013年, 270頁至281頁 (Mizuha Nobuo. "The Split Among Chinese Liberals: Hu Shi and Luo Longji in the 1930s." In *Hu Shi and Modern China's Pursuit of Ideas: Proceedings of the International Symposium to Commemorate the 120th Birthday of Mr. Hu Shi,* edited by Pan Kuang-che. Taipei: Showwe Information Co., 2013), 270–281.

歐陽躍峰。《唐廷樞：中國第一位近代企業家》。《安徽師範大學學報（人文社會科學版）》, 2004年第3期, 5頁至11頁。(Ouyang Yuefeng. "Tang Tingshu: The

first Modern Entrepreneur of China."
*Journal of Anhui Normal University
(Philosophy and Social Sciences).* 2004, no.
3, 5–11.)

談遠平。《中國政治思想：儒家與民主化》
。台北市，揚智文化事業，2004年。
(Tan Yuanping. *Chinese Political Thought:
Confucianism and Democratization.* Taipei:
Yang-Chih Book Co., 2004.)

薛暮橋，《中國社會主義經濟問題研究》，北
京，人民出版社，1979年 (Xue Muqiao,
R*esearch in Problems in Chinese Socialist
Economics* (Beijing: People's Publishing,
1979)).

韓承樺。斯賓塞到中國──一個翻譯史的討
論。編譯論叢。2010年9月，第3卷第2
期，33頁至60頁 。(Han Cheng-Hua.
"Spencer Comes to China—A Discussion
of Translation History." *Compilation and
Translation Review* 3, no. 2 (September
2010): 33-–60.)

闞雲平。《中國汽車工業的早期發展中國汽
車工業的早期發展（1920-1978年）》
。 上海人民出版社，2015年。 (Guan
Yunping. *The Early Development of
the Chinese Auto Industry (1920–1978).*
Shanghai: Shanghai People's Publishing
House, 2015.)

嚴復。《論世變之極》。《直報》，1985年2月
4日至5日。 (Yan Fu. "On the Speed of
World Change." *Direct Report*, Feb. 4–5,
1895.)

Index

CL Press

A Fraser Institute Project

https://clpress.net/

Professor Daniel Klein (George Mason University, Economics and Mercatus Center) and Dr. Erik Matson (Mercatus Center), directors of the Adam Smith Program at George Mason University, are the editors and directors of CL Press. CL stands at once for classical liberal and conservative liberal.

CL Press is a project of the Fraser Institute (Vancouver, Canada).

People:

Dan Klein and Erik Matson are the co-editors and executives of the imprint.

Jane Shaw Stroup is Editorial Advisor, doing especially copy-editing and text preparation.

Zachary Yost is Production Manager of CL Reprints.

Advisory Board:

Jordan Ballor, Center for Religion, Culture, and Democracy
Caroline Breashears, St. Lawrence Univ.
Donald Boudreaux, George Mason Univ.
Ross Emmett, Arizona State Univ.
Knud Haakonssen, Univ. of St. Andrews
Björn Hasselgren, Timbro, Uppsala Univ.
Karen Horn, Univ. of Erfurt
Jimena Hurtado, Univ. de los Andes
Nelson Lund, George Mason Univ.
Daniel Mahoney, Assumption Univ.
Deirdre N. McCloskey, Univ. of Illinois–Chicago
Thomas W. Merrill, American Univ.
James Otteson, Univ. of Notre Dame
Catherine R. Pakaluk, Catholic Univ. of America
Sandra Peart, Univ. of Richmond
Mario Rizzo, New York Univ.
Loren Rotner, Univ. of Austin
Marc Sidwell, New Culture Forum

Craig Smith, Univ. of Glasgow
Emily Skarbek, Brown Univ.
David Walsh, Catholic Univ. of America
Richard Whatmore, Univ. of St. Andrews
Barry Weingast, Stanford Univ.
Lawrence H. White, George Mason Univ.
Amy Willis, Liberty Fund
Bart Wilson, Chapman Univ.
Todd Zywicki, George Mason Univ.

Why start CL Press?

CL Press publishes good, low-priced work in intellectual history, political theory, political economy, and moral philosophy. More specifically, CL Press explores and advance discourse in the following areas:

- The intellectual history and meaning of liberalism.

- The relationship between liberalism and conservatism.

- The role of religion in disseminating liberal understandings and institutions including: humankind's ethical universalism, the moral equality of souls, the rule of law, religious liberty, the meaning and virtues of economic life.

- The relationship between religion and economic philosophy.

- The political, social, and economic philosophy of the Scottish Enlightenment, especially Adam Smith.

- The state of classically liberal ideas and policies across the world today.

www.ingramcontent.com/pod-product-compliance
Lightning Source LLC
Chambersburg PA
CBHW011833020426
42335CB00024B/2843